HAZEL SCOTT

Hazel Scott

The Pioneering Journey of a
Jazz Pianist from Café Society
to Hollywood to HUAC

KAREN CHILTON

THE UNIVERSITY OF MICHIGAN PRESS

ANN ARBOR

First paperback edition 2010
Copyright © 2008 by Karen Chilton

Published in the United States of America by
The University of Michigan Press
Printed and bound by CPI Group (UK) Ltd, Croydon, CR0 4YY

2016 2015 2014 2013   6 5 4 3

A CIP catalog record for this book is available from the British Library.

Library of Congress Cataloging-in-Publication Data

Chilton, Karen.
    Hazel Scott : the pioneering journey of a jazz pianist from Café
Society to Hollywood to HUAC / Karen Chilton.
        p.   cm.
    Includes bibliographical references (p.   ), discography (p.   ),
filmography (p.   ), and index.
    ISBN-13: 978-0-472-11567-9 (cloth : alk. paper)

    1. Scott, Hazel.   2. Pianists—United States—Biography.   3. Jazz
musicians—United States—Biography.   4. African American women
musicians—Biography.   I. Title.
    ML417.S427C45   2008
    786.2'165092—dc22
    [B]   2008011493

ISBN 978-0-472-03447-5 (pbk. : alk. paper)

For my Mother & my Sister

In memory of my Grandmothers

Contents

Contents

This is a song for the genius child.
Sing it softly, for the song is wild.
Sing it softly as ever you can—
Lest the song get out of hand.

—LANGSTON HUGHES

Each day that I have lived, thus far, has taught me something.
The sharing of pleasure; the loneliness of pain; the long hours
of waiting, for evidence of love; the brief, bitter, horror of hate;
the sad, misguided, misplaced trust; the fact of my own fallibility,
my own unworthiness. The greatness that has momentarily been
mine! The exalted seconds of genius, the immeasurable depths of
apathy. In each day of my life, there has been something of one
of these. Whether or not I shall be able to convey, in an interesting
manner, certain parts of the kaleidoscopic life that I have lived,
I truly do not know. All that I can do is attempt it.

—HAZEL SCOTT

Intro

In the winter of 1939, as New York's most famous poets and intellectuals, artists and celebrities descended upon Café Society, the city's first integrated nightclub, a nineteen-year-old relative unknown prepared for her debut.

Blues singer Ida Cox was scheduled to perform that night. When she was laid low by illness, Billie Holiday made a suggestion to the club's impresario, Barney Josephson: *"Hire Hazel Scott."* When he asked, *"Who is Hazel Scott?"* She replied: *"Just hire her."*

Josephson decided to take a chance.

She moved toward the piano with the grace and sophistication of a performer well beyond her years. She made good use of her full round shoulders and ample bosom, revealing luscious brown skin against a white satin strapless gown—a look that would later become her signature. There were fresh gardenias in her hair in homage to her friend and mentor, Billie Holiday. And diamonds, a precious plenty, to add extra sparkle at the wrists and décolletage.

The crowd had come prepared to hear Ida Cox's "Wild Women Don't Have the Blues"; what they got instead was a set that began with compositions by Bach, Liszt, and Rachmaninoff. Still, they indulged the young beauty, if for no other reason than their curiosity had been aroused.

Hazel played the classics with abandon, her expert hands racing across the keys. Then, in midmeasure, she added bass notes on the first and third beats, while steadily increasing the tempo, playing the original melody while introducing another, until finally each piece was transformed into something highly syncopated and swinging. The shift was stunning. Touches of Tatum could be heard in every chord. Over the applause, she continued, weaving improvisations and casting her fetching smile to soften the shock of it all.

It wouldn't be long before the club that featured such greats as Teddy Wilson, Albert Ammons, Meade Lux Lewis, and Mary Lou Williams made Hazel Scott its premier headliner, proclaiming her the "darling of Café Society."

It was her voice that I discovered first. Not from a song she recorded or a performance in a Hollywood film but from her candid opinions on various subjects, from jazz to democracy, motherhood to civil rights, all in the faded print of vintage *Ebony* magazines. Intrigued by the outspoken pianist who confessed, *"I've been brash all my life, and it's gotten me into a lot of trouble. But at the same time, speaking out has sustained me and given meaning to my life,"* compelled me to explore further.[1]

What I found was a woman of remarkable gifts—a Juilliard-trained classical pianist who had taken New York by storm back when Swing was "king," becoming a breakout success in the male-dominated world of jazz. A prodigy as a child, she soon rose to international stardom. She was the first black woman to host her own television show and one of the first to refuse to perform before segregated audiences. She negotiated lucrative contracts with Hollywood studios, becoming one of the highest paid performers of her era. Above all else, she was a black woman during a time of pervasive racism who refused to accept the status quo. Although she had grown up thinking of some of the biggest names in jazz as family—Art Tatum, Fats Waller, Billie Holiday, and Lester Young—her own name has been almost entirely lost in time.

Hazel's marriage in 1945 to Harlem minister and civil rights crusading congressman Adam Clayton Powell Jr. made them one of America's most high profile African American couples. Their extravagant lifestyle kept them constantly in the national press, as did her defiant stand before the House Un-American Activities Committee (HUAC) during the McCarthy era. So, I wondered, how could such a person, over the years, lose her place in history?

I learned that Hazel was a complex personality full of contradictions. The same woman who appeared onstage in sexy formfitting gowns would go home, put on a cardigan and kneesocks, and pick up her knitting needles or spend hours reading in one of the seven languages she spoke. She took her formal classical training, fused it with her love for jazz and blues, and spent the peak years of her career "swinging the classics," an act some believed undermined her real talent. And, while she never set out to wear "the activist tag" (as she called it), for a proud West Indian American infuriated with all forms of injustice, taking a stand was more a natural compulsion than an intention.

My curiosity about the life and career of Hazel Scott naturally led to me her son, Adam Clayton Powell III.

Together, we talked about his mother's life, rifling through old photos and sheet music, record albums and videotaped footage, through notes written on the backs of envelopes, and inside her personal phone books. In an act of incredible generosity, he entrusted me with Hazel's journal writings, transcribed from dozens of yellow legal pads; these pages represented what was to be her memoir, which she had planned to call "Scott Free."

Here, then, is the long overdue unearthing of Hazel Scott's legacy, the narrative of a life lived fully, bravely, and always on her own terms.

CHAPTER ONE

That Marvel of Marvels

Amid low-lying mountains and fertile valleys, where the sounds of African ceremonial drums fell in time with the sacred hymns streaming out from the cathedral and children danced to popular calypsos in the street, Hazel Dorothy Scott was born. She was graced by the natural beauty of this lush land on the northwest coast of Trinidad, where the songs of hummingbirds hung in the salt air, where emperor, d'abricot, and tiger butterflies cast an iridescent spell over the hillside, and the breeze off the Gulf of Paria cooled the brows of laborers in the cane fields. But island life for her family was far from paradise.

Hazel was the fifth child of Alma Long Scott and R. Thomas Scott but the first to survive beyond infancy. On June 11, 1920, the twelve-pound baby was carried from the hospital to their home on Richmond Street, a two-story brick house with a cast-iron veranda circling the top floor. In the first few months, she was watched carefully for any signs of failing health. But as young Hazel continued to blossom worries were set aside and replaced by the usual exuberance the birth of a newborn brings.

Two years later, when Alma became pregnant for the sixth time, the couple held fast to their faith, praying for another healthy child. They had a son. His life, however, would be brief, cut short by a doctor's dirty scalpel, which brought on blood poisoning.

Although Hazel was only two years old when her brother died, for years she would bear witness to the toll it took on her mother. "When she spoke of my younger brother her face crumbled a bit each time," Hazel remembered.[1] Alma spent many days pondering the deaths of her children. Oftentimes she would look at her little girl and say, "You are alive for some reason. Only God knows why you alone were spared."[2]

The hollow space between being *an* only child and *the* only child expanded with the years. A sensitive girl, Hazel began to believe it was her responsibility to restore happiness in the home. "I always tried to be a super-duper kid . . . to make up to her for the children that didn't make it."[3]

She relished the stories of her family's past, and throughout her life she would reproduce many of them in her journals, inserting her own observations and drawing her own conclusions. Hazel journeyed back as far as three generations, piecing together the fragments of her maternal family line.

Alma Long, Hazel's mother, was the daughter of Samuel and Margaret Long. Both Venezuelan natives, Sam Long had worked as a contractor for the Trinidadian government and was believed to have been directly involved in the construction of some of the island's landmark buildings, including the President's House. He was a man of means, with a commanding presence that was sure to leave a lasting impression. Everyone knew him. An amateur violinist, he knew how to use his instrument to attract attention. According to family lore, Sam Long left behind a trail of scorned women and illegitimate children. In her journal, Hazel wrote, "My grandfather, 'Old Long,' the patriarch Samuel, had single-handedly populated half the island of Trinidad before he met my grandmother."[4]

By the time Margaret crossed paths with Sam Long, he was in his early sixties and had slowed down considerably. Margaret, described by her granddaughter as a "small ivory-skinned hellion," was a far more serious creature than her husband-to-be, despite being only in her early twenties when they met. Margaret had married for love once, but suffered the loss of that husband in a tragic landslide accident when she was seven months pregnant, "throwing her into a state of shock," Hazel surmised, "that was to leave her a totally different human being than the one she had been till then." Margaret developed a tough exterior, and from that point on, concerned herself only with practical choices that could ensure a more secure future. After meeting Sam Long, she decided to negotiate the premium that was her youth, a shrewd move for the young widow and single parent of an infant daughter. She settled for the stability an older man could privide.[5]

Margaret and Sam had three children together—daughters Lilla and Alma and a son named Cyril. Maud, Margaret's daughter from her first marriage, Sam accepted as his own. The Longs lived in the style of middle-class island society, heavily influenced by the ways and customs of the British. The children were sent to parochial schools, given music lessons in piano and violin, and never missed a Sunday Mass. Margaret raised her children with a heavy hand, passing her own tough, steadfast nature on to them, insisting that they understand the importance of hard work. The difficulties of Margaret's own youth had made her sensitive to money matters and financial security. When Alma found a good, decent man to marry, Margaret was satisfied.

Catching Alma's eye took some doing. At the time that R. Thomas Scott introduced himself, she was completing her education at St. Joseph's Convent School, training to become a concert pianist, and was totally consumed by her musical aspirations. Thomas (called Tommy) arrived in Port of Spain from Liverpool, England, to teach. At that time, there were two prominent schools on the island from which he had to choose—St. Mary's College, an all-boys secondary school run by the Roman Catholic Church, and Queen's Royal College, whose alumni would later include the future prime minister of Trinidad and Tobago, Dr. Eric Williams; political theorist and writer C. L. R. James; and novelist V. S. Naipaul. Ultimately, Thomas secured a position at St. Mary's, where it is believed he taught English for four years.[6]

An accomplished scholar, Thomas Scott had a dignified countenance and a worldly air. But he was a difficult man to know. He was remembered as intense and introspective, revealing little about himself. Thomas Scott was of West African heritage, his forebears members of the Yoruba tribe of Nigeria and Benin. According to Hazel's recollections, he was raised in Scotland and educated in England, which suggests that his family was among the population of Africans who landed in Great Britain during the British slave trade, a population that, after emancipation, scattered throughout Scotland, England, and Ireland. Although most of the biographical details of Thomas Scott's life are shrouded in mystery, Hazel would nonetheless claim, with absolute certainty, a Yoruba heritage.

Thomas would always be an elusive figure in Hazel's life. Her impressions of him were drawn from snatches of time they spent together. She remembered him mostly as highly intelligent with an intense sense of pride. Thomas was articulate and well read with an interest in linguistics. He was fluent in several Chinese dialects. He pursued his academic career with tremendous urgency, believing that progress for black people was directly related to academic achievement. Later in life, Hazel would sum up her father in a word—"*square.*"[7]

Hazel's parents had grand expectations for their lives. Alma, who was only seventeen years old when she married, planned a career as a classical pianist. The young and ambitious Thomas intended to gain tenure as an English professor at a leading academic institution, preferably a traditionally black college in the American South. And, although their dream of a large family had been shattered, self-pity was not welcome in the Scott household. They turned their attention to the future, wondering if a better life and greater opportunity awaited them beyond Port of Spain.

By the 1920s, what had been known as Cumucarapo by the Amerindians and Puerto de los Hispanioles by the Spanish—what had been nothing more than a small port and trading post—was now the capital city of Port of Spain, a flourishing industrial town where every new structure was built of brick and mortar—an emphatic nod to England's colonial dominance. Trinidadians—by now a population of Africans, East Indians, Chinese, English, Spanish, French, Portuguese, Dutch, and Scots (and every imaginable racial mixture

THAT MARVEL OF MARVELS

thereof)—wrestled with their differences. As in many parts of the Caribbean, where the legacy of slavery was difficult to leave behind, class distinctions were drawn along the color line where visible signs of European blood meant greater entitlements—landownership, quality education, and a chance at a career in any number of industries. Subcultures were formed outside of the British tradition among ethnic groups wanting to hold fast to the social and religious customs of their original homelands. Hindus and Muslims worshipped according to their doctrines while many West Africans carried on tribal rituals, sending up prayers to Shango, the god of thunder, and celebrating with drums and dancing. Although decades of political struggle against colonization lay ahead, there existed a real movement to make Trinidad a country of some prominence and distinction.

It was through this struggle that Trinidadians nurtured their national pride. This connection to a past, a people, and a culture would remain important long after Hazel left the island. Throughout her lifetime, she would continue to follow the country's quest for independence.

Around 1923, the relationship between Alma and Thomas took an unplanned turn. Having grown weary of home life, Thomas began detaching himself—first emotionally, then physically—from the family. He'd leave home for long stretches of time, returning only briefly to check in on his daughter. Soon Thomas went even farther, leaving Trinidad altogether, and heading off for the United States alone.

With her husband gone, Alma was forced to work doubly hard. Leaving Hazel in the care of her mother, she found work outside the home, taking on odd jobs all over the island while continuing her training in classical piano. There is even some evidence that she ran her own small restaurant on the island for a time. Alma was, of course, her mother's daughter. In difficult circumstances, she persevered, and the work paid off. After years of disciplined training, weekly lessons, daily practice, and rehearsals, Alma was finally able to secure her first solo concert in Port of Spain.

The performance started off well. Alma quite likely enchanted the audience with pieces such as Liszt's "Valse Oubliee for Piano No. 1," Beethoven's festive "Piano Sonata No. 19 in G minor," and Bach's "Prelude in C sharp," gliding from one piece to the next. But almost halfway through the program Alma suddenly felt shooting pains from her wrists down through her fingers. The more she played the more excruciating the pain. She played until she could no longer endure the pain. The concert ended, abruptly.

Live performance revealed an unfortunate truth—Alma's wrists were too weak to sustain a full concert. She did strengthening exercises, sought medical attention, and even tried some home remedies. Nothing helped.

Alma had never entertained the idea of doing anything but playing music. Now she had no other choice but to contemplate a different future. Almost immediately after the disastrous debut, she began giving piano lessons to neighborhood children.

One afternoon three-year-old Hazel was at home with her grandmother, preparing for a nap after the midday meal. To get Hazel to fall asleep, it was Margaret's custom to sing her to sleep with a hymn. That day she sang:

Gentle Jesus, meek and mild
Look upon a little child
Pity my simplicity
Suffer me to come to Thee.[8]

But it was Margaret herself, not Hazel, who was lulled to sleep. Left alone to amuse herself, Hazel approached the piano. Following her own instincts, she played with both hands. When Grandmother Margaret woke from her nap and heard the music, she thought one of Alma's students had come by to practice. *"Who's there?"* she called out.[9] Hazel responded with a high-pitched: *"Me!"*[10]

Into the street, Margaret cried out for everyone to come and see the miracle that had taken place. For months, at nap time, Hazel had been making her grandmother sing the same hymn over and over. Little did Margaret know that the child was trying to memorize the song so she could play it. Hazel later wrote that "Until then, no one had paid any attention to me as I crawled off my potty chair, seated myself on the floor and using the seat of the chair as a keyboard, played away for dear life along with the students who were studying piano with my mother. They had been amused, but no one regarded my urge as latent talent. Even when the children would strike wrong notes and I would scream with displeasure were they aware of the sensitive ear I possessed . . . seated in place at that marvel of marvels . . . I knew that somehow I could find 'Gentle Jesus,' somewhere among those keys in front of me."[11]

As neighbors gathered in the doorway, Alma appeared among the crowd. Hazel repeated the performance. Even more surprising than the event itself was Alma's reaction to it. Hazel never forgot it. In her mother's eyes she saw a mix of disbelief, amazement, and anxiety—a maelstrom of maternal impulses that she desperately tried to unravel but never could. "Even now," Hazel wrote, "I can remember she had a deprecating smile. She was not nearly as impressed as everyone else. Even now, I can wonder why." It didn't spoil her enthusiasm for playing, however. Nor did it stop Alma from encouraging her daughter to play.

Before long, Hazel was performing at small gatherings. She played by ear, duplicating the popular calypsos performed by live bands in the streets of Trinidad during the pre-Lenten Carnival celebration. Alma would dress her up in pastel dresses of silk and satin and put matching ribbons and bows in her hair. While Hazel played, the crowd would dance and clap along. All at once, Hazel had fallen in love with the piano and the stage.

Around this time, Alma and Margaret began discussing the possibility of leaving Port of Spain. Like many West Indians searching for a better life, they considered the opportunities available across the Atlantic enticing. Margaret's eldest daughter, Lilla, had already left for New York City years before. The women's plan called for Margaret to go on ahead, secure employment and a place to live. How "Old Long" figured into their plan is not known. Given his age (he would have been in his eighties by this time), and assuming that he was still alive, it is quite likely that he was either not able or not interested in embarking on such a life-altering journey.

Once she got settled in New York, Margaret worked for nearly a year, saving what money she could from housekeeping jobs and sending it back to Trinidad for Hazel and Alma's passage.

On June 11, 1924—Hazel's fourth birthday—she and her mother boarded the *Maraval,* joining dozens of other West Indian families on the large passenger ship, sailing far away from the familiar and toward what was, for them, unknown and uncharted but ever so alluring.

CHAPTER TWO

A World Away

Thrilled by the roar of the ship and its rhythmic sway over the waves, Hazel traipsed up and down the decks unable to contain her excitement. After all, it was her birthday, and she expected to have a good time. Alma had been laid low by seasickness and could do very little to make their trip the festive time she had promised. While her mother slept, Hazel slipped out of the cabin and made her way around the ship alone, telling everyone she passed by, including the captain of the ship, that she had just turned four years old and she could play the piano. The captain, she recalled, was "enormously amused and set about making me prove my claim."[1]

Hazel played several calypsos for the captain and a small crowd of delighted passengers, reveling in the spotlight. Her birthday party was now in full swing.

Meanwhile, Alma awoke to find her little girl gone. There was no sign of Hazel anywhere in their section of the ship. Hazel quipped, "Years afterwards, I was to learn that we had not traveled romantic steerage as I had assumed but in the abominable middle class of the ship's caste system. I followed an inborn unerring instinct and mounted directly to first class!" When Alma found her daughter and demanded that she return to their cabin, a battle of wills ensued. Hazel insisted that her mother perk up and join her party. Looking back, Hazel concluded that this event signaled the beginning of their lifelong battle. She wrote, "In the next few minutes a pattern was established that was to prevail throughout our lives. On one end of the tug of war, I pulled the two of us upwards. On the other end, my mother, while wanting only the best for me, refused to share it with me."[2]

Upon arriving in New York City, Alma and Hazel made their way uptown to Harlem, knowing little of what they'd find there. Margaret had provided her daughter with some of the quotidian details, and information about the prospects of finding work, but Harlem in 1924 was more than just a place to live. A fervent energy had gripped the neighborhood, making way for the progressive activity of black social and political organizations, the publication of major black journals, and a flourishing black Arts movement that would define the decade. Harlem in the 1920s was the sound of Duke Ellington and Chick Webb, Fletcher Henderson and Ethel Waters, the writings of James Weldon Johnson, Langston Hughes, Jessie Fauset and Zora Neale Hurston, and the artistry of Aaron Douglas, Augusta Savage, and James Van Der Zee.

But, despite the blooming cultural scene, it was a trying time for Alma, who was unsure of just how she and her daughter were going to make it. Having only limited funds, she needed to find work right away.

Alma and Hazel bounced from place to place, living briefly in the Bronx neighborhood where Margaret worked as a domestic maid and at various addresses throughout Harlem. Yet the most vivid of Hazel's childhood memories come from the years she spent on West 118th Street at the home of her aunt and uncle.

Mother and daughter moved into one of the large rooms of the three-story brownstone, which was already full, top to bottom, of family and friends from Trinidad. Hazel recalled, "Half-sisters and half-brothers abound in the Long family, creating no end to the confusion. 'Here is your Aunt so-and-so' my mother would smile and present still another stranger. Third and fourth cousins continued to arrive even unto the fourth generation!"[3]

Most of central Harlem was steadily changing over from white to black. The Jewish and Italian families that had been in the area for decades were now moving to the outer boroughs—Queens, Brooklyn, and the Bronx. The transformation, or what some white landowners referred to as the "Negro invasion," happened rapidly. In fewer than ten years, Harlem became home to a diverse aggregate of black people—an educated black middle class, uneducated laborers escaping the "Jim Crow" South,[4] and Caribbean blacks from the colonized islands of the West Indies.

For all of its shocking differences from their home in Trinidad, Harlem did offer some familiar comforts. On every block there were black people speaking in a mix of tongues—Puerto Rican Spanish, Haitian French, British- and Dutch-accented English. The only cadence truly new to the Scotts' ears would have been the southern drawl of natives from the Carolinas, Georgia, and Virginia.

Margaret the matriarch laid down the house rules. She worked hard all week, cooking and cleaning for a paltry wage on Intervale Avenue in the Bronx. When Margaret made it back to Harlem, she expected her daughters to make sure that the scents of home met her at the door. Island tradition called for spicy and sweet combinations, dishes made with brown sugar, coconut milk and lime, garlic, curry, and Scotch bonnet peppers. Alma would scour the city to find the necessary ingredients. She prepared the meals; her sister Lilla served them. The family would sit down to spicy stewed chicken, or "pelau" with pigeon peas and rice, green plantains and fish, pastelles and callaloo—a vegetable mixture of dasheen leaves, okra, onions, and pumpkin. Sugar cakes and sweet breads with ginger lemonade provided Margaret the kind of welcome she required.

The most extravagant meals were saved for Sundays. Sundays were, in fact, the most memorable days of Hazel's childhood. She recalled the way her mother would lay out their clothes for Mass the night before, the food preparations for Sunday dinner that began on Saturday night, and their morning walk over to the Church of St. Thomas the Apostle. "There was wonderful food for Communion breakfast. Rich chocolate from Trinidad, homemade buttered bread, baked ham studded with cloves. I was glad to be alive," she gleamed.[5]

All of these family rituals were maintained for years and served to make their transition to life in the States smooth. Hazel's adjustment to her new environment was made easier by the presence of a piano in the house. With her love of showing off, she became the family's regular afternoon entertainment. Whenever one of their relatives from Trinidad paid a visit, the first request was, inevitably, to "hear the prodigy play calypsos."[6] One effect of receiving so much attention and approval from adults was that Hazel seemed to feel little need for the company of other children. With family members moving in and out and the stress of making ends meet, not to mention the social and emotional adjustment, the house was often full of conflict.

Witnessing the daily anxieties and problems of grown-ups, as well as the changing moods of a family of mostly women, only served to enhance Hazel's precociousness. She observed each of their personalities, their likes and dislikes, what set them off, what didn't.

Hazel never really knew what to make of her grandmother. Margaret's prickly personality usually kept her at a safe distance. "As loving as she could be, she was also capable of cruelty," Hazel remembered. She also noted how Alma's kindness and generosity were rarely reciprocated by other members of the family, which made her all the more desperate to please her mother.

According to Hazel, her Aunt Lilla was the most villainous. It was Lilla who intentionally and consistently withdrew her love and affection. "She spent most of her life seated by the window where she observed the goings-on of the neighbors," Hazel recalled. "She claimed that her heart was so bad that she could afford no exertion. Whatever she required, I had to fetch for her."[7] She and her husband owned the house. Family or not, as far as Lilla was concerned, everyone else was a boarder. She viewed Hazel less as her niece than as a useful nuisance, someone who could run errands. Other than that, she ignored her.

With the entire household, except for Lilla, going off to work in the morning, no one was there to witness how Hazel was suffering under her aunt's care. And Hazel chose not to tell them. Undoubtedly, she believed it would only make matters worse.

Having found her five-year-old niece to be a reliable errand runner, Lilla decided to see what else she could handle, eventually trusting her with the paying of bills. Whenever Lilla had to leave the house, she left Hazel in charge of paying any collectors who came by, tucking cash into the corresponding payment envelopes, and showing her the difference between the insurance, gas, furniture, and appliance bills. Surprised to see a little girl opening the door and handling business by herself, the bill collectors quite naturally talked about it, and word spread. Then the inevitable happened. One afternoon, a group of young men broke into the ground floor apartment window, grabbed Hazel and demanded to know where the money was kept. As her aunt had made her promise, Hazel wouldn't tell them. When their threats failed, the young men proceeded to beat her up. Neighbors heard her screams, and someone called the police. Lilla returned home to find her house filled with police officers. "She began to have hysterics," Hazel remembered.[8] When Alma came home from work and heard the news, she was mortified. Hazel remembered her mother's tears at the sight of her all bruised and bloodied. When a neighbor revealed the details about what had happened and how the whole neighborhood knew that Hazel handled the household bills, Alma promptly fainted.[9]

Days after the incident, every conversation was about Hazel's narrow escape, how the outcome could have been worse, and how, fortunately, there was no sexual assault. In that, at least, they could all be grateful. Every Harlem resident knew the neighborhoods' dangers. Racial tensions between blacks and the handful of whites who remained in the area had been mounting for years. The newspapers were full of stories of fights breaking out, confrontations in the street, robberies, and muggings. The adults had attempted to shield Hazel from the ugliness of it all, changing the subject when the child entered the room. Now their outrage could hardly be quieted. Hazel heard it all. "Each time the story was repeated, emphasis was placed upon the color of the boys. Those horrible 'white' ruffians. The brutes who could beat up a small girl."[10]

Another aspect of the incident, equally distressing to the family, was the fact that their home was now associated with the sirens and commotion of a police appearance. That their brownstone could be pointed out as the scene of a crime was unbecoming to an upstanding, hardworking family.

Thomas Scott lived in New York but exactly where and with whom was information that changed often. If he resided a few blocks away or in another borough altogether, it didn't matter much. His visits were few. When he did show up to spend time with his daughter, instead of strolls through Mount Morris Park or a trip to the Bronx Zoo, he lectured Hazel on social issues and current events, speaking candidly about the kinds of injustices he'd endured. It was a quantum leap in learning for Hazel. And Alma was none the wiser. In fact, she might have put an end to the visits had she known how father and daughter were spending their time.

Over the years, Thomas had paid more than cursory attention to the teachings of the Jamaican-born black nationalist Marcus Garvey. Adjusting to life in the city, Thomas looked for answers. Nothing in his background had prepared him for the kind of treatment he received from his white bosses. His pride prevented him from doing menial labor, which left him, more often than not, between jobs. Profoundly confused by the uselessness of his intellectual prowess, he had yet to find employment equal to his education. But when Thomas heard Garvey speak—a black man, an immigrant like himself—it helped ease the bite of discrimination that had met him at the shores of the Atlantic upon his arrival in America.

His afternoons with Hazel had included, at least once, a meeting at the Universal Negro Improvement Association headquarters on 135th Street. Thomas joined Garvey's UNIA and became a full-fledged "Garveyite," a staunch supporter of the black nationalist movement. Walking into Liberty Hall, the fervor of race pride streaming out of the building was impossible to ignore, and the message clear: "One God! One Aim! One Destiny!" Inspired by the example of the southern black leader and educator Booker T. Washington, Garvey's electrifying speeches captivated the black masses in major cities across America and abroad. Hazel's eyes widened as she glanced around the big hall. It was pure pageantry—the Universal African Black Cross nurses standing shoulder to shoulder in their starched white uniforms, immaculate men in the full regalia of a military of their own making, and Garvey himself, "the magnificent man in a black uniform with gold epaulets."[11]

Marcus Garvey's impassioned speech impressed upon Hazel's five-year-old mind ideas that she could hardly comprehend. When he cried out, "I am a man!" Hazel thought he was stating the obvious. She sought explanation from her father.

I remember my father's eyes filling with tears as he told me: "That's just it, my child, I'm afraid there are people who cannot see that he is a man."[12]

While other black leaders, namely, W. E. B. DuBois, wanted black people to fully integrate into the larger society and reap the same rights and privileges as their white American counterparts, Garvey's grand ambition was to establish a separate, independent black nation. And for a large number of black people, especially the West Indians who represented his base, this was a call to action so fantastic, so far-fetched that just hearing it made it feel possible.

Growing up around such conflict—social, political, racial, and cultural—made an indelible impression on Hazel. Whatever efforts her mother made to protect and shelter her, and her father to enlighten and prepare her, Hazel was beginning to form her own opinions about the differences between black and white.

Around this time, a major news story broke involving a wealthy white man from a prominent East Coast family, Leonard "Kip" Rhinelander, who was suing his wife for fraud. Rhinelander claimed that he didn't know his fair-skinned wife, Alice Beatrice Jones, was actually a "colored" woman, the daughter of a white mother and a black father. Daily accounts of the trial were printed in all the major tabloids. Although Hazel could read quite well, no one around her had taken notice. When they saw her walking around with the *New York Daily News,* she was told "not to make a mess of it, to keep it tidy for the grown-ups."[13] But one evening, encouraged to entertain visitors, Hazel asked the guests—to the shock and horror of her family—what they thought of the Rhinelander case.

After that, Alma and Margaret decided to keep the newspaper hidden from the child. But what they didn't realize was that lazy Lilla sent Hazel out every day to pick up the paper, and there she would linger at the newsstand just long enough to get an update on the Rhinelander affair before returning home.

Yet Hazel's education on race matters was only beginning.

One day, she was playing outside of her brownstone with a neighborhood friend, a small white girl her own age. They were playing "house." Hazel was the child, her friend the mother. A huge excavation had been dug in the front of the brownstone, as the city made preparations for a new subway line that would eventually become the "A" train. The girls were playing nearby when her friend told Hazel, "Turn around, so that I can brush you off and send you to school." Then, the little girl pushed Hazel into the ditch.

Workmen rushed to pull her out, "a crumpled, bloodied mess."[14] "The first thing that startled me was the look in their eyes," Hazel recalled. "Fear. Fear and guilt. They, too, were white. They had witnessed the horrible act. They were involved and they resented it and me."[15] The girl took off running and was never questioned. Thinking about the incident many years later as an adult, Hazel resolved that a child of any race could have done the awful deed, but the fact that this little girl was white was significant to her. She internalized this experience as an error on her part; turning her back to the white child and trusting her was a mistake she vowed never to make again.

Once again Alma had to explain the inexplicable to her little girl. This time she told Hazel that she would simply have to learn to defend herself, to be tough and resilient. But Alma knew that Hazel wasn't like the other children in the neighborhood. She didn't have the hard edge of city kids, the kind of street-smart scrappiness that urban living often cultivates. Hazel was sensitive and introspective. She was a girl who dreamed, spending hours at the piano or alone in her room making up imaginary games to pass the time.

Alma used Hazel's interest in music to turn her attention away from the Harlem streets. She listened closely when Hazel played, and noticed how she approached the piano with enthusiasm, how at ease she was with the instrument. She realized that the piano was not merely a pastime, not simply an attention getter for her daughter, but something more.

The piano would be the salve for the string of unfortunate events. Music would place them both on a firmer footing.

CHAPTER THREE

Paraphrasing Rachmaninoff

Under Alma's direction, Hazel learned the fundamentals of the piano. Her ear was so keen that she could play, almost immediately, whatever she heard. But Alma wanted her to learn the proper technique. She organized a daily schedule of formal instruction, beginning at the beginning—hands-alone training to hands together, proper fingering, scales, sight-reading. "It was my first encounter with true discipline and as I was to do all my life—I promptly rebelled," Hazel said. "Instead of the dull five finger exercises that had to be repeated interminably, I would break into *Hold'em Joe—Me Donkey Want Water! Calypso* was much more fun than Every-Good-Boy-Does-Fine."[1]

Alma ignored Hazel's five-year-old antics. Strict and serious, she was much more interested in how quickly her daughter was absorbing the lessons. Hazel's progress was swift, and she enjoyed the rapid pace. They soon discovered she had perfect pitch. Beat by beat, Alma counted out the measures while Hazel's small hands flew across the keys, stretching and gaining strength daily. "Learning to read music took no time at all," Hazel recalled. "Forcing myself to practice strengthening exercises was the real chore. I detested it."[2] Alma taught Hazel the easy pieces all beginning piano students learn—minuets and sonatinas, Beethoven's "Für Elise" and "Moonlight

Sonata," Mozart's "Fantasia in D Minor." It wasn't long before she was playing classical compositions of varying degrees of difficulty.

Alma now knew without question that Hazel possessed "the gift." With this realization, she set about constructing a path for her daughter's life, passing along not only her knowledge of music but her own dashed dreams of a concert career. She decided it would be Hazel who would become great.

Their lessons intensified with greater attention placed on technique, style, and performance. Alma instructed Hazel on poise and presentation: *Face forward, head up, shoulders relaxed, flat back, hands spread gracefully over the keys.*

Alma and Margaret cautioned Hazel to be conscious of her hands—not to injure, hurt, scratch, or burn them. Her hands, she was told, ensured her future.

Once Hazel reached a level where she had learned and memorized a repertoire of classical works, Alma began seeking out venues where she could perform publicly. Her first appearances took place in the church. Sundays at St. Thomas the Apostle were replaced by visits to Baptist, Methodist, and Pentecostal churches all over Harlem. Up until then, all Hazel knew of church was the solemnity of the Catholic Mass. She didn't know what to make of the boisterous preaching and spirit-filled "Hallelujahs!" and "Amens!" that swelled in these sanctuaries. Performing was no problem, but the stomp and shout of the Protestant black church scared the child half to death. She wrote, "Mother sat next to me in the pew of the small unfamiliar church. Each time it was a different church. The minister, unlike the priest, was black. He shouted. It was unfamiliar and frightening. Why was he angry?"[3]

Pressed up against her mother, Hazel sat quietly in the pew, hands folded neatly in her lap. She waited to be called to play. Alma gave the cue with a gentle nudge to her side, then she hopped up and made her way to the piano. Delighted by the sight of the cute little girl all dressed up in satin and chiffon frills, the congregation grew still as she approached. Amid the surprised murmurs, she played Gounod's "Ave Maria" and Bach's "Jesu, Joy of Man's Desiring." Joyous music. There were shouts of "Amen" and applause as she quickly curtseyed then rushed back to Alma.

Alma had been steadily scoping out piano competitions and auditions for Hazel. When she discovered a children's program being held at New York's famed Town Hall, she submitted Hazel for an audition, understanding fully that a debut there would give her daughter's career a tremendous boost.

In 1925, Hazel performed her first professional recital. Although the program, the selections she played, and the reception she received are details now lost, it is easy to imagine how she must have sparkled that day as her mother and grandmother looked on, sitting proudly in their seats, an afternoon when Hazel assumed her position among Manhattan's young musical elite.

Once word of Hazel's performing around town reached her Harlem neighborhood, much was made of the young pianist. When she entered the neighborhood elementary school, she was recognized by her schoolmates as "the little girl who plays the piano." Suddenly, it seemed, Hazel was popular among other children. She was praised by their parents for her talent and discipline. Yet for Hazel the very early years of performing were far less exciting than most people assumed. She experienced a great deal of loneliness, the desperate need to fit in, the pressure to perform. Her gift for music set her apart from other children. She was different, a realization she found quite unsettling.

Recounting in her diary the events of an afternoon children's party, she paints precise images of the children in attendance, their personalities, their talk and laughter. "It was happy birthday for the tiny girl, with the long, long curls. She was surrounded by laughing friends," Hazel wrote.[4]

Hazel remembered sitting alone along the wall, observing the other children, not participating. Fearing that she wouldn't belong, having had so little experience (and several bad experiences) in the company of kids her own age, it took the adults to encourage her to join in the fun. So she played party games and ate "coconut cake and strawberry ice cream, soda pop and grape punch."[5] Things were going well until one of the adults decided it would be a nice treat if

Hazel played the piano. Before she knew it, she was surrounded by all the guests. All except the girls, who drew away to the other side of the room.

That afternoon the boys sang the lyrics as Hazel played one pop tune after another. The girls stood on the sidelines offering only cold stares. As Hazel rose from the piano bench, everyone applauded. Then the birthday girl approached. Hazel wrote:

> She leaned towards me and whispered, *"We only invited you so that you could play the piano!"*[6]

For a girl at such a tender age, the idea that she had no real identity apart from playing the piano was terrifying. Loving the attention she received when she performed, Hazel was ill-equipped, emotionally, to deal with the indifference she felt when the applause stopped. She questioned the value of her talent, wondering what it was all worth if it came at the cost of those things that all pubescent girls cherish—friendship, love, and acceptance. A misfit, she began picking herself apart and determined that there was very little to like. Her face she found mousy and uninteresting; her full lips were the source of ridicule. "The sensual lower lip that later was to attract many a male was looked upon as a sign of ugliness in our house," she wrote. "Teased about it, I caught it in my teeth and went around holding it that way." Her hair wasn't to her liking either; she lacked the long tresses she envied on the little girls in picture books and magazines. And "no amount of Shirley Temple curls all over my head or huge ribbon bows helped," she confided.[7]

She'd receive no sympathy from her family, however. Hazel knew full well that with this identity crisis she was absolutely on her own. Surrounded by such prideful women, a pity party for such a gifted child was never to be entertained.

When she could no longer make sense of the world around her, Hazel withdrew. She read books, wrote in her diary, daydreamed. She referred to her search for clarity and understanding—"the maze"—the tricky, winding paths of emotion where boundaries intermingle between reality and the truth, where, for most of her childhood,

Hazel would wander. "The maze had taken form. The search had begun," she would write, repeatedly.[8]

In 1928, when Hazel was eight years old, Alma took her to the
Juilliard School for an audition. Although the requisite age for en-
trance was sixteen, Alma was undeterred. She marched down to the
Juilliard building, which was located at that time near Columbia
University's campus at 120th Street and Claremont Avenue. Exactly
how she convinced the auditioners to make an exception and allow
Hazel to be heard one can only imagine.

Hazel chose one of the most popular of Rachmaninoff's twenty-
four preludes as her audition piece, the "Prelude in C Sharp Minor."
Because her fingers could not reach the full octave of the minor
chords in the composition, Hazel played them as sixths to accommodate the minor tonality. (Rachmaninoff himself may have found
it an amusing irony considering that his extremely large hands
could cover an interval of a thirteenth, a span of nearly twelve
inches on the keyboard.) Dismayed to be hearing—through an open
door down the hall—someone improvising a classical masterpiece,
Dr. Frank Damrosch, the venerable head of Juilliard, stormed into
the room, interrupting Hazel's audition.

Known in academic circles as something of a terror, Damrosch
demanded, *"Who is that paraphrasing Rachmaninoff?"*[9]

When he saw the little girl with bows in her hair and legs dan-
gling from the piano bench, he was shocked. "I explained that I was
only reaching the closest thing that sounded like it, not even knowing what a sixth was at that age," Hazel revealed.[10] She played on.
When she finished the piece, Professor Oscar Wagner spoke quietly:
"I am in the presence of a genius."[11]

Both Wagner and Damrosch agreed that the child's gift was rare
and worthy of cultivation. But a scholarship for someone as young
as Hazel was not possible. Instead, Professor Wagner made a special
arrangement for her entry, offering to teach Hazel himself.

Hazel Scott was admitted to Juilliard as Wagner's private piano
student, matriculating within the halls of one of the country's most
illustrious schools of musical training. This uncommon arrange-

ment exemplified the school's commitment to providing superior musical education to exceptional students. As most of the student body was over the age of sixteen, and predominantly white and male, Hazel was likely the youngest person enrolled and one of very few African Americans.

Professor Wagner became both mentor and manager to Hazel. During the intense years of working one-on-one, he sought out opportunities to showcase and hone her performance skills. He remained convinced of her ability to become a great pianist. And soon Hazel, too, developed a greater appreciation of her talent.

During a children's piano competition at Carnegie Hall, Wagner asked the judges if Hazel could play something of her own choosing rather than the preselected piece, Beethoven's "Minuet in G." Their response was that the Beethoven composition was sufficiently challenging for any gifted child. "Yes, that's just it," Wagner said. "Hazel is a genius! I mean, something harder would be easier for her!"[12]

The days of her youth were full. Hazel attended regular classes at public school, then it was off to Juilliard for several hours of piano training. Back at home there were household chores, homework, and more practice. She rebelled against the strict routine and used the school grounds to exert control over her daily life. "In school, I was popular because all the kids loved to hear me play the piano." Ironically, in music appreciation class, where she should have easily excelled, Hazel was met with disdain by the instructor, who seemed to make a habit of not calling on her.

The other students would beg the teacher to allow Hazel to play; the teacher responded by making snide remarks about "popular junk."[13] This went on for the duration of the school year until one day Hazel decided to challenge the teacher. "If you would like to hear something *besides* popular junk . . . I'll be happy to oblige," she said, as she tore into Chopin's "Etude in C Minor."[14] Outraged, the teacher dismissed the class and escorted Hazel to the principal's office, which was fast becoming her second home.[15]

With all of Alma's efforts to make Hazel a refined young lady, she had to compete with the Harlem streets. And there was only so much sheltering she could do. Policemen patrolled the area. There were fights on and off the schoolyard. At school, away from the watchful eyes of her mother and grandmother, Hazel carried on the kind of bad behavior that never would have been tolerated at home.

On one occasion, when she was in the fourth or fifth grade, Hazel decided to give her homeroom teacher a gift for the Christmas holidays. The teacher, whom Hazel described as "a typically bourgeois, fair-skinned 'middle-class Negro' type . . . riddled with color prejudice and class consciousness," apparently favored the light-skinned students and was dismissive of all the others.[16]

Hazel had noticed how much this teacher paid attention to the care of her own hair, which was "thick, curly hair that she plastered to her skull in an attempt at straightening out the rebellious curls," and how she'd fawn over the girls with fine, long locks.[17] Using her own meager savings, Hazel purchased a metal hair-straightening comb, (a "hot comb" as it was commonly called), wrapping it nicely, along with a card that read: *"To you, dear Mrs. R. Merry Xmas. Now you can throw away the stocking cap!"* Hazel signed her full name.

Her brave admission of guilt failed to impress Alma. Her mother simply wanted the antics to stop. She didn't have the time or patience to make constant trips to the school.

Whatever pleasure Hazel took in acting up, she found no joy in her mother's reprimands, which typically left her feeling sad and full of regret. Recurring fears would haunt her—that she wouldn't be loved, that she would somehow lose her mother's favor. She was torn "between the desire to please and feeling that she must have loved the boy who had died more than she loved me."[18]

Hazel would retreat to her bedroom, where she created an imaginary world of lovely characters and happy endings. Yet her mother's words replayed in her mind, words Alma spoke when she, too, was feeling low:

He would have played the violin. . . . What a thing that would have been. You two would have played duets.[19]

24

CHAPTER FOUR

Women's Work

On October 24, 1929, "Black Thursday" brought a hush to the roar of the twenties. And everything went dark for a while. Following the stock market crash, relief applications among blacks in Harlem quadrupled. It would be just a matter of months before breadlines became a regular feature of the landscape. Women lined up underneath the Third Avenue elevated train tracks hoping to be chosen for a day's work of cooking and cleaning. Men scrounged up what they could to make the weekly rent.

Caught up in jazz and blues, swinging at the Savoy, the sparkle and flash of Harlem nightlife, no one saw it coming.

Margaret and Alma were well aware that in order to sustain themselves they had to make sound decisions. In 1930, they decided to make a move. After six years of scrimping, the two women purchased a brownstone at 79 West 118th Street, just one block from Lilla and Sydney's. As Harlem's population was growing faster and larger with each passing year, the overcrowded conditions and high demand for housing gave many landlords license to overcharge for apartments. Home ownership would give them some stability.

Their brownstone was a few doors down from the corner of Lenox Avenue, a busy thoroughfare lined with florist shops, fruit stands, delicatessens, and storefront churches of various denominations. Their new address was close enough to Lilla and Sydney's that

Hazel could run over anytime she wanted, which she did frequently now that the couple had given birth to a little girl. When Olympia was born, Hazel observed a change in her aunt's disposition. "Lilla was tender with her own daughter; a lot more gentle than she had ever been with me."[1]

On the mortgage loan papers, Alma listed her occupation as "housemaid for private home," but her enterprising nature resisted a life of servitude. It had never been her intention to come to the States to live anything less than the middle-class lifestyle she'd left behind in Trinidad. Now, with the added responsibility of making monthly payments on their $12,500 mortgage, and with Margaret getting older and working less, she set out to create new sources of income.

She opened a tailoring shop on the premises. "By descending two steps from the street, and walking a few steps further, you would find yourself in an immaculately clean, well-appointed, cleaning and dying establishment, with an enormous pressing machine that my dear mother had not the remotest idea how to operate!"[2] Witnessing Alma's struggles, a Jewish tailor who owned a shop on Lenox Avenue came over and tried to help. But Alma still didn't trust herself. Feeling more secure with an electric iron, she would press her customers' clothes in the back of the apartment away from prying eyes.

When the tailoring establishment folded, Alma decided to open what must have appeared as the most unlikely of businesses, a Chinese restaurant. But given Trinidad's large Chinese population, the cuisine was, in fact, quite familiar. And food, Alma figured, would be a simpler undertaking. "Anything that came out of a kitchen was her province—from kreplach to Cantonese chicken!" claimed Hazel.[3] As for this new culinary experiment, Alma had learned "at the elbow of a trusted family friend, whose brother had married one of her half-sisters."[4] She employed some of the neighborhood boys to pick up supplies. Hazel recalled seeing rows of boys lined up in the backyard with big trays filled with white rice, separating the flawed grains. "She was a marvelous, gifted cook, my mother, and until she had been held-up and robbed three times, and had become discouraged, she had done rather well with the restaurant."[5]

The entire time Alma was crafting plans for her entrepreneurial ventures, she'd been suppressing the urge to return to music. Though she longed to play, she had not figured out a way to make a living in music aside from teaching. And even teaching in the middle of the Depression would prove difficult; few families were able to afford the luxury of piano lessons for their children. Yet, living in Harlem, it was impossible for her not to know who and what was popular, the jazz bands, the touring vaudevillians, the composers and musicians whose stars were on the rise. She took a special interest in the women performers—Ethel Waters, who had followed up her appearance in *Africana* on Broadway with a record deal on Black Swan Records and a promotional tour with Fletcher Henderson and the Black Swan Troubadours; and Josephine Baker, who began her career as a dancer with a traveling troupe, *The Dixie Steppers,* and once in New York tore up the Broadway stage with her comedic charms in Eubie Blake and Noble Sissle's hit musical revues *Shuffle Along* and *Chocolate Dandies.*

Then there was the young and gifted Florence Mills. Before her untimely death, Mills was one of the biggest names in show business. She began as part of a sister act on the vaudeville circuit. When she replaced Gertrude Helen Saunders in the role of "Ruth Miller" in *Shuffle Along,* she became a recognizable talent in New York, hailed by critics as one of Broadway's newest finds. Her effervescent stage presence and winsome soprano earned her billing as the "Queen of Happiness." She went on to appear in Sissle and Blake's *Chocolate Dandies* and Lew Leslie's *Plantation Revue* and *Dixie to Broadway,* but it was her performance in *Blackbirds* that she would be remembered for. When she sang the hit tune from the show, "I'm a Little Blackbird Looking for a Bluebird," fans swooned. *Blackbirds* opened at the Alhambra Theater in Harlem in 1926 and then toured in Paris and London. Upon her return from Europe, Florence Mills had become one of the first black women to achieve international fame. Then, in 1927, she died suddenly from tuberculosis at the age of thirty-one, darkening Harlem's spirits. At the Mother Zion African Methodist Episcopal (AME) Church, a crowd five thousand strong paid their respects to the beloved songstress, while a flock of blackbirds was released from a low-flying airplane as the funeral progression moved down 145th Street.

Along with "black Broadway" and Harlem's burgeoning community of musicians and theater and literary artists, all-women orchestras came in and out of town, featuring women as bandleaders and instrumentalists who could swing with the best of them, playing everything from trumpets to trombones, crossing gender lines, and expanding the expectations of their male counterparts.

It wasn't a new phenomenon; all-women bands had been around for years, though few had achieved a real national presence. Many of them toured on the TOBA circuit—the Theater Owners Booking Association (commonly referred to by performers as "Tough on Black Asses")—a booking agency that provided black entertainment to a network of white-owned theaters across the South, the East Coast, and a few states out West. Designed for black audiences, "Toby Time" shows were made up of black musical comedy acts, dancers, singers, and musicians. The work conditions at the TOBA theaters were typically substandard, and the treatment of the artists was usually poor. Nevertheless, many great performers began their careers on the TOBA circuit, including Bessie Smith, Ethel Waters, Fats Waller, and Sammy Davis Jr.

During the 1920s, all-women orchestras were crisscrossing the country, touring through big cities, small southern towns, and the Midwest. Popular among them were Bobbie Grice's Fourteen Bricktops; Dyer and Dolly Jones, the mother-daughter trumpet-playing duo; and pianist/bandleader Lovie Austin and Her Blues Serenaders, a Chicago-based mixed ensemble that became known for accompanying blues singers Ida Cox, Alberta Hunter, and "Ma" Rainey, and for its recordings with veteran jazz musicians such as Kid Ory and Johnny Dodds.[6] The Dixie Sweethearts, the Melody Maids, and "the Blonde Bombshell of Rhythm" Ina Ray Hutton and her Melodears hit the road in the 1930s. The Harlem Playgirls were quite popular for a time, featuring tenor saxophonist Viola "Vi" Burnside and trumpeter Ernestine "Tiny" Davis, both of whom went on to make their mark years later in "America's #1 All-Girl Jazz Band," the International Sweethearts of Rhythm.[7]

All of this got Alma thinking.

Months of contemplation led her to a choice that was as unlikely as it was unexpected. The saxophone. She would learn to play the saxophone. Without further consideration and very little discussion, she went down to a local music shop, rented a tenor sax, and sat down to teach herself the instrument. "My mother started to learn the saxophone and she would practice in our tiny living room," Hazel recalled.[8] Her grandmother would bring relatives over to watch. "[Alma's] cheeks would puff out and her face would turn red, and they hooted with laughter. 'Oh God! She's going to explode!' They rocked, holding their sides."[9]

Putting aside a few dollars a week for lessons, Alma studied saxophone with the Donawa Brothers, whose music school was nearby. Hazel would accompany her on pieces such as "Laughin' Sax" and "Cryin' Sax." Alma endured rigorous drills to perfect her embouchure and learned to relax her throat, tongue, and facial muscles. Fingering, breathing, proper head position, and the variances of jaw and lip pressure were all skills specific to reed instruments that she now had to master.

Where volume, rhythm, and pitch were concerned, her classical training was a definite help, but Alma was off to a rather bumpy beginning. Almost everyone close to her thought her saxophone playing was ridiculous. It made no sense to Margaret that she would take such a huge financial risk in the middle of the Depression. Neighbors who caught wind of it were curious. "The neighbors were always eager to find out what my poor mother was up to," Hazel wrote.[10] "A woman without a man to support her, she constantly intrigued men and women alike with her resourcefulness."[11] When Alma was unfairly criticized or attacked, Hazel would rush to her defense. But Alma was unmoved by the criticism. It mattered little that the saxophone was considered unbecoming to the feminine frame and was a difficult instrument for a woman to play. This was about survival.

Hazel was dismayed by her family's lack of support. When she'd had her fill of all the ridicule, she would lash out, at will, despite her mother's admonitions. Fights with family members gave what would become Hazel's characteristic outspokenness its first spark. She declared, "Everybody in this family lives at the top of his lungs— in self defense!"[12]

Alma remained focused. She pinched pennies for fabric to make nice dresses to audition in. She spent countless hours practicing her horn. The sooner she was able to refine the quality of her playing and develop her own "voice" on the instrument, the sooner she could begin to look for work. It wasn't only the technical aspects of the saxophone that were a concern, however. When Alma made the transition from piano to saxophone, she also had to shift her interest from classical music to jazz.

She walked onto the scene when the sound of Swing, with its intoxicating rhythms and uptempo melodies, was sweeping the nation. And the music went hand in hand with the dance. From Chick Webb to Count Basie, Duke Ellington to Jimmie Lunceford, a big band's popularity was often decided by how well dancers could move to its music. In order to "swing" her sax with the same confidence she had playing classical piano, Alma needed to gain a true understanding of jazz music—its blues and ragtime roots, where it was headed and where it had been.

Months passed before Alma had the chops to hit the audition circuit. But once she was ready, she didn't stop searching until she found herself a gig, eventually joining Valaida Snow and the Berry Brothers.

Valaida Snow came from a musical family out of Chattanooga, Tennessee. A statuesque beauty, Valaida could sing, dance, and play nearly a dozen different instruments. She had been taught by her mother, Etta Washington Snow, who had been educated at Howard University, to play the trumpet, saxophone, and clarinet, as well as the cello, bass, violin, mandolin, harp, and banjo. She would ultimately become known for her trumpet playing and vocals. She was a rare commodity among musicians, one of a scarce few female jazz instrumentalists with a name in the business whose tremendous skills had brought her some measure of fame.

Following cabaret performances at Barron Wilkin's Exclusive Club in 1922, and work onstage in *Chocolate Dandies, Rhapsody in Black, Blackbirds,* and Will Masten's *Revue,* Valaida's eclectic journey as trumpeter, arranger, bandleader, and vocalist took off. Globetrotting, Valaida took her music to Europe, the Far East, and Russia. European fans called her "Little Louie" because of the traces of Louis Armstrong's sound in her style. Her bravado won fans over—she could hit a high C on her horn, break into a tap dance combination, then belt out the bridge of the tune. Like Josephine Baker, European audiences found Valaida Snow exotic and captivating, making it easy for her to book long-term engagements at concert halls and cabarets overseas.

In between her stints abroad, Valaida returned to New York and organized an all-woman band. Alma auditioned and won a spot in the reed section and began readying herself for an upcoming tour with the Berry Brothers.

James and Ananias Berry's flash act was perfected in Harlem clubs and vaudeville theaters. The Berry Brothers—James, the singer and comedian; Warren, the trained dancer and acrobat; and Ananias (called Nyas), the master of the Cakewalk Strut—began their dance act performing in church. They molded themselves after the legendary vaudevillians Bert Williams and George Walker (originally known as the Two Real Coons), whose musical comedy shows *Clorindy, The Origin of the Cakewalk, Sons of Ham, Bandana,* and *In Dahomey* redefined black theater and paved the way for generations of black entertainers. The Berry Brothers had already achieved several milestones in their young careers by the time Alma met them—appearing in Hal Roach's original film shorts, the *Our Gang Comedies;* performing for the opening of the new art deco architectural marvel Radio City Music Hall; and eventually booking a five-year gig at the Cotton Club as the opening act for Duke Ellington and his orchestra.

Their steady flow of work piqued Alma's interest, and she immediately began looking for a way to get Hazel in on the act. She proposed to the boys' father that Warren, the youngest brother, team up with Hazel, but it never materialized. "I really believe that the old man had always wanted to keep his three boys together in one act. Finally, this is what happened, and the world saw one of the greatest dancing acts in show business," Hazel recalled.[13]

Touring with the Berry Brothers and Valaida Snow in nightclubs along the East Coast was Alma's chance to test her chops. She found herself energized by Valaida's dynamism. Valaida's example gave

Alma a glimpse into what was possible. She was making decent money. And, while most Americans were hungry, jobless, and truly suffering, entertainers, by providing audiences a momentary escape from the drudgery of day-to-day concerns, were quite often financially solvent. As Warren Berry remembered, "During the terrible time of Depression, we were living the height of luxury compared to the average Joe."[14]

While on tour, Alma was able to send money home to Margaret and Hazel, make the monthly mortgage payment, and still tuck small sums away.

But, as it turned out, Alma's time with Valaida Snow would be brief. Not long after Alma joined the act, Valaida fell in love with Ananias Berry and the two were married. The all-woman band disbanded, the Berry Brothers broke up, and Ananias and Valaida moved ahead with plans for a duo of their own.

Still, Alma's experience with the band was valuable. Having honed her skills on the road, she was soon able to find other work, and soon joined Lil Hardin Armstrong's all-women band. As Hazel recalled, "Lil Hardin Armstrong, one of Louis' former wives, was a nice, friendly woman who played a mean piano."[15] Memphis-born Lillian Beatrice Hardin was trained in classical piano and organ and raised in the gospel tradition of the black church, but her family's move to Chicago in 1918, when she was a teenager, fueled an interest in jazz and blues. After a successful stint with King Oliver's Creole Jazz Band, and tremendous efforts to help build up the career of her husband, the inimitable Louis Armstrong, (urging him to go solo, and playing piano on his legendary "Hot Five" and "Hot Seven" recordings), in the 1930s she took up the role of bandleader.

In the latter part of 1931, Alma joined the Harlem Harlicans, one of Lil's early ventures as the leader of an all-women swing band. Lil had put together an ensemble of talented female musicians, including the classically trained trumpeter (and wife of Fletcher Henderson) Leora Meoux Henderson, violinist Mae Brady, and Dolly Jones, whose reputation as one of the best female trumpet and cornet players was already established.[16] By now, Alma had become quite proficient on the saxophone. Hazel wrote, "She was beautiful with a strong way of playing. Most of the men are pretty rough about that. Invariably some man would come up to the bandstand and say, 'Lady, you play that thing just like a man.' And she would say, 'Mister, you carry your children just like a lady.' "[17]

Hazel got in on the act one night, surprising her mother and the other members of Lil's band. The venue was the Apollo Theater on 125th Street. While Lil Hardin's group was onstage playing, Hazel, to the shock of her mother and the rest of the women in the band, stepped out to sing. "I was supposed to be in bed," she wrote. "Mother jumped up in her chair. She later said to me, 'You're running around here singing pop tunes. Well, if you like that sort of thing (she was still a classicist at heart), here's how it should sound.' And mother went and played an Ethel Waters record for me."[18]

After her all-women orchestra dissolved in the mid-1930s, Lil led an ensemble of mostly men, all former members of violinist Stuff Smith's band, which was based in Buffalo, New York. But Lil kept Alma on tenor saxophone. She did a brief stint with the new band, touring upstate New York, Detroit, and Chicago before returning home to Harlem.

When she was eleven years old, Hazel attended Julia Ward Howe Junior High School on West 120th Street, an all-girl middle school just a few blocks from her house. She had matured into a studious and disciplined student. She loved to read and had developed a real interest in learning different languages. In her spare time, Hazel studied Spanish, French, and German language books and would buy newspapers printed in as many languages as she could find. Alma believed Hazel's uncanny ability to pick up languages quickly was a gift she inherited from her father.

In 1933, through the many contacts she had made, Alma began arranging concert bookings for Hazel at uptown venues. A small headline in a neighborhood paper read, "Recital and Dance—Mrs. Alma Long Scott presents her 13-year-old daughter, Little Miss Hazel Scott—Child Wonder Pianist, Friday Eve., November 24, 1933, at the

Alhambra Ballroom." To supplement her studies with Professor Wagner at Juilliard, Alma had hired a private coach, Margaret Kennerly Upshur, to prepare Hazel for the concert. Little is known about the teacher except that Hazel held her in very high regard. She wrote, "I gave my first full recital by working with Margaret Kennerly Upshur. Mrs. Upshur was a fantastic influence in my life."[19]

Hazel also remembered Nora Holt Raye, an accomplished musician, scholar, and critic, who attended that particular concert. A Kansas City native, Raye was the first black American to receive a master's degree in music, in 1918. Her thesis was an orchestral composition entitled *Rhapsody on Negro Themes*. A cofounder of the National Association of Negro Musicians, Raye had traveled throughout Europe and Asia for twelve years, performing as a singer in nightclubs. She returned to the States to become the music critic for the *Chicago Defender* and later for Harlem's *Amsterdam News*. The first black journalist to be elected to the New York Music Critics Circle, Raye was an early supporter of Hazel's career, never missing her concerts ("not if she was within 100 miles!"), a gesture Hazel would never forget. Having the endorsement of someone of Raye's stature imbued Hazel, in the early stages of her career, with a sense of belonging and legitimacy in the music world.

Now that her daughter's career was under way, Alma continued to dream. She had learned plenty from both Valaida Snow and Lil Armstrong—how to organize a band, arrange bookings, and budget the finances. Confident now in her decision to return to music, Alma was filled with renewed ambition. She set her sights even higher.

CHAPTER FIVE

Crescendo

"Overnight, I had become a slender, provocative creature."[1]

Summer had come, and Hazel's budding figure had outgrown all of her clothes. Grandmother Margaret took her shopping, complaining that Alma had left her "woefully unequipped as to a wardrobe."[2] They went shopping on 125th Street where Margaret, uncharacteristically, allowed Hazel to pick out whatever she wanted—"Pretty, form-fitting, cotton-frocks; a smart, pale green linen suit and a pair of pumps with spike heels."[3] Yet, her newfound freedom was quickly reined in. Margaret had allowed her granddaughter to buy mature-looking clothes, but Hazel was rarely permitted to go out wearing them.

Margaret's stern rules made life a rather mundane affair for the teenager. According to Hazel, her grandmother had become more contrary with age. "Each day," she wrote, "I grew further away from the possibility of a warm loving relationship with her."[4] Nonetheless, Hazel didn't stray from the daily routine Margaret charted for her, a routine that allowed for very little excitement. Occasionally, she'd catch the eye of a few young fellows and turn a few heads before reaching home. Her full-time job at Mabel Laws Horsey's Dance Studio kept her busy enough. She played for the ballet and modern classes and on occasion, switched roles from accompanist to dance student, slipping in a few dance lessons for herself. Coming out of the Lenox Avenue subway at 116th Street provided some daily thrills—"the walk from the subway entrance to our house was a joy," she remembered.[5] "Boys appeared from nowhere to walk along with me; boys who had known me all my life!"[6] But Hazel knew better than to step foot on her block in their company. "When we would arrive at my corner . . . making sure that the old lady was at her usual spot looking out the window, I would walk, alone and solemn, crossing directly in front of the house to look up at her innocently."[7] Her self-confidence was buoyed by this new attention, attention elicited from something other than playing the piano. "At fourteen," Hazel wrote, "I had suddenly become a swan."[8]

When Alma was in town, the house became "a mecca for musicians."[9] She had made many friends on the circuit, some of them among jazz music's elite. Frequent guests included two of the world's most acclaimed pianists—Fats Waller and Art Tatum.

Fats's easy laugh and ready smile was always welcome. He treated Hazel like a niece, and she would often refer to him as her uncle. Many an afternoon was spent with the two of them seated together at the piano, Hazel soaking up as much knowledge as she could, paying very close attention to his barreling left hand and the whimsical right.

The chubby kid with the lovable sobriquet had been taught by the very best stride pianists, James P. Johnson and Willie "The Lion" Smith. He'd come a long way since his days playing at uptown rent parties, after-hours jam sessions, and as the house pianist and organist at local theaters. Throughout the 1920s and 1930s, he was one of the most popular entertainers in the country, appearing regularly on the radio and recording a string of successful hits for the Victor label with "Fats Waller and His Rhythm."

Fats had studied classically but could not resist the urge to indulge in the blues-based boogie-woogie music that was all the rage in the 1930s. It wouldn't be long before Hazel would follow his lead.

Art Tatum was a relative newcomer on New York's jazz scene, having come from Toledo, Ohio, in 1932, but he had quickly made a name for himself, battling against the best pianists around in "cutting contests" where each tried to outdo the other with their skills, "cutting" into the middle of a performance and dominating it with even greater pianistic leaps. News of his phenomenal pianistic skills preceded him into every nightclub, barroom, and rent party. Tatum had a singular style. Never venturing too far from a tune's original melody, he'd put his inimitable stamp on it, adding his own unique flourish—sparkling glissandos and thrilling runs, constantly changing chord progressions. His fiercely inventive style of playing was the sound that emerging jazz pianists of the era would try to emulate.

Hazel learned her own Tatum-inspired swing at the hands of the master. The hand speed and dexterity she had developed from her classical training facilitated her quick grasp of the technical aspects of "stride." Tatum encouraged Hazel to follow her natural inclination to experiment with contrapuntal forms, creating harmony among several contrasting melodic lines. Because her musical interest was now leaning toward popular music, he advised her to concentrate on the blues; a true understanding of its structure, and the soul and feeling of the music, would give her interpretations greater color and texture.

Given Hazel's tendency to indulge in the lively, up-tempo tunes she heard on the radio and in Harlem's streets, Tatum's advice proved sound.

From the start, he and Hazel were like father and daughter, Hazel calling him "Papa Daddy."[10] It was a connection that would last throughout their lives. Alma loved him just as much, greeting him regularly with home-cooked meals and a case of Pabst beer.

Soon word began to spread that the great Art Tatum was spending a lot time at the Scotts'. Next thing they knew, fans and musicians were coming by, hoping to get a glimpse of the great pianist or, even better, to hear him play. Neighbors sometimes huddled out front or slowed their pace as they walked by the brownstone. Hazel remembered, "One afternoon the bell rang, and there was a girl about eighteen-years-old standing there. She said, 'I've heard Art Tatum is gonna be here in a little while. May I come in?' It was Carmen McRae."[11]

Lester Young and Billie Holiday, a tight-knit pair themselves, were also like family to Hazel and Alma. Both were already prominent figures on the jazz scene, well on their way to becoming icons in the jazz world.

Hazel and Alma were drawn to Lester Young's kind, easygoing nature. Hazel had fond memories of him and her mother standing in the middle of the living room floor, taking turns on the tenor sax.

At this point in his career, Lester Young (called "Pres," as in "President of the tenor sax") had played with the big bands of Fletcher Henderson, Andy Kirk, and Count Basie. Known for his remarkable solos, his improvisations would inspire generations of saxophonists to emulate his cool sound and style.

If Art Tatum was a father figure and Lester Young a favorite "uncle," then Billie Holiday was most definitely a big sister to Hazel. Alma and Billie met on the jazz circuit and had become close friends. "I would put a nickel in the local jukebox and hear Lady Day sing," Hazel said, "then come home and find her sitting in the kitchen with my mother. And they'd say, 'Get outta here! We're talking. Get away, get away.'"[12]

Billie Holiday played an active role in helping to find ways to move Hazel's career forward. In such discussions, Hazel was always a willing participant. Her exchanges with her mother often involved her pressuring Alma to take her to one audition or another. "I was the stage mother in the family," she confessed.[13] It was her custom to inform Alma of auditions she had heard about. And if Alma didn't jump on the information quickly enough she'd demand: "What are you trying to do, undermine my career?"[14]

One of Hazel's important early auditions was for the famed bandleader, composer, and lyricist Noble Sissle. Coming off the success of *Shuffle Along* and *Chocolate Dandies,* Sissle was planning a new revue that Alma hoped would include a role for Hazel.

Hazel maintained a calm countenance in the audition, rattled neither by nerves nor high expectations. She played for Sissle the same way she had been playing in church, in Harlem theaters, and at home for guests. "Mr. Sissle was waiting for us at a rehearsal studio," Hazel remembered. "Seated on a stool near the piano, with a bored expression on her face, was the most beautiful girl that I had ever seen. Her mother was there too, and I could see that there was tension in the air."[15] Hazel played piano while the other young performer sang. Sissle asked them to try different songs and suggested several changes as Hazel played. When they were done, Hazel introduced herself and discovered that the other performer, whose "breathtaking" features had her mesmerized the entire time, was Lena Horne.[16] Although the show was never mounted, the paths of these two young women would continue to cross.

After Lil Armstrong had gone back to Chicago and made it her base of operations, Alma played for a brief time with Chick Webb's band at the Savoy. She was the only female instrumentalist in the band at the time, a major accomplishment, though a little-known fact, and quite a progressive move for the bandleader.[17] But Alma wanted more control over her work situation. She had been thinking about putting together an all-women band of her own, and in the mid-1930s she did precisely that, forming Alma Long Scott's American Creolians. Although little is known about the roster of musicians whom she employed, Alma led the band on club dates throughout the United States and the Caribbean.

Meanwhile, Hazel was dying to get out from under her grandmother. "I was fourteen, and had badgered my mother into allowing me to play in her orchestra."[18] She wrote, "I told her very calmly then, 'I cannot stay home with people who aren't in the business—they want to make a little lady out of me.' I said if she didn't let me play in the orchestra I would become a juvenile delinquent. She was upset—she wanted me to play the classics—but she relented."[19] After Alma made peace with the idea, she taught Hazel to play trumpet, which she played during some of the Creolians' early gigs. Not long after, however, Alma worried that she would develop the bruised and chafed lips of a trumpet player. So Hazel settled in as the band's principal pianist.

The group worked regularly at a neighborhood tavern on Grand Street in Brooklyn. Hazel enjoyed the adult atmosphere, where people drank, smoked cigarettes, got drunk, and cussed out loud.

Things were going well for the American Creolians until one night a union delegate showed up at the club and noticed right away that Hazel was underage. Membership in the American Federation of Musicians was required for working musicians, but the minimum age to join at the time was eighteen. Consequently, Alma had to make an appearance at the Local 802 office and explain the situation to the union head. Hazel begged her mother to do whatever she could to keep her in the band, even if it meant she'd have to lie about her age. Alma convinced the officials that her daughter was a serious musician, an integral member of the band. Her argument was persuasive, and when it appeared that she did not intend to leave their office until they allowed her to add a few years to Hazel's age on the records, they finally gave in. The following afternoon Hazel was the proud possessor of a union card.

Onstage, Hazel was a ham. She created a stir during the band's rehearsals and performances—flirting with her eyes, playing suggestively, and improvising at will. The other women in the band became increasingly annoyed by all the attention the gifted ingenue was receiving. They quickly tired of her antics, complaining that she was getting "too cute" during concerts. Alma realized that her precocious daughter required a bit of humbling. With the help of a booking agent, "Feets" Edison, Alma sought out a solo opportunity for Hazel.

Around that time, the Count Basie Orchestra was appearing at the very grand and enormously popular Roseland Ballroom. Located in the center of the Broadway district, Roseland called itself "America's Foremost Ballroom," where Fletcher Henderson and his orchestra held fort, where dancers could cut loose on the quarter-acre dance floor, and out-of-town bands from Kansas City or Chicago could cut their teeth. "Every musician within a radius of two-hundred miles made it to Roseland to hear William Basie and the fantastic sounds of that orchestra," Hazel remembered.[20]

Booking Hazel as a solo act at Roseland gave Alma the excuse she needed to kick her daughter out of the American Creolians. The Roseland booking undoubtedly took some doing, considering that Hazel Scott's name was mostly known only in Harlem. It was to be her baptism of fire and one of the critical turning points in her young career. She would be appearing on the same bill as the Count Basie Orchestra.

"There I stood in the wings . . . staring round-eyed at the beautiful young men out on that stage playing incredible jazz and began to shake. My teeth all but chattered and I was ready to call it a life right then and there!" she remembered.

"Do you really expect me to follow THIS?" Hazel asked her mother. "She smiled, patted my hands, warmed them between hers and began to adjust my white lace dress."[21]

The Basie band swung into "One O'Clock Jump." Herschel Evans went into his solo, and "the crowd surged toward the bandstand."[22] Hazel distinctly remembered that "young Bill Basie, smooth, sharp and relaxed," looked in her direction and gave her a wink. When the song was over, he set the microphones in place for her.

Terrified, the fifteen year old stumbled onto the stage after some friendly nudging from Lester Young and drummer Jo Jones, who were on hand to offer moral support.[23] Nerves aside, Hazel knew that everything in her musical life, from her formal training at Juilliard to her informal education at the side of her mother, Fats Waller, and Art Tatum, had prepared her for this occasion.

Hazel's memories of that auspicious night, as noted in her personal journals, reveal that she gave a solid performance and won over the audience with upbeat boogie-woogie numbers. More importantly, she confessed to gaining an even greater appreciation for her musical gift. She wrote, "The desire to reach an audience, to communicate a beauty that has been entrusted to your care, should not fill you with dread."[24] Humbled by the extraordinary opportunity she'd been given, the teenager adopted a more mature view of her career, vowing to always approach the stage and her performance with deference.

While Hazel's career began to flourish, her father was dying in a Long Island hospital. Just twelve years after settling in the United States, R. Thomas Scott passed away. Losing him wasn't a new feeling; Hazel felt she had lost her father long before. Referring to him by his name only—not "Father" or "Dad"—she wrote matter-of-factly:

> When I was fifteen, Tommy Scott had quietly expired after a long miserable illness. During the years that he held on to a drab thread that was all that remained of the colorful tapestry of his life, Alma faithfully made the long journey to the hospital far out on the island.
>
> At the end he barely knew her and scarcely realized what his surroundings were. He would prattle on in one of the Chinese dialects he had picked up.[25]

Hazel remained respectfully ambiguous about her father for the rest of her life. As her popularity grew as a musician, press reports filled in the biographical gaps as it related to Thomas Scott. Stories were embellished and many presumptions made. Some allusions were made as to his desire to teach at a traditionally all-black university in the South; it is unclear whether or not that dream ever materialized. One reference in *Collier's* claimed that Thomas Scott had witnessed a black man's lynching in the South and "came home for Christmas a beaten man."[26] Others falsely concluded that he was a doting father and husband who supported his family until his dying day and only after his death was Alma forced to go out and get work as a musician. They also assumed that her father's death was a tremendous loss to the family. In the press, Hazel would make comments such as "My father was a scholar. He was very quiet and withdrawn. He was a very defeated man by life."[27] She would typically add that he never liked her being in show business. "He took me to see *The Merchant of Venice* because he wanted me to be a lawyer. And I came out and announced that I was gonna be an actress. I saw the expression on his face. He hated the thought of my being involved with anything to do with performing, showing yourself to the public."[28]

After his death in 1935, Hazel rarely mentioned his name.

Alma was always very private about her relationships with men. Aside from Thomas Scott, Hazel mentioned only one man whom she remembered Alma spending time with—"Eddie the marvel, who made everyone adore him within minutes."[29] She remembered the soft-spoken minister as an extremely nice man whose courtship of her mother was short but intense. Eddie passed away not long after they began dating. Alma never remarried.

After just one year, the American Creolians disbanded for a variety of reasons, mostly financial. The lack of a steady flow of bookings made it difficult to stay on the road. As was the case in many of the all-women orchestras, changes in the women's personal lives inevitably led to constant personnel changes, as band members left to get married and start families or to pursue more stable careers. Now that Hazel was maturing, her mother placed greater demands on her to contribute to the household income. Alma had always made it clear that playing piano was a profession not a pastime or form of refinement. That kind of luxury they simply could not afford.

All around them the frustration and despair of unemployed neighbors, half-starved children, the sick, and the poor spilled out into the streets. Tensions ran so high in Harlem that it took little or nothing to incite violence. On March 19, 1935, a riot broke out as a rumor spread that a Puerto Rican youth had been caught stealing a pocketknife at the Kresge's store on 125th Street and had subsequently been taken to the basement and beaten to death by store employees. Within hours, stores in the area were looted and set afire, dozens of arrests were made, and one innocent teenager seen running away from the commotion was indiscriminately shot by police. By the time the child who was supposedly beaten to death appeared in public to refute the story, the riot had taken on a life of its own. In the *Nation*, Oswald Garrison Villard made a prescient observation: "The nerves of a considerable portion of a community of 200,000 people snapped because of five and a half years of depression, with an unemployment average of no less than 70 per cent in certain areas, because of economic and social discrimination and prejudice."[30]

Danger in the streets made Alma more wary about Hazel's safety. She kept close tabs on her daughter's whereabouts. She rallied an entire crew of people to watch out for Hazel, particularly on nights when she was working at a nightclub. Her manager was instructed to keep grown men at bay. If anyone got too close, he'd shout, "Leave this girl alone, she's a virgin!"[31] Hazel was insulated by Alma's friends, including Billie Holiday, who was given the job of looking after her whenever Alma wasn't available.

Vividly, Hazel remembered being fifteen and playing one night with a swing band on 57th Street. At the end of the night, she was hanging out with the other musicians outside the club doors. One of the guys asked her how old she was; she told him she was eighteen. "Then I heard a scream that was absolutely primeval. A roar came out of the shadows where Lady Day was crouching—*'You lying little heifer!'* I took off and Lady took off after me, with one shoe in her hand. She chased me down the street, through the cars, and into the subway."[32] Hazel finally stopped and begged Billie's forgiveness. " 'You're not going to tell my mother are you?' I asked. 'Tell her?' said Lady. 'I'm going to sit there and watch her knock you down!' "[33]

Ken and Juanita Harrison were also part of the team Alma assembled to help guide and protect her daughter. Hazel adored Juanita. She was close to her age but had married young and already had two children. Her husband Ken dabbled in show business and was always on the lookout for new talent. After hearing about a piano competition whose top prize was a radio show on WOR, he sought out Hazel. "Ken Harrison could smell an audition better than a pointer could smell a quail!" she wrote.[34]

Ken nervously escorted Hazel to the audition, giving her all kinds of advice on what to play, how to play it, and how to behave toward the auditioners. When they reached 42nd Street and Broadway, Hazel told him firmly, "Ken! Kindly do not tell me how to conduct business! We will go to the audition and I will play and sing, as I have been doing for eleven years!"[35]

Hazel auditioned, played several ballads, and walked out with the job, beating out hundreds of hopefuls.

At WOR, Hazel was given a six-month contract along with the freedom to select her own program. She played the classics, announcing each piece before she began. Hazel specifically chose pieces that demonstrated her hand speed and mastery of complex compositions. In order to capitalize on the success of the radio show, Hazel and Alma decided to release her manager from his duties. They realized that "Feets" Edison didn't have what it took to move Hazel's career forward. "Good ole Feets. A decent man, but he wasn't big time. . . . Feets couldn't really get me off the ground."[36]

For the next few years, they relied on their own resources. Hazel posed for one of her first professional publicity photos with the distinguished Harlem photographer James Van Der Zee. She continued performing for uptown crowds in afternoon recitals as well as in some of Harlem's nightclubs.[37]

In September of 1938, Hazel was cast in the Broadway musical revue *Sing Out the News* at the Music Box Theatre. The producer was Max Gordon, a Broadway hit maker who'd already had box office success with dozens of shows, including Clare Boothe's *The Women*, *Ethan Frome*, *The Jazz Singer*, and the musical comedy *Jubilee*, which made Cole Porter's "Just One of Those Things" and "Begin the Beguine" standards in the American songbook, and introduced audiences to a fifteen-year-old future matinee idol Montgomery Clift. With music and lyrics by Harold Rome, *Sing Out the News* featured Hazel in the chorus, singing "Franklin D. Roosevelt Jones," which told the story of a black child born in "New Deal" America and the high hopes his family held for his future.

When he walks down the street
Folks will say "Pleased to meet,
Mr. Franklin D. Roosevelt Jones."
What a smile, and how he shows it.
He'll be happy all day long, what a name,
I'll bet he knows it.
With that handle, how can he go wrong?[38]

Onstage, Hazel's lively rendition of the tune stood out, grabbing the critics' attention and garnering her good notices. The show's producers increased her salary from sixty-five to one hundred dollars a week.

She followed up her Broadway debut with a part-time gig at the

Yacht Club on 52nd Street. As the intermission pianist for the popular lounge singer Frances Faye, Hazel was "low man on the totem pole."[39] She may have considered it a thankless job, but the experience marked a major shift in her playing.

It was Frances Faye's custom to have her dinner during the intermission, and she would eat among the crowd, not in her dressing room, so she could sit in on Hazel's performance. "Whenever I'd start something that got the audience's attention—one of the popular tunes of the day—she'd send the busboy over. He'd say, 'You can't do that number. Miss Faye does it in the show.' Finally, one day, I had had enough. I said, 'I know, I'll play the Bach Inventions and I'll syncopate them, really up, up tempo, and see if she does THAT in her show!'"[40] This style of syncopating classical music required a command of the classics, an understanding of swing, and the ability to invent jazz riffs spontaneously. Said fellow pianist Dick Hyman, "Jazzing the classics was not a new practice, nor have we stopped doing it. This kind of treatment has been fairly common since ragtime days."[41] The celebrated pianist and radio host Marian McPartland commented, "The very first time I heard it, I thought it was a very hip thing to do. Later on, I changed my mind, and thought that it was really a show business kind of thing. But I wouldn't put it down. When I was a teenager, whenever I heard it, I thought it was pretty fantastic. It was very impressive."[42] Dr. Matthew Kennedy, a classical pianist who also trained at Juilliard in the late 1930s and later became the longtime director of the acclaimed Fisk Jubilee Singers, concurred: "It involved a lot of interpretation. And a special feel for it, a very special talent, which Hazel Scott had."[43]

But the very idea of bastardizing classical music was appalling to Alma. The Inventions, Bach's collection of short pieces, were written to fine-tune young pianists' technical agility and enhance their understanding of composition. They were to be treated with reverence not impertinence. Hazel argued that she was fulfilling that intention wholeheartedly and clearly understood the pieces well enough to take them to a boogie-woogie extreme. "My mother hated it. She was a purist—liked her jazz straight and her classics straight. She'd just shake her head," Hazel mused. When Alma reprimanded her about her blatant improvisations at the Yacht Club, Hazel insisted, "This is self-defense, believe me when I tell you."

Art Tatum liked what he heard in Hazel's playing. In his estimation, she now had a well-seasonsed sound and her style was very polished. He gave her the ultimate nod of approval when he asked her to take over his post at the Famous Door on 52nd Street in March of 1938. She wrote, "Papadaddy" was very kind. He was more than kind. He was *devastating*."[44] At eighteen, Hazel was playing between sets of the Louis Prima Band.

Tatum was also generous enough to teach Hazel his rendition of Vincent Youmans's "Tea for Two." It was an extraordinary interpretation of the song. In Maurice Waller's biography of his father, he described Tatum's approach, how he started out by making slight alterations to the melodic line. His real innovation, however, began as "Tatum's left hand worked a strong, regular beat while his right hand played dazzling arpeggios in chords loaded with flatted fifths and ninths. Both his hands then raced toward each other in skips and runs that seemed impossible to master. Then they crossed each other. Tatum played the main theme again and soared to an exciting climax."[45] This was the challenging arrangement Hazel had learned. She would perform the tune not only during her Famous Door engagement but throughout her career.

That same year, Ken Harrison organized the Hazel Scott Band (also promoted as Fourteen Men and a Girl), and they played the State Palace Ballroom in Harlem to solid reviews. The band's personnel included Gus McClung, Bernard Flood, and Edward Anderson on trumpet; John Horton, Faunley Jordan, and Needon Hurd on trombone; Roger Boyd, Alvin Moss, Raymond Hills, and Eric Miller on saxophone; Andrew Jackson on guitar; Larry Hinton on drums; Selwyn Warner on bass; and Eddie White on piano. Hazel was billed as "the glamorous darling of Harlem." According to the small blurbs that appeared in the local press, it was during these engagements that Hazel began incorporating vocals into the act, as well as one of her early boogie-woogie compositions, "A Swingy Serenade."

The press was intrigued. The headline in one local paper read: "New Fem Batoneer, Only 18, Sings Pop Tunes Seven Ways!" Reporters wanted to know her background, her hobbies, and how she spent her time off the jazz circuit. One of them wrote, "She plays fair trumpet, writes short stories, does noteworthy etchings and designs her own hats, taking time out occasionally to read papers printed in Yiddish, French, Italian, Spanish, German, Chinese and English."[46]

The Hazel Scott Band was short-lived, however. A feature article in *Collier's* reported, "Hazel was too girlish to give her band the thought and time it required. She preferred roller skating and polishing her nails." She told her fellow band members, "You're all wonderful characters and I'm awful. I'm spoiled, irresponsible, selfish—unworthy to have a band of my own. Therefore, you're all fired."[47]

Her lack of interest could have easily been a result of working so hard for so long. Her schedule was grueling. She spent her nights playing in nightclubs; then she would wake up early for school in the morning. Dragging into Wadleigh High, four blocks from her house on West 114th Street, she'd arrive with her lessons incomplete and half faded from memory. When she got home from school in the afternoon, she'd sleep for a few hours and then prepare for work later that night.

In spite of everything, Hazel graduated from high school on time and with honors. Her Juilliard training ended soon after when Professor Wagner became too ill to continue teaching.

Hazel admitted candidly, "All these things exacted a frightful toll. . . . There were times when I thought that I just couldn't go on."[48]

She had seen a lot, accomplished plenty, and experienced more at eighteen than those twice her age. She had grown up in an adult music world where she played for pay. It wouldn't be long before Hazel became the family breadwinner, her youth devoured by adult responsibilities and the demands of a great talent.

CHAPTER SIX

Hazel's Boogie-Woogie

With its leftist political leanings and integrated club policy, which applied to both performers and patrons, Café Society was a truly novel idea. The venue opened in the winter of 1938, proclaiming itself "the wrong place for the Right people." Starting with its name, a cunning play on the label usually given to the fashionable elite, Café Society parodied upscale Manhattan nightspots and their clientele. Satirical murals were painted on the walls, and the waitstaff dressed casually; there was no special guest list, no color bar, and no preferential treatment. Decidedly unpretentious, the club was a natural haven for artists, poets, writers, and actors. Small but hip, it had a short bar and cocktail tables for two in the middle of the floor. Amid the haze of cigarette smoke, the jazz, comedy, and cocktails, there sat Paul Robeson and Langston Hughes, Leonard Bernstein and Nelson Rockefeller, Lillian Hellman and Eleanor Roosevelt engrossed in lively conversations on art and politics that went deep into the night. Everyone felt that what was happening at Café Society, though long overdue, was still ahead of its time.

Barney Josephson, the club's owner, was in his mid-thirties when he decided to enter the nightclub business. The son of Latvian Jewish immigrants, Josephson was the youngest of six children. His father, a cobbler, died when he was two years old; his mother worked as a seamstress in a ladies' tailoring shop. The Josephsons were a close-knit clan, raised to be enterprising, liberal-minded and hard-working. Two of his brothers, Leon and Louis, became lawyers, and one owned a shoe store, where Barney Josephson worked after graduating from Trenton High School in New Jersey. On his nights off, he would make frequent trips to Harlem to hear the jazz music he loved. After seeing Duke Ellington and other great acts at the Cotton Club, he was shocked to find that black patrons were refused entry and black performers were forced to use the back entrance. Such barefaced bigotry infuriated him. It was this kind of experience that prompted him to do what had never been done in New York.

Josephson had been intrigued by the idea of a political cabaret since visiting similar clubs in Prague and Berlin. But he knew nothing about running a nightclub. He solicited the help of his brother Leon, who helped him raise the six thousand dollars needed to secure a location in Greenwich Village. Helen Lawrenson, a journalist, was called in to assist with promotion and marketing. "It was our first political nightclub," Lawrenson wrote.[1] "From the beginning, it was completely integrated: black and white performers, black and white patrons. This had never happened before, outside of a few Harlem places where whites got the best tables. Not at Café Society they didn't!"[2] In her book, *Whistling Girl,* she credits herself with coming up with the club's clever name and slogan. "I helped to start it," she wrote. "I gave it its name; I did all the early publicity and wrote the advertisements; I auditioned a few of the performers; and for the first months I acted as an unofficial hostess, sort of a B-girl de luxe."[3]

Josephson told the artists hired to paint the mural, "You guys paint anything you want."[4] He promised to pay each of them $125 and a due bill for another $125 so they could come in and eat and drink whenever they wanted. The artists, a collective of painters, cartoonists, and muralists from the government's Works Project Administration—Anton Refregier, John Groth, Adolph Dehn, Ad Reinhardt, Syd Hoff, Sam Berman, Abe Birnbaum, Peggy Bacon, and William Gropper—created mocking caricatures of "café society" types in upscale social settings.

John Hammond was in charge of the music. A highly successful record producer, music critic, and talent scout, Hammond was credited with having discovered Billie Holiday and Bessie Smith and bringing a number of jazz orchestras to the forefront, including the big bands of Count Basie and Benny Goodman. When he joined the team of Café Society devotees, his impeccable taste in artists became the club's most valuable asset. A Yale dropout and heir to the Vanderbilt family fortune, Hammond forfeited Park Avenue privilege to become purveyor of all things jazz and blues. He used his own money to fund artists in recording and promotional ventures. For Café Society, he worked gratis. He took on the job with his usual enthusiasm, scouring the country to find talented musicians and vocalists to fill the club's roster.

"Hammond was mad about Negro music: blues and boogie-woogie," Lawrenson remembered, "not Uncle Tom spirituals or furrowed-brow intellectual jazz, but the black gutbucket music from the whorehouses, honky-tonks and gin mills of New Orleans, Chicago, Kansas City."[5] He found blues singer Ida Cox in a burlesque house in Jersey City. Blues shouter Joe Turner and pianist Pete Johnson ditched their Kansas City digs for the big city, and one of the best piano-playing duos of the period, Albert Ammons (the father of jazz saxophonist Gene Ammons) and Meade Lux Lewis, left their respective taxi-driving and car-washing jobs in Chicago to join Hammond in New York.

Shortly before Café Society's opening, Hammond produced a historic concert event at Carnegie Hall, tracing the musical roots of black music. "An Evening of Negro Music: From Spirituals to Swing" was dedicated to the memory of Bessie Smith, who had died a year before. As a board member of the National Association for the Advancement of Colored People (NAACP), Hammond approached them first to underwrite the concert, but the organization's conservative leadership declined. It took time to find a sponsor as black music, at the time, was generally considered appropriate for nightclubs and ballrooms not the concert stage. Ultimately, Hammond was able to convince *New Masses,* a prominent Marxist magazine, to provide full financial support.

The eight-part program began with spirituals and hymns sung by

Mitchell's Christian Singers and Sister Rosetta Tharpe followed by a "Soft Swing" segment featuring the Kansas City Six with Lester Young, Buck Clayton, Jo Jones, Freddie Greene, Walter Page, and Eddie Durham. "Harmonica Playing" introduced Sanford "Sonny" Terry, a blind musician from North Carolina, while the "Blues" were left to pianists James P. Johnson and Pete Johnson, blues shouter Joe Turner, Ida Cox, and blues singer and guitarist Big Bill Broonzy. Other vocal numbers were performed by Helen Humes and Jimmy Rushing. "Boogie-Woogie Piano Playing," featuring Albert Ammons and Meade Lux Lewis, was such a hit that their performance is credited as the official beginning of the boogie-woogie craze in America. Sidney Bechet's clarinet and saxophone represented "Early New Orleans Jazz," and "Swing" was swung courtesy of Count Basie and his orchestra.

From Spirituals to Swing was the first concert of its kind, one in which the music of black Americans was presented in a formal setting in a major concert hall before an all-white audience. It was a statement of cultural, social, and political import that presupposed the music's relevance in the American mainstream. The concert was such a monumental success that Carnegie Hall decided to host it a second time the following year. Many performers on the bill gained more exposure that night than they had received in their entire careers. Café Society was on the receiving end of their success, as most of the performers were offered regular engagements at the club.

With the comedian Jack Gilford as emcee, Café Society opened its doors, on New Year's Eve 1938, to the sound of Frankie Newton's six-man band, Teddy Wilson's sparkling piano, and the hauntingly gorgeous vocals of Billie Holiday. Now a star in the jazz world, having toured with Artie Shaw and Count Basie, Billie Holiday's name alone gave Café Society a certain cachet. Opening night it wasn't only her presence that would set the tone for the club but her performance of the one song that was sure to create a stir.

"Strange Fruit," whose lyrics depict in vivid detail the brutal lynching of a black man in the South, was one of the first protest songs with an antilynching motif. It originated as a poem written by

HATZEL'S BOOGIE-WOOGIE

Abel Meeropol, a schoolteacher, poet, and closet communist from the Bronx. Written under the pen name Lewis Allan, once set to music the song was sung around town by various people in small settings. But it was Barney Josephson who introduced the tune to Billie Holiday. Her rendition was so powerful that people assumed Meeropol had written the song just for her; others believed it was her own original composition.

The staging of Billie's performance was intentionally dramatic. When she sang the song, Josephson insisted that no food or drinks be served. Nothing was to distract from the impact of the performance. In dimmed light, with only a spotlight on her face, Billie sang:

Southern trees bear a strange fruit,
Blood on their leaves, blood at the root,
Black body swinging in the Southern breeze,
Strange fruit hanging from the poplar trees.[6]

Perfectly still, arms akimbo, eyes closed. The lyrics shocking everyone into silence. Tears would occasionally stream down Billie's face. "The tears would come and knock everybody in that house out," Josephson remembered.[7] Her delivery added to the drama, her voice was the embodiment of rage and sorrow.

At the end of the song, Billie made a graceful exit without as much as a bow (per Josephson's instructions). "Strange Fruit" was saved as the last song of the evening, after which audiences would file out of the club, stunned.

Reactions to Billie Holiday singing the politically charged song were variously supportive and disparaging. Some felt it gave the singer greater depth as an artist while others believed she was taking significant risks with her career. John Hammond, in particular, was against it. He considered the song "artistically the worst thing that ever happened" to her.[8] He feared that Holiday's raw talent would somehow be defiled, becoming too polished, too sophisticated. "I think she began taking herself seriously, and thinking of herself as very important. . . . As soon as pop artists think they are contributing to art, something happens to their art," Hammond stated bluntly.[9] He also believed that aligning herself with left-wing intellectuals would do irreparable damage to her career. It was no secret that some of the artists and investors of Café Society had strong communist ties. Leon Josephson, in fact, was an avowed member of the Communist Party.

"What everybody doesn't know is that the club was founded to raise money for the Communist Party," Helen Lawrenson admitted. Her participation in the club, she claimed, was solicited by Earl Browder, then head of the American Communist Party.[10]

Still, Billie Holiday's nightly shows were a tremendous push for Café Society. Hearing her sing "Strange Fruit" was the new hot ticket in town. "Jazz and politics were what it was all about," Lawrenson recalled. "Some people hated it; others were all agog. It was the most exciting spot in town and the proving ground for more remarkable talent than possibly any similar place before or since."[11] Although it was a well-known fact that Josephson didn't pay much, what an artist could gain in exposure made Café Society a favorite performance venue among musicians and vocalists. It was where comedians Jack Gilford, Zero Mostel, and Imogene Coca perfected their routines and Lena Horne, Josh White, Georgia Gibbs, Mary Lou Williams, "Hot Lips" Page, and Teddy Wilson all became recognizable talents.

Throughout her career, Hazel would credit Billie Holiday for her breakout success at Café Society. It was Billie who got her the gig by introducing her to Josephson, and demanding that he hear her play. When Billie left her scheduled engagement three weeks early, she insisted that only Hazel replace her. All of this maneuvering, Hazel believed, was Billie's way of crafting a future for her young protégée. Billie knew firsthand what kind of publicity Hazel would receive at the popular nightspot. She also knew that Hazel was the kind of performer Café Society audiences would appreciate.

Hazel's popularity at the club grew so rapidly that it wasn't long before she became its premier headliner. Josephson, impressed by her overall package—her undeniable skills as a pianist and vocalist, her glamorous image, and her ability to work a crowd—saw in

Hazel a huge business opportunity. Her swinging the classics drew steady crowds, but it was her stage presence and sensual delivery that made Hazel a marketable commodity. *Time* magazine called her the "Hot Classicist," reporting, "But where others murder the classics, Hazel Scott merely commits arson. Classicists who wince at the idea of jiving Tchaikovsky feel no pain whatever as they watch her do it. . . . Strange notes and rhythms creep in, the melody is tortured with hints of boogie-woogie, until finally, happily, Hazel Scott surrenders to her worse nature and beats the keyboard into a rack of bones."[12]

Aside from the big career boost the gig offered, it also provided Hazel with the social outlet she so desperately wanted. At work, she could commingle in the late night hours with other musicians and sign autographs for fans. Particularly on Sunday nights, considered *the* night at the downtown hotspot, jazz musicians and thespians, celebrities and savants about town would converge upon the club for late night laughs, good music, and fun.

She developed a devoted following of prominent artists and dignitaries—Paul Robeson, Duke Ellington, and Eleanor Roosevelt, among others. Hazel remembered, "When I was nineteen years old, I stood on tiptoe to kiss Paul Robeson's chin. It was a moment that I shall always cherish. His laughter rang out with the richness of a huge bell. Here was all this magnificence, all the legendary greatness, and he was so dear, so approachable!"[13]

Living above the club in an apartment on the top floor was British jazz critic and record producer, Leonard Feather. After seeing Hazel's show, Feather became an instant fan and offered his immediate support. "I first saw her there and arranged to produce her first record session," he said.[14] He organized a pickup band of three English musicians from the London-based Bert Ambrose band, Danny Polo (clarinet), Pete Barry (bass), and Albert Harris (guitar), and three musicians of West Indian descent, with Pete Brown on alto sax and trumpet, Arthur Herbert from Coleman Hawkins's band on drums, and Hazel on piano and vocals. Called the Sextet of Rhythm Club of London, the group recorded four sides, all composed by Leonard Feather, for the Bluebird label.

On the up-tempo boogie-woogie numbers, "Why Didn't William Tell?" and "Calling All Bars," which she opens with a rhythmic cadenza before introducing the brass Hazel demonstrates her great dexterity. She plays the unison melody, employing sequencing between solo improvisations. For the first time on record, Hazel's vocals are featured on "You Gave Me the Go By" and "Mighty Like the Blues." She meticulously balances her vocal phrasing with the piano, never attacking a note but subtly leaning into it. Hazel's mature rendering of the blues belies her youth as she sings:

> I was full of the joy of spring
> Now I've lost my faith in everything
> Can't believe he's gone
> But still I'm gonna spread the news
> I'm through with love forever
> 'Cause it's mighty like the blues.[15]

This early recording helped Hazel attain a legitimate place in the jazz world, exposing her to a wider audience as well as bringing her to the attention of other well-known musicians. The legendary saxophonist Coleman Hawkins, known for his forward thinking and willingness to adapt to the changing sounds of jazz, was impressed with Hazel's technique. After leaving Fletcher Henderson's orchestra, Hawkins spent five years performing throughout Europe. When he returned to the States in 1939, he organized a big band that played the Golden Gate Ballroom, the Apollo, and the Savoy among other venues across the country. Around this time, he hired Hazel to write arrangements for the new band. It was a newsworthy acquisition. "Newest star to sign with Coleman Hawkins is lovely Hazel Scott, pianist and singer, whose work around New York has been attracting much attention of late," a local newspaper announced.[16] Although few details are known about her collaboration with Hawkins, working alongside one of jazz music's greatest innovators had to have been an essential part of Hazel's growth as a musician, not to mention an indication of the level of respect her talent now garnered.

Opportunities like these came about through the persistence and hard work of Leonard Feather. Acting as her publicist and producer, he pushed to get major news outlets interested in her, a job he found constantly challenging. Hazel's obvious talent and popularity did little to change editors' minds about featuring a black woman inside their pages much less on their covers. When she had performed at the World's Fair of 1939 earlier in the year, her sold-out shows received only marginal notice. Like most black performers of the period, Hazel's early publicity came from the black press, including the *Amsterdam News,* the *Chicago Defender,* and the *Pittsburgh Courier;* in later years, magazines such as *Ebony* and *JET* would be an invaluable source of national exposure for black entertainers. Still, Feather remained steadfast. Like Barney Josephson, he was convinced of Hazel's star potential. He believed it was just a matter of time before her Café Society appearances would bring her the national recognition she deserved. "No other club could have provided as suitable a springboard for the career of a Hazel Scott," Feather would write years later in the *Los Angeles Times.* "She suffered no indignity there."[17] Indeed, in just a few short years Hazel Scott would become one of most popular American artists of her generation.

With packed houses every night, no one would have believed that Café Society was losing money. Josephson blamed it on the location. A more upscale locale would bring in a wealthier clientele; cocktails and cover charges could increase. He considered closing the downtown club, but his press agent, Ivan Black, convinced him otherwise. Instead they used the news of a second club to promote the first, running advertisements that claimed the expansion was necessary to take care of the overflow of patrons who were breaking down their doors downtown. Café Society Uptown opened in October of 1940, two years after the first club. It was located on Manhattan's East Side at 128 East 58th Street near Park Avenue. As Josephson and Black had hoped, people flocked to both clubs to see what all the hoopla was about. Within three months, Café Society was in the black.

Hazel was swept up in the storm of publicity as well, with Josephson giving her top billing at the uptown location. And, while avid fans romanticized the notion that the new club must have been built especially for her, it was here that Hazel became a star.

Although the ambience of the new club was more luxurious, the idea remained the same. Anton Refregier painted another mural on the two-story walls, slightly less satirical and in softer hues. John Hammond, once again, supplied the musical acts. Opening night was an extravagant affair, featuring some of the very best musicians in the business. The Boogie-Woogie Boys—Ammons and Lewis—ripped away on two pianos, Teddy Wilson's orchestra played, and "sultry, curvesome, Trinidad-born Hazel Scott . . . played Bach and Liszt on the piano, first straight, then hot," wrote *Time*, "as the authentic afflatus descended upon Café Society."[18]

The evening's entertainment also included a surprise performance by the world famous bandleader Benny Goodman, who'd been standing at the back of the club unnoticed. He walked up to the bandstand unexpectedly, clarinet in hand, and started blowing "Somebody Stole My Gal."

It was a successful opening for Barney Josephson and a great showcase for Hazel. The clientele was more upscale, but its affection for Hazel's talent equaled, if not surpassed, that of the bohemian downtown crowd. She received even more exposure, garnering offers from concert halls all over the country, glowing reviews from music critics, and favorable notices in the national press. Hazel was, as Luther Davis wrote in *Collier's*, "the unquestioned princess" of Café Society Uptown, among a crowd that he depicted as "representatives of Hollywood's greats, the Social Register's city dwellers, and Dun & Bradstreets more frivolous tycoons."[19]

At the downtown club, other outstanding female talents replaced Hazel, most notably Mary Lou Williams and Lena Horne.

Born in Brooklyn in 1917, Lena Horne had performed as a Cotton Club dancer, as a singer on Broadway in Lew Leslie's *Blackbirds of 1939,* and as the female lead in an obscure film, *The Duke Is Tops,* opposite the Apollo Theater's emcee, Ralph Cooper. She'd sung in nightclubs all over New York and toured with the Charlie Barnet Orchestra. Even with her years in the business, she had never experienced anything quite like Café Society.

> I kept expecting something violent to happen when I came out to sing and saw one or two Negroes at a table of white guests or several tables of Negro guests threaded throughout the audience. But there was never an explosion. The waiters never refused to serve anyone, and no guests ever shoved back their chairs and stormed out, as Barnet's boys had done with me. Instead, the guests not only remained for dinner and the show, but, white and Negro, they invited the performers to join them at their tables.[20]

By the time Mary Lou Williams debuted at Café Society, she was already considered the doyenne of jazz, the most accomplished female instrumentalist on the scene. Like Hazel, at three or four years old, she climbed onto the bench next to her mother who was playing a tune on a small pump organ. She repeated the melody easily after hearing it, and from then on, great attention was paid to cultivate her natural gift. Born Mary Elfrieda Scruggs in Atlanta, Georgia and raised in Pittsburgh by her musician mother, Mary Lou was playing professionally at eight years old. As "the little piano girl of East Liberty," Mary Lou performed around town until joining the vaudeville circuit at age 13 as the pianist in Buzzin' Harris and His Hits and Bits. She eventually married the band's saxophonist, Johnny Williams and joined his small ensemble, The Syncopators. She followed him to Kansas City, making a name for herself in Andy Kirk's Twelve Clouds of Joy. She was a key component of the band's success, writing original compositions and arrangements that led to the group's recording of over 109 sides, including "Walkin' and Swingin," "Scratchin' the Gravel," and "The Lady Who Swings the Band." Mary Lou was approached by many of the top bandleaders in the country for her arranging skills. She wrote "What's Your Story Morning Glory?" for Jimmy Lunceford; "Roll'Em" and "Camel Hop" for Benny Goodman; and for Duke Ellington, she wrote the hit tune "Trumpets No End" (adapted from the Irving Berlin tune "Blue

Skies"). "Mary Lou . . . is the only person who can still play boogie-woogie and make boogie-weary ears perk up in attention and flap with pleasure," Bill Gottlieb wrote in the *Washington Post*.[21]

Accustomed to the interaction of a bandstand full of musicians, Mary Lou found that playing with only a bassist and a drummer took some getting used to. She confessed, "After being with a big band, I felt so alone."[22] But as the weeks progressed she grew to appreciate the stability of a nightclub engagement, stating, "Being in one place was quite to my liking."[23]

Meanwhile at Café Society Uptown, Hazel was making more money than she'd ever made before. Not exactly known for his generosity when it came to salaries, Josephson raised Hazel's pay from several hundred to fifteen hundred dollars per week.

In these more upscale surroundings, Hazel's "mommy-made" gowns with the puffed sleeves and satin sashes were tossed aside. Now she wore elegant, formfitting gowns from New York's finest shops. Her act was finely tuned—the music, her performance, her look. She wore diamonds and strapless gowns. Depending on where a guest was seated, she may have looked nude behind the grand piano. So appealing was her overall package that the press often focused more on how Hazel looked than what she played. About the strapless gowns, she said, "They thought it was a style, but I needed the arm freedom and it was convenient."[24]

Josephson made sure that all of Hazel's personal needs were met. "I had a dressing room big as an apartment," she said. When her good friend the vocalist Mildred Bailey appeared at the uptown club, Hazel insisted that she share it with her. Hazel recalled with pleasure Bailey's way of sizing up the audience: "Mildred would come backstage, and I would ask, 'How's the crowd?' She would answer, 'The assassins are out there tonight.' If it was an especially awful audience, she would say, 'They brought knives.' Or 'They brought hatchets, or axes.' Only if the crowd was very quiet and loved ballads did Mildred think they were a good audience."[25]

In this sophisticated world of jazz and Manhattan nightlife, Hazel, mature well beyond her nineteen years, projected a veteran's air, assured of her place among the best New York had to offer. The work ethic instilled in her by Alma kept her grounded. It also gave her a growing reputation as a no-nonsense performer. Her girlhood insecurities were now gone. Her carriage was regal. Her manner of speech was up front and uncompromising. It was easy, at first glance, to mistake Hazel's bristling self-confidence for haughtiness, which some whispered was due to her West Indian heritage. Helen Lawrenson tells the story of once bumping into Hazel in the ladies' room and asking her about an after-hours spot where she and a friend could commingle with some black male musicians; Hazel snapped, "I don't know any places like that in Harlem. I live with my mother and I never go out."[26] "She snubbed me," Lawrenson said.[27]

Despite her detractors, Hazel poured everything she had into her performance. She gave herself over to her audience and she expected the same in return. The level of intensity she brought to her performances was palpable. The exchange between performer and spectator was especially important to Hazel; it was what fueled her onstage. "But the bright-eyed jubilance with which she performed could freeze in an instant," Leonard Feather remembered. "Nobody who ever saw her will forget her habit of stopping suddenly, transfixing any noisemaker with an icy glare and waiting for total silence before she resumed. Some thought her arrogant; others knew that she simply demanded respect."[28]

In 1940, Alma and Margaret sold their brownstone on West 118th Street and moved into a swank new apartment on 92 St. Nicholas Avenue near 115th Street, with large rooms and a nice view. Alma gave piano lessons in their new place to the handful of well-to-do families that hadn't been knocked down by the Depression and could still afford lessons for their children. Hazel brought in the lion's share of the household funds, although she preferred not to deal with money matters. She turned her pay over to Alma and rarely had a dime in her possession.

Away from the nightclub, she reverted to her girlish ways. She wore ankle socks and oxford loafers around the house, long skirts, cardigan sweaters, and no makeup. She rarely did her own shopping. She left that to her mother as well. When Alma would return with new dresses and gowns for her club act, it was always a surprise, "like getting gifts on Christmas," she'd say.

Hazel's popularity in Manhattan nightclubs could only be rivaled by her popularity at home in Harlem. Neighbors were proud to say they lived near the Scotts. She had taken to sewing and designing her own clothes; mostly brightly colored pantsuits that she would wear on casual occasions. She could be seen in them often, walking up and down Harlem's sprawling avenues running errands with her mother or on Sunday mornings on their way to church. She began calling them her "Hi, Hazel!" outfits, because whenever she wore them she was immediately recognized. Harlem residents considered her one of their own. She returned the favor by appearing in popular uptown clubs where local residents could hear her play.

Hazel recorded her first solo album for the Decca label in December of 1940. *Swinging the Classics: Piano Solos in Swing Style with Drums* features songs from her Café Society repertoire. Each tune she transforms into a highly improvisational variation of a classical theme. She takes compositions such as Spanish composer Manuel de Falla's "Ritual Fire Dance" out of the classical idiom rhythmically and makes it swing. While maintaining the integrity of the flamenco-inspired composition, Hazel introduces boogie-woogie elements. Opening with a rhythmic trill, she plays in cut time with the drums providing the ostinato throughout. Liszt's "Hungarian Rhapsody No. 1 in C Sharp Minor," which she had performed as early as her Juilliard audition at the age of eight (and no longer had to paraphrase), is clearly her favorite. She plays the introduction dramatically, as it was written; then, after only a few bars of the slow section of the composition (the "Lassan"), she allows her right hand to run wild with the melody, turning the austere, somber mood of the piece into a romp, while pounding away with the left hand, creating a "stride" that is reminiscent of Fats Waller. In the original composition, the second section (the "Friska") is written in direct contrast to the first and is to be played fast. Hazel chooses to expand on this theme throughout by playing the entire piece exuberantly. Bach's "Two-Part Invention in A minor," Chopin's "Waltz in D-flat Major," and Grainger's "Country Gardens" all demonstrate the kind of crowd-pleasing boogie-woogie interpretations that would be Hazel's claim to fame.

Swinging the Classics was a sellout. Breaking recording industry sales records that year, it sold thousands of copies in its first few weeks. Raved one reviewer, "Miss Scott's talent is peculiarly adaptable to the jazz medium. Her left hand technique is strong and forceful, her right hand nimble and driving. She is the only woman pianist I have heard who can be classified with Mary Lou Williams."[29]

A few years later, the Leeds Music Company transcribed her swing arrangements of the classical tunes and published them under the title "5 Piano Solos from Boogie Woogie to the Classics as played by Hazel Scott."

In the spring of 1941, Barney Josephson hosted a Café Society concert at Carnegie Hall. He rented Carnegie Hall (a common practice in the early days of its history) for an evening of entertainment by the club's premier acts. A benefit concert for the Musicians' Union Federal Local 802, he called it "From Bach to Boogie-Woogie." Lena Horne appeared on the bill under her early stage name, Helena Horne, singing renditions of "Embraceable You," "There'll Be Some Changes," and "Summertime." Art Tatum played a varied program of classics and standards—Dvorak's "Humoresque," "Get Happy" by Koehler and Arlen, and the immensely popular Cole Porter tune "Begin the Beguine." Other performers on the program included the Golden Gate Quartet, Pete Johnson, Albert Ammons, and Henry "Red" Allen and his orchestra.

Hazel opened the second half of the concert, performing tunes from *Swinging the Classics*. John Cleveland wrote for *Collier's*, "On the stage appeared a lovely colored girl of an even twenty years, a dusky beauty with large flirtatious eyes, a pouting mouth, a quietly confident grin. She wore a strapless gown, and it was a dressmaker's dream; her mere appearance won applause."[30] Once Hazel went into her boogie-woogie, some audience members laughed nervously, others squirmed in their seats, uncertain of the appropriate response. Hazel was swinging, and soon, so were they.

"It was the most impudent musical criticism since George Bernard Shaw stopped writing on the subject," commented one reviewer. "It was witty, daring, modern, but never irreverent. I think Liszt would have been delighted."[31] Hazel was kept onstage for several encores as the exhilarated crowd applauded, begging to hear more. In the middle of the uproar, there was one guest, however, spotted by journalists, who was seen storming out of the hall in disgust during Hazel's performance. When Hazel was told, she didn't become defensive, instead she said, "I'm inclined to agree with him. I know lots of people have good reasons why it's all right to swing the classics, but—well, I wish I didn't do it. I just can't help it. My stuff is hybrid," she concluded. "I'm not grim enough for the classics. As for swing—well, I'm not sufficiently aboriginal."[32]

What had begun as an act of pure rebellion at the Yacht Club years before had now become her "hook," the culmination of all of her training, formal and informal. "Jazzin' the classics" was what audiences came to expect from Hazel Scott. And for a while this unconventional aspect of her piano performance suited her, appealing to the entertainer in her, who loved nothing more than to excite a crowd. "She had a great personality. . . . Hazel was a showperson in her playing, style, and presence," pianist Marian McPartland recalled.[33]

The concert ended with "the loudest jam session ever heard in the hall."[34] There were three bands—six trumpeters, five drummers, and nine pianists who shared three baby grands—all playing the quintessential Basie tune "One O'Clock Jump."

Hazel maintained a rigorous schedule with her regular weekly engagement at Café Society Uptown along with other bookings at Boston's Ritz-Carlton, the Paramount, and the Roxy in New York. She made numerous guest appearances on radio shows and was now in demand for interviews with major music journals such as *Downbeat* and *Discography*. Josephson handled her contracts, seeing to it that all of them met Hazel's conditions, among them her refusal to play before segregated audiences. Her contracts called for immediate forfeiture if the audience was separated by race when she arrived—she would be paid but there would be no show. This, of course, limited the cities where she could be booked and negatively affected her income, but she would have it no other way.

Occasionally, Hazel played for charity events, many at the request of Josephson, some of which were sponsored by leftist organizations. Hazel's free concert at the Hebrew Home for the Aged in the Bronx was touted in the *New York Herald Tribune*. The article reported that she sang "Eli, Eli," "Kol Nidre," and "Yiddishe Mama" while old men and women wept.[35] The event was equally nostalgic for Hazel, giving her an opportunity to sing songs she had learned as a child while living in a predominantly Jewish area on Intervale Avenue.

Josephson's designs for Hazel's career were carefully crafted. He placed her at high-end hotels and concert halls, billing her as the "Darling of Café Society." She was in such high demand, it was not uncommon for club owners to try to steal her away from him. The Waldorf Astoria offered her double what Josephson could pay, but Hazel insisted, "Why should I work for any other night club in town? I'd be a jerk."[36]

In February of 1942 Hazel returned to the studio to work on her second album—*Hazel Scott: Piano Solos with Drums*. She was accompanied by drummer, J. C. Heard. She had been spending more time composing and included two original compositions on the recording, "Hazel's Boogie-Woogie" and "Blues in B Flat." Both were standard twelve-bar blues played straight, without affectation, but containing what had become a common quality in all of her music—a sense of fun. In live performance and on records, she gave the impression that no one could possibly be enjoying themselves more than she. It wasn't with errant disregard, but with a lighthearted touch, particularly on the up-tempo numbers; never frivolous, but definitely whimsical. One of her most requested numbers at Café Society was her rousing rendition of "Dark Eyes," which she also included on the new release. She gives the tune her exciting and inventive Scottian treatment, employing various embellishments—syncopated rhythms, and changes in tempo and mood. Also included are "Hallelujah," from the musical production *Hit The Deck*, and Gershwin's "Embraceable You."

"Hazel has something to offer which, unlike the work of so many swing performers, is not aimed solely at the jazz specialists. As the present album reveals even more fully than the first," Leonard

Feather wrote in the liner notes, "[s]he has learned how to combine an innate musicianship and orthodox technique with an unusually commercial quality which is aural as well as visual." Feather further insisted that this recording should establish Hazel as "no mere stunt artist" but a legitimate swing pianist. His notes hinted at the ongoing debate over the legitimacy of "swinging the classics," versus straight-ahead jazz.

But for those critics who were categorically opposed to the idea, this sophomore effort only reinforced their opinion of Hazel Scott's piano playing as purely commercial. Critic Bill Gottlieb not only blasted Hazel's performance, he criticized the critics who liked it. In his "Swing Sessions" column in the *Washington Post,* he wrote, "Despite unqualified praise by unqualified critics like Walter Winchell and Brooks Atkinson, Hazel remains a beginner with flashy, ambitious ideas but with too many thumbs and too little soul."[37]

There was great debate among jazz critics and aficionados over how Hazel's style compared to Mary Lou Williams's pure jazz and blues aesthetic. Hazel's breakout success gave critics cause to question why she had surpassed Mary Lou Williams in terms of recognition and opportunity. Aside from the fact that they were from distinctly different backgrounds, personally and musically, they were also a generation apart. Mary Lou Williams was ten years older than Hazel. She was a pianist and an accomplished composer and arranger. Hazel was primarily a pianist and vocalist with an attractive performance style and undeniable commercial appeal who had only just begun writing her own compositions.

Yet critics chose to direct their attention at their most obvious differences. The two women were compared on every point, from their pianistic styles to their physical appearance. Hazel was sultry and flirtatious onstage; Mary Lou was guarded and reserved. Hazel's medium-brown skin was considered more of an advantage than Mary Lou's dark skin. In a *Newsweek* article entitled "Hep Hazel," one journalist tried to make sense of the differences drawn between the two women: "True, the very very hep hepcats writhe in agony at her antics and point bitterly to the relatively unsung genius of one Mary Lou Williams at Café Society Downtown in New York City. True, too, there is also the matter of Miss Scott's undeniable café au lait charms. 'In a strapless evening gown,' Earl Wilson recently wrote in *The New York Post,* 'she makes most sweater girls look underfed.' Miss Scott's public, however, is tolerant to the degree of frenzy. . . . Hazel is an entertainment classic."[38]

Without mentioning her name, another critic cast aspersions on Hazel, in an attempt to give Mary Lou Williams her due. The article entitled "No Kitten on the Keys" began with the usual parlance: "If you shut your eyes you would bet she was a man. But last week's audiences at Manhattan's Downtown Café Society had their eyes open. They heard a sinewy young Negro woman play the solid, unpretentious, flesh-&-bone kind of jazz piano that is expected from such vigorous Negro masters as James P. Johnson. Serene, reticent, sloe-eyed Mary Lou Williams was not selling a pretty face, or a low décolletage, or tricksy swinging of Bach or Chopin. She was playing blues, stomps and boogie-woogie in the native Afro-American way—an art in which, at 33, she is already a veteran."[39]

As a teenager, Hazel recalled hearing Mary Lou's early recordings with Andy Kirk's band. "I stole an Apollo Theater placard from a dry cleaners window with her picture," she said.[40] Her example as a successful female jazz musician and composer who was well respected and admired by her peers was a continual source of inspiration for Hazel, especially in the early years of her career. Hazel idolized Mary Lou Williams, as did most of her female counterparts. To her dissenters, Hazel played coy, saying, "I know I'm not the best girl pianist I ever heard."[41] She, like many others, placed Mary Lou at the very top of the profession.

Leonard Feather recalled of Hazel, "She was as much a jazz fan as a musician. I never heard her make a derogatory comment about any fellow pianist."[42]

When Barney Josephson badgered Mary Lou to be more of an entertainer, like Hazel, by adding some extra flourish to her performances, wearing low-cut dresses and more jewelry, and connecting with the audience, she understandably reacted angrily. She resented the request, finding it ridiculous and insulting. Mary Lou was a musicians' musician. For her, it was only about the music. She had no interest in using her personality to entertain the audience. As far as she was concerned, that was the job of the music. Still, she understood that there were different kinds of musicians and entertainers. She never judged or criticized Hazel's performance style, even though she had no intention of replicating it.

"There was never any jealousy between those two women," said Mary Lou's manager, Fr. Peter O'Brien. "Both of them were extremely intelligent. Hazel was a lot of fun and more extroverted, while Mary was very serious, more interior. Now, Mary would get very, very angry about musicians [who] were highly touted who couldn't play. But she loved Hazel. She was very proud of her."[43]

There was a great deal of camaraderie among female musicians at the time. They were in such small numbers that they could hardly afford infighting. It was a struggle for women instrumentalists to gain ground in the male-dominated world of jazz music. They struggled for the same respect, the same pay, decent jobs, and safety on the road. It was altogether a risky undertaking. Typically, jazz women were expected to dress up prettily and sing with the band not *play* with the band. But Hazel only had to look at her mother's example to feel confident that there was a place for her in the industry. She had no reason to think otherwise, having been surrounded by women musicians all her life.

Neither Hazel nor Mary Lou allowed professional criticism and comparisons to interfere with their personal relationship. They would share a friendship that endured their entire lives.

In March of 1942, Hazel returned to Broadway for a run at the Paramount Theater. *Priorities of 1942* was a vaudevillian revival with comedic acts and plenty of singing and dancing. The show's producer, Clifford C. Fischer—who had brought the *Folies Bergere* to Broadway—decided that a return to vaudeville was what wartime audiences needed to keep their spirits lifted. The cast featured comics Lou Holtz and Willie Howard, and Paul Draper, a graceful dancer of international renown who tap danced to Bach, Scarlatti, and Mozart. Hazel performed "Black Eyes" and "Tea for Two." During its six-month run, Hazel's reviews were stellar. Brooks Atkinson, the famed drama critic for the *New York Times,* who could make or break a career with the flick of his pen, wrote of Hazel's performance, "She has the most incandescent personality of any one in the show, and she is dressed and turned out to make the best possible use of it. There is not a dull spot in her number. Every moment counts as she intends it to."[44]

Stardom suited the twenty-two year old. She loved the limelight, and it loved her back. She had her hands insured by Lloyds of London, fell in love with expensive fur coats, and had all of her jewelry—diamonds mostly—custom made by the celebrated jeweler Harry Winston. In fact, she was noted for having one of the most famous jewelry and fur collections in show business—two minks, a silver fox, a Russian sable, a beaver, a white fox, an ermine wrap, a stone marten cape, and a Persian lamb.[45] Her jewels were rare pearls, a diamond and clip necklace valued at twelve thousand dollars that could be broken down into several clips and pins, ruby rings, and a seventy-six-carat aquamarine ring. Some pieces she designed herself and others were made by Madison Avenue designer Victoria Stone.[46]

Her circle of friends included some of the most popular talents in the business. Hazel could be seen gallivanting around town with Leonard Bernstein on one arm ("Skinny Lenny" she called him) and Frank Sinatra on the other.

Fondly, she recalled her early impressions of Sinatra: "The first time I saw him his hair fell down his forehead in ringlets. That's how young we were. His eyes were a blaze of sky unknown to any cloud. His body a wire that was never still. He vibrated animal magnetism and women and girls sold their souls for a glance from him."[47]

In her first encounter with the great crooner, Hazel was prepared to dislike him, however. He had replaced Jack Leonard as the male vocalist in the Tommy Dorsey Orchestra. And Leonard was a friend to many musicians. "His dismissal had been abrupt and we were unhappy," Hazel wrote. At the Paramount Theater, on Frank's opening night, a gang of fellow musicians gathered to "sit in judgment of the new singer." She remembered, quite vividly:

A young man with a face shaped like an Egyptian cat came on-stage. He opened his eyes and in the spotlight they were brilliantly blue. He opened his mouth and began to sing and it was all over![48]

Hazel was intrigued by Sinatra musically. She recalled, "His phrasing was so different from anyone I had ever heard. He reached down and slid up into the notes of the scale with his own ingenuity using his voice as the musical instrument it is. His delivery was direct and he exuded confidence."[49] From that day forward, Hazel was not only a devout Sinatra fan but the two became close friends.

Between shows, Hazel would run over to the Riobamba on East 57th Street to catch a few minutes of Sinatra's set. Sinatra would return the favor, as the two seemed never to get enough of watching one another perform. "When he was through with his performance, he would come around the corner to see me."[50] A witness to their running back and forth between clubs was the actor and composer Walter O'Keefe, who shared the bill with Sinatra. One night he finally told Hazel, "What you two need are a couple of pairs of roller skates!"[51]

As with many professional entertainers, their friendship was interrupted by the constraints of time and distance as their careers moved them in different directions. Over time, they saw less and less of each other. Hazel remembered their last gathering. She was hanging out with Frank and his wife Nancy at the Riobamba. "Nancy was pregnant with 'little' Frank," Hazel recalled. They shared light-hearted conversation, but in the back of her mind Hazel knew her days of romping around Manhattan with her old buddy were numbered. Frank Sinatra was on his way to Hollywood and journeying closer to true stardom. "He had the world by the tail," she said. After that night, they would see each other very rarely.

Since the Café Society downtown club was closed on Mondays, musicians went to the uptown club to hang out. It was the one place where they knew they could find one another. Teddy Wilson, Duke Ellington, Billy Strayhorn, and Art Tatum passed through, as did Eddie Heywood, Doc Cheatham, and Bud Powell. There were Lena

Horne, Carol Channing, Canada Lee, and Joe Louis, and the list went on and on. And there was Hazel at the epicenter of the Monday night milieu. She became, in her own words, "a truly spoiled baby."[52] And Hazel's peers reveled in her success. Her name was now synonymous with that magical time, not only in the club's history, but in New York's musical past.

With the money she made from her albums and concert dates, Hazel purchased her first home in upstate New York. Leaving their Harlem digs behind, she and Alma moved to 25 Monroe Place in White Plains. Although she had treated herself to many extravagances, she loved more than anything that she now could afford a place where her mother would be happy. She even bought Alma a fur coat. It is unclear whether or not Grandmother Margaret came along or maintained the apartment on St. Nicholas Avenue. But Alma was right there to help with the decorating and to tend to the victory garden.

Hazel also bought a car and hired a chauffeur to make the forty-five-minute drive into the city for her engagements. At the end of the night, after the final number, the last autograph, and the hugs and kisses with celebrity guests and musician friends, Hazel would fall into the car exhausted. Three little words to her chauffeur would put her closer to rest and relaxation: "Home, Charlie, honey."[53]

CHAPTER SEVEN

Seeing Stars

Summer 1942. It was the season of Hazel's introduction to Hollywood.

With all its cinematic allure, the gray-toned glamour and illustrious tales of girl meets boy and good over evil, Hollywood held no mystery for the astute young pianist. Up until that time, few black performers had escaped the poor treatment handed down by studio bosses, directors, and producers. From Butterfly McQueen in *Affectionately Yours,* with lines such as "Who dat say who dat when you say dat,"[1] to Louis Armstrong portraying a savage character in *Rhapsody in Black and Blue,* dressed in leopard skins ("when you're down under six feet, no more fried chicken will you eat"), there in the archives lay irrefutable evidence of the crass stereotyping of gifted black performers who dared to pursue a film career.

Hazel had seen what a mockery Hollywood made of so many black actors, relegating them solely to the roles of maid, butler, servant, or fool. Vowing never to don a maid's uniform or a washerwoman's rags, vehemently she wrote, "From *Birth of a Nation* to *Gone with the Wind* from *Tennessee Johnson's* to *My Old Kentucky Home;* from my beloved friend Bill Robinson to Butterfly McQueen; from bad to worse and from degradation to dishonor—so went the story of the Black American in Hollywood."[2] She added, "If anyone seeing the great dancer Bill 'Bojangles' Robinson made the fatal mistake of assuming that 'Uncle Bo' was an Uncle Tom, let me also set the record straight where he is concerned."[3]

> When "Uncle Bo" made a picture with Shirley Temple, Negroes were proud! The fact that this brilliant, talented man, this dancer without peer, this world famous star, had to become a servant in order to appear on screen was a thorn in the flesh to very few people. It was *not* a joyous experience for Bill Robinson however! He had no illusions about a Black man's privileges. He knew that *only* as her butler, her trusted servant, could he take the hand of the little golden haired child and teach her to dance.[4]

Blacks in Hollywood had to play the game according to studio rule, which typically meant at the cost of their dignity and pride. This bitter reality made Hazel exceedingly cautious when inking the fine-lined details of her film contracts. By her early twenties, she had developed a thick skin, and the quick tongue she'd always had grew quicker still. It wouldn't take long for studio bosses to learn what those on the concert and nightclub circuit already knew—that she would not pander or kowtow. With Hazel Scott, there would be no obsequious smiles, no hunched shoulders, downcast eyes, or shuffling of any kind. She was her own woman. And rubbed the wrong way she would conspire against any enemy with a vengeance.

When Josephson began discussing the possibility of her working in Los Angeles, Hazel made several decisive demands. In her outspoken (and sometimes reckless) way, she made it clear from the start that she would just as soon walk off the set than suffer even the slightest indignity. Her film contracts were to include a clause that gave her final approval of her musical numbers. If it provided a wardrobe that was anything less than flattering, she would wear her own clothes. Finally, she insisted that no matter who was in the cast, no matter what the story line, she would not play a character. Her credit would read "Hazel Scott as herself."

While she and Josephson hashed out the final details of her contract, she was offered several roles—four different opportunities to play a singing maid. Naturally, she refused them all.

In a deal initiated by Orson Welles, Hazel signed with RKO Pictures. In her first film, which centered on the history of jazz, she was to costar with Louis Armstrong. It was an exciting idea, but the picture would never come to pass. It was a casualty of the falling out between the studio and Welles, whose critical successes but box office flops (*Citizen Kane, The Magnificent Ambersons,* and *Journey into Fear*) and catastrophic productions (*It's All True*) were more than RKO was willing to bear.

Around the same time, another high-profile opportunity had come and gone for Hazel. She was given serious consideration for the role of the pianist in the film classic *Casablanca,* but the producers ultimately decided they wanted a male to play the part, and cast actor, Arthur "Dooley" Wilson.

While on a talent hunt in New York, director Gregory Ratoff discovered Hazel at Café Society Uptown and offered her a small part in the film *Something to Shout About,* a backstage drama featuring the music of Cole Porter and starring Don Ameche, Janet Blair, Cyd Charisse, and William Gaxton. Ratoff filmed a few sequences of Hazel that he planned to take back to Hollywood and insert into the film. When Columbia executives viewed the footage, they found Hazel captivating and decided to expand her role, asking her to join the rest of the cast on the Columbia Studio lot in California.

Alma didn't want to leave New York, but she had no intention of sending Hazel out to Hollywood alone. In her place, she sent a chaperone, Mabel Howard, to "keep an eye on her." Hazel would joke years later, saying, "And I may have needed some keeping an eye on!"[5] Mabel was a handsome woman, stout and stern, with a quiet countenance. She could impose her authority with just a look. Hazel liked and respected her. The pair would grow close in time, as Hazel looked to Mabel as a reliable and trustworthy friend.

Something to Shout About is the time-honored tale of a young girl from Altoona, Pennsylvania, who decides to give the big city a go, featuring Cobina Wright as the rich divorcee "Donna Davis," a talent-free chanteuse who uses newly acquired cash from her divorce settlement to stage and star in a vaudevillian musical. After a sad performance before audiences, she is cast off and replaced by the small town girl who just happens to be an extremely gifted ingenue, "Jeanie Maxwell," played by Janet Blair. Hazel is a standout in the film as the girlfriend of an aspiring drummer and hoofer named "Chuckles" (James Walker). They live in a boardinghouse filled with artists, where they jam regularly on an old upright piano in the common room of the house. She is introduced by Don Ameche, the male lead, as "Hazel Scott, the singer's best friend, also the best pianist in the business." Impeccably dressed in each scene, with lovely dresses, coiffed hair, and full makeup, Hazel wrote "I wore my personal wardrobe for the nightclub and theatre scenes and the studio furnished street clothes. I wore my own jewels; rubies and diamonds, matching the jeweled embroidery of my gowns."[6] Hazel almost looked out of place in the dive where the artists were supposedly experiencing hard times, waiting for their big break. And if "Chuckles" hadn't been a great performer it would have taken some stretch of the imagination to believe they were a twosome. Hazel's lines (or perhaps it was her delivery of the lines), alluded to the fact that she was "slumming." When Janet Blair asks where on earth she learned to play the piano, Hazel responds in jest, "Very simple. You start picking with one finger at three, you study for years and you go to conservatory. Finally, you graduate and you wind up playing for Chuckles."[7]

Hazel sings "I Always Knew," a different song from the one she was originally given. The first tune Cole Porter had offered was something Hazel decided she "couldn't feel." Preferring the risk of insulting him to turning in a lackluster performance, she asked him to give her another number. "He stared at me coldly, nodded once, abruptly, and handed me another song without a word."[8]

"You'd Be So Nice To Come Home To" was the tune Hazel turned down. Instead, Janet Blair sang it in the film, with Hazel providing piano accompaniment. Nominated for Best Original Song in the 1944 Academy Awards, the song went on to become a big hit for Porter. And years later, when Dinah Shore recorded a cover of it that was met with similar success, Cole Porter—who Hazel now considered a good friend—still remembered what had happened, joking, "But *you* can't feel it!" "The funny thing is," Hazel wrote, "I *still* don't feel it! The idea of some guy lolling around the house waiting for *me* to come back from a hard day's work is singularly unattractive!"[9]

Cole Porter's film score also included the tunes "Through Thick and Thin," "Lotus Bloom," "Hasta Luego," and the title song, "Something to Shout About." Teddy Wilson and His Band appeared in the vaudeville sequence, though shot from such a distance that only their sound was recognizable. Ina Ray Hutton, conducting her all-male band, appeared as well and received critical notice for her "distinctly individual personality and technique."[10]

Although reviews of the film were mixed at best, Hazel's individual performance was well received. "Hazel Scott's amazing piano technique would be a brilliant decoration of any picture," wrote Nelson B. Bell in the *Washington Post*.[11]

Back in New York, Josephson was planning an anniversary celebration in honor of Hazel's third year as Café Society's headliner. "Café Society Uptown . . . is 'swingphony' hall to Hazel. To it, and to one of the most faithful followings ever assembled by an entertainer," wrote *Look* in its coverage of the event.[12] Musicians from the downtown club came uptown that Monday night in November of 1942 to toast Hazel: Teddy Wilson, Helen Humes, Joe Sullivan, and Connie Berry. Eddie South and John Kirby's band provided the music. Art Tatum was there along with Benny Goodman, Woody Herman, and Count Basie. As noted in *Time*, "Celebrities regard her with reverence, movie stars ask her for autographs."[13]

Much attention was paid in the press to the huge sums of money Hazel was making. Her annual salary in the early 1940s was upward of twenty thousand dollars, which included her Café Society cash plus other concert appearances. She was fast becoming one of the highest paid black entertainers in the industry. *Look* reported, "The sprightly-looking Miss Scott burst into the big money by playing the works of the masters as they had never been played before—in swing time, with a boogie beat, faster than the boys around Carnegie Hall ever thought they could be played with a high-heeled slipper pounding the floor and the cash customers wondering if all this could be really true."[14] Hazel's personal possessions fascinated the media; they kept count of how many furs and diamonds she owned. Her "traveling wardrobe" was reportedly "a mink coat and stole, three gowns, three dresses, Fath and Dior suits."[15]

In the handling of her film contracts, Josephson made sure that she was paid handsomely. He claimed that he never took a manager's commission from Hazel's film earnings but used those bookings as leverage in her work at Café Society, where she was expected to appear regularly and for a base salary. Always with an eye on business, Josephson knew an appearance by one of Café Society's biggest names in a major motion picture would be the best form of advertising for his nightclubs.

Hazel's next film project was a Metro-Goldwyn Mayer production. In *I Dood It*, directed by Vincente Minelli, Hazel teamed up with Lena Horne, who had a seven-year contract with MGM. Josephson negotiated a weekly salary of $4,000 for Hazel. When the financial details of her contract were publicized, the studio was shamed into raising Horne's salary to $900 per week with annual raises of an additional $100 per week.[16] Considering the times, as well as the competition, Hazel fared far better than many of her contemporaries. *Newsweek* had already revealed that for *Something to Shout About* she had drawn "a nice $2000 a week while Lena Horne was struggling along in Hollywood on a reputed $450." The beautiful and talented Dorothy Dandridge, who Lena Horne once described as "our Marilyn Monroe," had been performing in films since the mid-1930s, and by the time she starred in her Oscar-nominated role as "Carmen Jones" in the 1954 film of the same title, she was earning $1,800 a week. Hattie McDaniel, winner of the Academy Award for Best Supporting Actress in *"Gone with the Wind,"* was making $700 a week, primarily playing maid roles. Although she may have been underpaid and underappreciated, McDaniel managed to be philosophical about it, stating, "I'd rather play a maid than be a maid."[17]

Lena Horne arrived on the *I Dood It* set having performed small singing roles in *Panama Hattie, Cabin in the Sky,* and *Thousands Cheer*. But it was her performance as Selina Rogers in *Stormy Weather* that made her one of the biggest black film stars of the period. White producers and directors considered her fair skin and keen features palatable; casting her, they believed, would not upset the status quo. This did not, however, preclude her from some of the same injustices that other black performers suffered. Like Hazel, she recoiled at Hollywood's characterizations of black women as "Topsy" and "Sapphire," and refused to play roles resembling either.

Their shared determination to bring about change in the industry created a common bond between Hazel and Lena Horne. As the two young women continued to work together in films and on the nightclub circuit, they eventually became good friends. Hazel admired Lena's accomplishments. Her great talent and her beauty, Hazel believed, would ultimately have some impact on how black women were portrayed in film. "Until the powers that be at M.G.M. stood Lena Horne up against a white pillar in *As Thousands Cheer,* as far as Hollywood was concerned, the women of our race were a bunch of dogs. There had been one or two exceptions but on the whole, we were relegated to the kitchen and back stairs," Hazel wrote.[18]

I Dood It was another of MGM's lighthearted musicals, a musical comedy full of misunderstandings and mistaken identities leading to funny and uncomfortable situations between the two stars, Eleanor Powell and Red Skelton. (The film's title came from Skelton's own comedic phraseology.) Hazel and Lena performed a big musical number, strategically placed in a stand-alone sequence that could be easily edited out for distribution in the South, a standard practice during the period.

When Hazel enters the scene about three-quarters of the way into the film, she appears with a small entourage of men at her side draped in a full-length white fur coat and black sequined gown. The scene is staged as a "producers audition" where she and Lena Horne are trying out a new act. She plays a lovely and languid rendition of "Taking a Chance on Love." As she steadily increases the tempo of the tune, the camera closes in on the keys to catch her fast fingering. The arrangement makes use of various styles, moving from ballad to boogie-woogie and back again. Hazel's piano sets the stage for Lena Horne's grand entrance. She waltzes in with her white satin gown sweeping the floor and a three-quarter-length sable coat, which she tosses, casually, to one of the men in the chorus. She breaks into "Jericho" with Hazel accompanying her on the piano. A black chorus stands behind the "wall of Jericho," which tumbles to the ground after a few blows from a solo trumpeter. When the wall falls, Hazel takes over, transforming the tune into an up-tempo boogie-woogie while the jubilant ensemble swings to the beat. The entire sequence is beautifully lit. The men are all in tuxedos and the women are in elegant dresses, bejeweled, some with flowers in their hair—progressive costuming given the times, indicating a slight shift in Hollywood's characterization of black Americans. Surely, black audiences must have been pleased, if not utterly surprised, to see a screen full of black performers, well coiffed and well dressed.

The critics raved over the two women on the screen. "Hazel Scott and Lena Horne, with an all-Negro ensemble, chip in with one of the film's most rousing periods of sensational syncopation, something called 'Jericho' being the medium of their unique virtuosity. The piano must have been invented with the ultimate glorification of itself and Hazel Scott in view. Lena Horne adds her tip-top vocalizing to the combination with devastating results," Nelson B. Bell wrote.[19]

Hazel's next project was based on the Jerome Kern and Oscar Hammerstein II's Broadway musical *Very Warm for May*. Directed by Roy Del Ruth, *Broadway Rhythm* is a musical about making a musical, featuring Ginny Simms, George Murphy, Charles Winninger, Gloria De Haven, Lena Horne, Eddie "Rochester" Anderson, and the Tommy Dorsey Orchestra.

Hazel and Lena Horne were exquisitely gowned, all dolled up in their short scenes, which included a big song and dance number for Horne as "Fernway De La Fer." In "The Jungle Room," she sings "Brazilian Boogie" with conga players and an ensemble of black dancers scantily clad in primitive costumes. She later gives a lovely performance of George Gershwin's "Somebody Loves Me." Hazel's scene could have come straight out of Café Society. A vision in a canary yellow sleeveless dress with yellow marabou feathers about the neck, she plays a jazzed up version of Chopin's *Minute Waltz*. She tosses coy smiles to the audience, bouncing on the piano bench as if overtaken by the boogie and unable to control the rhythm pouring from her hands. It's a hot two or three minutes, just enough to make audiences stand up and take notice.

Hazel was now working both coasts, completing four films in a year's time and flying from California to New York and points in between to fulfill her concert date appearances. She would perform on radio shows in New York such as NBC's "For the Record" and "The Million Dollar Band," appearing with the likes of Frank Sinatra, composer Deems Taylor, and radio conductor Raymond Paige. Then she'd hit the road to Chicago to perform a "Bach to Boogie" swing concert at Orchestra Hall heading back to the West Coast just in time to shoot her next film. There is also some evidence that she was even booked once or twice in Las Vegas, which during the 1940s would have made her one of the first black women to perform there.

A mention in *Current Biography* stated, "In Hollywood, when her daily chores on the lot are done, Hazel assuages her homesickness for Café Society by taking a turn at the Mocambo, a Hollywood nightclub."[20] The Mocambo wasn't just any nightclub, it was *the* place to be, where celebrities were seen and stars were made on their stage. After leaving Tommy Dorsey's Orchestra, Frank Sinatra made his solo debut at the Mocambo. Errol Flynn, Judy Garland, Janet Leigh, Bogart and Bacall, and Gable and Lombard were among the Mocambo's regular guests.

Hazel's shows at the Mocambo were a lucrative side gig for her away from the drudgery of daily film shoots. She was paid fifteen hundred dollars per week for an extended run at the club. Gossip columnist Hedda Hopper exclaimed in print, "I don't wonder Gregory Ratoff is shouting about Hazel Scott. . . . She's dusky, dynamic, daring, and talented."[21]

In the summer of 1943, Alma finally made it out to the West Coast, giving Mabel Howard a break and a chance to return to her own life and affairs. At last, Hazel had her mother by her side. Between her engagements, she introduced Alma to California living. They were invited by western star Harry Carey and his wife Olive to stay at his ranch in the San Fernando Valley. Carey taught Hazel to ride horseback western style. Every morning they'd wake up early and ride far into the hills while Olive and Alma spent the afternoons sharing the latest gossip.

But Hazel's vacation was cut short as plans for *The Heat's On* got under way. Gregory Ratoff had followed through on his promise to cast Hazel in his next film, which was designed as a vehicle for the legendary Mae West with William Gaxton and Victor Moore as her costars. Xavier Cugat and his orchestra performed the musical score, written by John Leipold.

On set, Hazel described Mae West as "shrouded in mystery." She appeared only when Ratoff would respectfully tap on her dressing room door: "Miss Vest, Ve are vaiting!"[22] "Like Maurice Chevalier," Hazel wrote, "Ratoff's accent grew thicker every year. You couldn't exactly call it an affectation—but it certainly did not do any harm; adding to the mystique! It was what he wanted to project, his Russian-ness."[23]

In her scene, Hazel plays and sings one of the hits from the film's soundtrack, "The White Keys and the Black Keys," a standard eight-to-the-bar tune, written by Jay Gorney with lyrics by Henry Myers and Edward Eliscu. Dressed in a long black gown with black and white accents and a plunging neckline, she plays with great velocity, pulling out her arsenal of inventive harmonies and trills. It's a showy number designed to tantalize viewers. Her performance is very presentational in the elaborate style of the old Hollywood musical. She rarely looks at the keys but directs her attention toward the two "producers" in the audience as she sings. When she hits the bridge, the camera pans over to a trumpeter, who plays with his right hand covered by a hand puppet. The puppet gets most of the screen time, gesturing as if *it* is playing the horn. When the trumpet solo winds down, the lights are dimmed to reveal only Hazel, in a white version of the black gown she wore earlier, seated between two concert grand pianos—one black and one white. With her back turned away from the audience, she increases the song's tempo to a heart-pounding pace; her left hand bangs out the bass line on the white piano, while her right hand rips away at the melody on the black one. She spins on her chair from one piano to the next, turning just slightly to smile at the audience. The song ends with both lids of the pianos rising as she plays the two-handed finale on both pianos. It is a virtuosic performance, full of fun and pianistic acrobatics, and one of the most memorable sequences in the film.

In her next and final scene, the "Caisson number," designed as a tribute to the soldiers fighting overseas in World War II, Hazel is first heard singing "When the Caissons Come Rolling Along." She then appears in a Women's Army Corps (WAC) tailored uniform seated at the piano. The soldiers march center stage in full uniform, with rifles in tow, to Hazel's upbeat piano playing, while their women sway behind them. In midstep, Hazel belts out: "Attention! Let's boogie-woogie!" The soldiers break into a full dance number; Hazel jumps up from the piano and joins them. She cuts a few steps then lays out the dance number that sends the couples into a rousing "Lindy Hop." Then, on Hazel's word: "Attention! Right Face!" the soldiers march off to war as their wives wave them farewell. The scene ends solemnly with Hazel and the chorus standing, saluting the soldiers as they march off to war.

From the looks of it, the scene comes off without a hitch. The dance number is tight; the music is great. But there was some behind- the-scenes drama that had Hazel seething. On a day when Gregory Ratoff was absent from the set due to a sudden illness, an unexpected series of events unfolded. Dancer and choreographer David Lichine, whom Hazel had worked with on *Something to Shout About*, began working on the film's dance sequences and in Ratoff's absence had taken over the reins as director. It was then that he and Hazel went to battle on set. It was a culture clash of sorts that had serious repercussions. Hazel would speak about the incident openly in the press throughout her career, referring to the episode as "On Strike in Hollywood."[24]

By now, Hazel had grown accustomed to Ratoff's acquiescence to her every request. When she requested that only Phil Moore arrange her music for the film, he gave the usual reply, "Give the Baby, what she wants."[25] "I was to drill eight young men in a rhythmic routine after which we left for war. This was at the height of the war effort and everyone was awash with patriotism," Hazel wrote.[26] Eight women were in the scene, playing the role of the soldiers' sweethearts. Walking from her dressing room, Hazel noticed Lichine in conference with the costume designer, Walter Plunkett, who had costumed *Gone with the Wind* and was well-respected in the industry. Lichine, it turns out, had a problem with the crisp, white aprons the women were wearing. He thought they looked too clean. So he asked the makeup department to spray them with oil and dirt. Hazel was outraged: "Am I to understand that these young women are to see their sweethearts off to war, *wearing dirty Hoover aprons?*"[27] Lichine answered, "What do you care? You're beautifully dressed. What's it to you?"[28]

> The next thing I knew we were screaming at each other and all work had stopped. He insisted that we were going to shoot the scene the way he saw it. I insisted that no scene in which I was involved would display Black women wearing dirty aprons to send their men to die for their country.[29]

Finally, Hazel shouted: "Have you ever seen any Negroes other than your own domestic servants?"

Those were the words that brought the entire production to a halt. Lichine immediately reported to Harry Cohn (sometimes called "King Cohn"), president of Columbia Pictures, that "the Scott" was throwing temperamental fits.[30]

Hazel staged a three-day strike on the set, refusing to show up until the costumes were changed. "Until my fight at Columbia, no Black person had ever dared oppose the Establishment. You either kept your mouth shut and took the roles you could get or you remained out of work," she declared.[31]

After their three-day standoff, Lichine realized that he was fighting a hopeless battle. It was clear that Hazel was willing to risk her reputation and even her career to make her point. "He finally agreed and the girls were told to report the next morning, dressed in their own frocks for the scene, ready to go at nine o'clock," Hazel recalled.[32]

Hazel gathered all of the women in her dressing room and gave them their instructions: 'Tonight I want every one of you broads into the hairdresser's. Tomorrow morning at nine, I want you on this set, immaculately turned out."[33] She had put her career in jeopardy for what she believed in, and if nothing else, she wanted them to and appreciate the gesture. She remembered their silence as they filed out. "Each of them looked at me as if they were taking a last look before the lid was closed for the last time. I had antagonized the head of Columbia Pictures—in short, committed suicide!"[34]

Harry Cohn was apprised of everything that took place between Hazel and Lichine. When Hazel was given the chance to explain her position to him, she realized, "It was useless to attempt an explanation. It was impossible to declare my racial pride. All he could see was what he considered my treachery. I was costing him money."[35] And there was no one there to back her up. "There I was, out on a limb of race pride," she wrote, "and Harry Cohn swore that he would chop it off."[36]

As for Lichine, Hazel concluded that he was "not really a vicious man. He was behaving in what he believed to be a normal manner. He had never known any Negroes. If he had ever seen any in the flesh, they were domestic servants. It is a reasonable assumption that he could not conceive of black people in any other role! Since black people were always servants on screen as well, what else could he have expected? My attitude was completely alien to him."[37]

Hazel's fight was not all for naught. In the final cut of the film, the women are not wearing dirty aprons. In fact, they're not wearing aprons at all, only pretty floral print dresses.

Before Hazel completed her work on the film, one of the actresses on the Columbia lot pulled her to the side and gave her some interesting inside information. It may have been hearsay or simply actress gossip, but Hazel was so riled up that she was liable to believe anything. The actress told her that Harry Cohn thought very highly of her. "He thinks you are the most unusual girl he has ever seen," she said.[38] Evidently, prior to Hazel's "strike" Cohn had showed her a side of himself that he rarely revealed. He was kind to her. Even though she was a newcomer to Columbia's lot, her dressing room was nicer than all the others. Cohn would leave his office to walk with her down the studio streets between takes. Hazel had thought nothing of his behavior. In fact, she enjoyed their conversations, as Cohn always seemed interested in her opinions. The actress also told Hazel that Harry Cohn had big plans for her, but warned, "If you refuse him, you will have made a terrible enemy! He's made no secret of his feeling for you. You might just be through in this town if you refuse him!"

Instead of this information providing some hope that Cohn would excuse her strike on set, it made Hazel even more cynical about the whole ordeal. She wanted to leave town immediately. What the actress had told her could have easily been a pack of lies, but Hazel was impetuous. Her patience with Hollywood had run out. She went straight to her mother and told her to get packed. She was done. Most of her scenes were complete; all that was left was a few long shots that would be used for intercutting. Alma questioned her daughter's decision, but Hazel was too furious to supply her with a satisfactory answer. They boarded a train that very day and left for New York.

When *The Heat's On* was released, it fell short of critics' expectations. The press had a field day playing off the title, writing that the "heat" was most definitely off. It was Mae West's last film during Hollywood's studio days; she returned to the Broadway stage and to her writing career. She didn't make another film until *Myra Breckenridge* some twenty-seven years later.

Hazel waited for repercussions from the West Coast. "But there was stony silence from Columbia and Harry Cohn. Ratoff said nothing either and I was baffled."[39] Months later she would find out that Harry Cohn made only one statement with regard to her strike, a fateful promise that would haunt her for years to come: "She will never set foot in another movie studio as long as I live."[40]

When Hazel returned to the East Coast, she was scheduled to appear at Carnegie Hall in a "Barney Josephson–Café Society presents" benefit concert for the Ambijan Committee, a pro-Soviet organization based in the United States that supported the Jewish Autonomous Region in a remote area of eastern Russia, Birobidzhan. The creation of this settlement was the Communist Party's attempt to create an alternative to Palestine for secular Jews who upheld socialist principles. Funds from the concert would contribute to the development of the settlement. That evening, the Hazel Scott Trio included Sid Catlett on drums and Johnny Williams on bass. Swinging the classics, they played Bach's "Invention No. 1 in C-Major" and Shostakovich's Preludes Nos. 10, 13, and 24. The performance ended with her popular original composition, "Hazel's Boogie-Woogie."

This return to New York and the concert stage was refreshing but brief. Prior to her falling out with Cohn and Columbia Pictures, Hazel was contracted to appear in Jesse Lasky's upcoming film, *Rhapsody in Blue*. With great trepidation, she returned to Hollywood.

Directed by Irving Rapper, *Rhapsody in Blue* is a biopic of the great pianist and composer George Gershwin, whose untimely death from a brain tumor at thirty-eight sent the entire nation into shock and mourning. The film starred Robert Alda as George Gershwin, Herbert Rudley as Ira Gershwin, along with Joan Leslie and Alexis Smith. Hazel had a gem of a scene. Her sequence begins as George Gershwin shows up as a guest in a posh supper club where Hazel is the headliner. The scene opens with her singing, in French, "The Man I Love." Her white gown is fitted with white fringe draped around the bustline that shakes when she shakes. Her bijoux is her usual selection of diamonds, earrings and bracelets on both wrists, but this time she adds a tiara. In French, Hazel announces to the crowd that one of the leading composers of the day is seated in the audience, "Welcome to Paris, Mr. Gershwin," she says. "And now, in your honor . . ." She belts out "Clap your hands! Slaps your thighs!" and then breaks into a swing medley of "Fascinating Rhythm" and "I've Got Rhythm," slowing down the tempo in the last few bars of the tune for her big finish.

With the crowd now center stage on the ballroom floor, Hazel, draped in a white feather boa is replaced by another pianist so she can do what she rarely had the opportunity to do—stand center stage and concentrate only on the delivery of a great vocal performance. She sang a soulful "Yankee Doodle Blues."

Hazel returned to New York after shooting her scene In the film happy to be home. She thought long and hard about what had transpired with Harry Cohn. She had a sneaking suspicion that the five films she had made in a year and a half's time would be the extent of her film career.

Cohn would make good on his promise. Hazel would receive no further offers, no scripts, no calls from directors. In retrospect, she wrote:

> It is not that I object to having had to give up my Hollywood career—although it was productive. The loss of my burgeoning career was a small price to pay for my self respect. If it became a question—as it did—of fame and fortune through acceptance of existing standards; or oblivion due to my embattled stand, there was no contest. There was never, and there could never be enough money in the world to compensate for the loss of one's dignity.[41]

Hazel looked upon her Hollywood days with some semblance of pride. All of her performances had lived up to her professional standards. She had done nothing that she would be ashamed of later. In an interview with *Ebony* she commented, jokingly, "There's one thing about being typed as myself. When people ask me what my favorite role is, I can answer with all modesty—Hazel Scott."[42]

Later in life Hazel confided in Leonard Feather about her work in film: "The only one that wasn't too horrible to talk about was 'Rhapsody in Blue' because it was a period film, set in the 1920s. I had to play and sing the way they did then, and I had a little bit of French dialogue. But all the others—forget it, please!"[43]

As World War II raged on overseas, musicians stateside did their part for the war effort. Hazel was among those who recorded V-discs ("V" for "Victory") of popular tunes for special release. Songs designed to keep hopes high were placed on twelve-inch, 78 rpm discs and sent abroad to soldiers and sailors. In New York and Los Angeles, artists gathered in designated theaters and movie lots for recording sessions. Her sides typically began with a sultry intro: "Hello fellas . . . this is Hazel Scott." In a New York session in August of 1943, she recorded "Body and Soul" and "People Will Say We're in Love." Accompanied by drummer Sid Catlett, she also recorded a disc performing Fats Waller's "Honeysuckle Rose" and Duke Ellington's "C Jam Blues."

The Army/Navy Screen Magazine, a short film program that included newsreels, cartoons, and staged performances of popular singers and musicians, featured Hazel onstage in full regalia singing a lively rendition of "It's Going to Be a Great Day."[44] She played in service hospitals and at the Stage Door Canteen on 44th Street, a club solely for servicemen on leave. She was known to perform even in contagious disease wards; she would wear a mask and carry a portable keyboard to play for the infirm. As one writer observed, "Whether playing at Café Society or in a hospital ward for veterans, her affect on men is the same—terrific. She makes the wolves whistle and the wounded wiggle."[45] She also appeared along with actor Frederic March and bassist-bandleader, John Kirby in the National Urban League's "Salute to Freedom," a show broadcast on NBC Radio to honor African American military personnel.

Hazel received more than a dozen unit citations from numerous service branches, and her war bond efforts were acknowledged by the Treasury Department.

Hazel's early recordings were hot commodities during the war. Along with Lena Horne and actress Dorothy Dandridge, Hazel Scott was a favorite pinup among military men; she answered thousands of letters and sent even more autographed photos overseas.

But, despite her success, the year ended on a sad note. In December of 1943, her longtime friend Thomas "Fats" Waller passed away of bronchial pneumonia. He was thirty-nine years old. Known to be overindulgent, the gregarious entertainer ate and drank himself into an early grave.

Dozens of musicians converged on Carnegie Hall's stage to pay tribute to the much-loved pianist and entertainer in "A Salute to Thomas 'Fats' Waller." Count Basie and His Orchestra played along with the Al Casey Trio, Sid Catlett, and Xavier Cugat. Ben Webster, Josh White, Oscar Pettiford, and Mezz Mezzrow all performed. Among the vocalists were Billie Holiday, Jimmy Rushing, Mildred

Bailey, and Thelma Carpenter. Pianists J. C. Johnson, Teddy Wilson, Willie "The Lion" Smith, Mary Lou Williams, and Hazel Scott performed Waller's brilliant compositions.

Although it was a somber homecoming, Hazel was glad to be back on familiar ground. Much ado was made over her return to Café Society. With a fan's passion, a writer from *Newsweek* described seeing her live show: "When she closes her eyes and looks enraptured as she plays the Chopin Waltz in C sharp Minor as it was written, the audience looks impressed and enraptured too. When Hazel sighs, says 'Ah, yeah,' softly to herself and begins a beat which would bounce Chopin right out of his grave, her public grins and starts tapping the table. And by the time Hazel's really hot and her face glistens under the tiny spotlight which is the room's only illumination, everybody's happy."[46]

CHAPTER EIGHT

Adam

He was the only son of Mattie Shaefer Powell and Adam Clayton Powell Sr., pastor of the century-old Abyssinian Baptist Church. A privileged child, Adam Clayton Powell Jr. was born on November 29, 1908, in New Haven, Connecticut, surrounded by all the comforts of middle-class living. The joy of his elder sister, Blanche, young Powell was bright, precocious, and inquisitive, a constant amazement to his family. He grew up in Manhattan's Tenderloin district, where he ran the streets with schoolmate—and future Scott family friend—Fats Waller. The old red brick church on 40th Street was their stomping ground until the Powells moved uptown as the foundation was being laid for Abyssinian's new home in Harlem.

Reverend Powell was a stern patriarch, a pillar of the community, and wholly dedicated to his family and the church. Mattie Powell was a consummate caretaker, a dutiful wife and nurturing mother who carried out her cherished role of minister's wife with ease. "I can still see her in a wide-brimmed Dolly Varden hat, with maybe an ostrich feather, a voluminous dress of that period, with cloth topped high-buttoned shoes, and always her impeccable white kid gloves," her son remembered.[1] There to provide additional doting was the nanny, Josephine, who shared a special bond with her young charge.

The family was close-knit and spent countless hours around the dinner table engaged in lively debates, each member sharing his or her perspective on the issues of the day. Quiet reflection and time spent studying Scripture was part of the family's daily routine. "What a home should be was all there," Powell Jr. recalled.[2]

It wasn't long after they moved to Harlem that young Powell had his "first brush with racism."[3] His fair complexion confounded neighborhood kids. On errands for his mother, he was often confronted by gangs of black children on one block and Irish and Italians on the other, both demanding to know if he was black or white, where the wrong answer meant an immediate pummeling. Although many members of the Powell family were very light-skinned, of African, European, and Native American ancestry, they never considered themselves to be anything other than Negroes. But, for the sake of his own survival, Powell Jr. "became what his friends wanted him to become, white in white crowds, black in black crowds," biographer Wil Haygood surmised.[4] It was nothing more than a game to the naturally charismatic youngster, an opportunity to exploit his powers of persuasion.

As a high school student at the prestigious Townsend Harris Hall, he showed signs of a keen intellect and the ability to lead. He organized an all-male youth group at the church called the Young Thinkers, where Powell and his cohorts could gather together to express their ideas on everything from politics to economics, and oftentimes from girls to sex, but always with Powell Jr. directing the conversation.

In 1926, Powell's beloved sister Blanche, only in her midtwenties, died from a ruptured appendix. Her death set him adrift. His schoolwork suffered badly, and he was eventually expelled from City College in his freshman year. He ran the streets looking for trouble, participating in every manner of vice he could find. He turned his back on the God of his father, the God he had been taught was with him always. He determined, angrily, that "God was a myth, the Bible a jungle of lies. The church was a fraud, and my father the leading perpetrator, my mother a stupid rubber stamp. The smiling good people of the church were grinning fools."[5]

His spiral downward was tolerated for a while. When a sufficient amount of time had passed, a family friend, Charlie Porter, intervened. He recommended, rather bluntly, that Adam get away from his family and its "holiness attitudes."[6] He suggested the prestigious, all-male Colgate University in Hamilton, New York. Calls were made, and arrangements were set in place for his admission.

Once he arrived on campus, Adam Powell Jr. realized that he was one of only five other black students, all of whom were athletes. The handsome, six-foot-two freshman was a curiosity to most. None of the students, black or white, were sure of his race. Amused by their befuddlement, he would neither confirm nor deny their suspicions. He lived in the dormitory designated for white students. He had a white roommate. He even tried to pledge a white fraternity. There are several different accounts of how his race was discovered. The fraternity's policy of conducting background checks on all potential pledges would be a likely explanation. Word had also gotten around that he was the son of a popular New York minister, whose identity would have been easy enough to uncover.[7] But in his memoir, *Adam by Adam,* Powell Jr. claimed that it was the arrival of his father on campus that unveiled the truth. His father had been invited to speak at Chapel; the topic of his speech, like many of his sermons, was on race relations. Afterwards, Powell Jr.'s roommate, Howard Patterson, from Brooklyn, wrote him a note: "I can't live with you any more because of the way your father defended Negroes today—you must be a Negro!"[8] It came as a shock to him when the university sided with Patterson, removing Powell from the room. Ostracized by the white students, who didn't appreciate being duped, and written off by the black students, who accused him of trying to "pass," this was his proverbial day of reckoning. He immediately sought alliance with his fellow black students, henceforth dispensing with his game of racial ambiguity. In an effort to win back their favor and demonstrate his race pride, Powell went out for the football team (despite the fact that he didn't have the necessary brawn to withstand the hard-hitting plays) and offered to tutor one fellow in German. He even joined a chapter of the black fraternity Alpha Phi Alpha on another college campus to impress them.[9]

Despite all of his social maneuvering, Powell performed well in his freshman year classes. The following semester, however, he slipped back into the kind of behavior that had gotten him kicked out of City College. Adam the playboy resurfaced. He flaunted his knowledge of New York City nightlife, the Harlem club scene, and showgirls while his grades plummeted and his popularity soared.

Powell Sr. was having none of it. He kept a watchful eye on his son's academic progress. He made it clear that nothing less than superior grades were to be tolerated, and during summer breaks he was expected to work and earn his own money.

In his final two years, Powell Jr. did eventually settle down, excelling beyond his father's expectations.

His parents had never pressured him to pursue a religious career. Their only wish was that he receive a solid education and follow a career path of his own choosing. And so it came as a great surprise when Powell Jr. announced his plans to enter the ministry.

Late one winter evening, while studying at his desk, "Suddenly there came a voice . . . , 'Whom shall I send? Who will go for me?' And there in that room in that quiet, for the first time in my life God talked to me."[10]

On Good Friday night of 1930, Adam Clayton Powell Jr. preached his first sermon before an unlikely crowd that he described as "all the girls from the Cotton Club . . . bootleggers, gamblers, all the fantastic array of acquaintances I had accumulated through the years."[11] Thirty-seven people were so moved by his "How many will walk just a few feet tonight for Jesus?" sermonizing that they joined the church that very night. One week later, Powell Sr. granted his son the license to preach. He was made the church business manager and his father's assistant minister.[12]

After graduating from Colgate, Powell came home to a Harlem he hardly recognized. "As the result of the Depression, 63 percent of the schoolchildren in the Abyssinian Church neighborhood were suffering from malnutrition, while I lived—and lived well—in our ten-room penthouse," he recalled.[13] He immediately joined his father's efforts to help residents in need. He organized church-sponsored relief programs that provided temporary jobs to thousands of Harlem's homeless and unemployed.

Work relief was his first and most pressing task. With a staff of volunteers and funding from the Emergency Work Bureau, he set up operations in the Abyssinian Church basement. On Saturdays an armored truck would drop three thousand dollars in cash at the church. Powell would then assign jobs—cleaning, painting, teaching—to those in need of work and divvy up the funds accordingly. "Thousands would line up every day," he wrote, "asking for just 'something' to do for a few dollars."[14]

With a thousand dollar gift given to him by his father, Powell Jr. set up a free food kitchen in the church gymnasium. He and his staff asked for donations from local grocers and meat markets. During its existence, the free kitchen provided over thirty thousand meals.

Around the same time he enrolled in graduate school at the Union Theological Seminary. He was overextended but resisted the idea of doing less. When his schedule kept him out of class, he coaxed the church secretaries to sit in on the class for him and take notes. Once the school officials discovered what he was doing, his enrollment at the school came into question. He finally decided to leave the seminary after a prayer he'd written for class was returned by the instructor with the comment: "Of no value." He was furious: "I asked myself then how any man could decide on what was or was not of value concerning another's man's conversation with God."[15] Powell Jr. left the school and began directing his full attention to the needs of his community.

He marched his first picket line on behalf of five doctors at Harlem Hospital—Conrad Vincent, Marshall Ross, Sidat Singh, Peter Marshall Murray, and Ira McCown. The doctors' complaints were many: racist hiring practices; unsanitary conditions; a lack of beds, equipment, and medication; and a segregated nursing staff. Harlem residents had never been satisfied with the hospital's service, referring to it as "the butcher shop" and "the morgue."

Adam Powell Jr. declared, "For the first time I heeded the call of the masses and became part of the struggles of the people of Harlem."[16]

He pursued the cause with "sustained indignation," refusing to give up until the doctors' demands were met. He organized a task force—the Committee on Harlem Hospital. Six thousand people showed up for the fight at the Board of Estimate and Apportionment armed with nothing more than "the massive strength of our unity." Initially, the board members refused to meet with him, but the organized masses gathered outside of their building left them few options. Powell was heard. After stating the doctors' demands, an immediate investigation was launched.

Ultimately, the facility was given a thorough cleaning, the Nursing School was revamped, and a new women's pavilion was planned. "This victory was very heady wine for a youngster of twenty-two," Powell Jr. proclaimed. "All my life I had been preparing for this moment and yet had never been conscious of it."[17]

Fueled by his first civil victory, he would take on New York's electric company and the telephone company, demanding fair and nondiscriminatory hiring practices and threatening mass boycotts if they did not comply. He organized the Coordinating Committee for Employment, joining the "Don't Buy Where You Can't Work!" campaign that had been sweeping through major cities across the country, most successfully in Chicago and Detroit. The committee's first order of business was to picket all of the stores on 125th Street "from river to river."[18] The group took on one store at a time. Blumstein's, one of the largest stores on the block, where blacks shopped in droves but were consistently denied employment, was first on the committee's hit list. Hundreds marched outside the store's front doors.

The plan worked. "One Saturday alone we closed ten stores that later signed contracts with us overnight," remembered Powell.[19]

In 1937, after nearly thirty years of service, Rev. Adam Powell Sr. turned over leadership of the church's ten-thousand-member congregation to his son. Now up in age and ailing, he trusted that his son would keep his vision for Abyssinian alive. "I built this church," he said, "but my son will interpret it."

Adam Powell Jr. solidified his new position as senior pastor of the church with a graduate degree in religious education from Columbia University's Teachers College. Meanwhile, the old guard at Abyssinian Baptist braced itself for the young reverend's impetuous nature.

Powell was known to march straight from the pulpit, through the church doors, right into the street. His minister's robe bellowing in the breeze, he would walk into local barrooms, tapping patrons on the shoulder and letting them know they'd missed church service that morning. "He would walk up and down Seventh Avenue and speak to everybody," remembered Esther McCall, a former Abyssinian church secretary. "People loved him and they knew him and he would speak to those that would try to hide from him, you know, if they were drinking or something or not looking too good. And then he'd say, 'Come out from behind there.'"[20]

In 1938, during a speech at the Shaw University commencement ceremony, where he received an honorary doctorate of divinity, Powell spoke against intraracial prejudice. "We've got to streamline our race and come to realize that mass action is the most powerful force on earth," he said.[21] It was evident from this speech, and others he gave at the time that he had a broader vision for his work as a minister, a vision that would place him far beyond the pulpit. Soon public office beckoned.

In November of 1941, Adam Powell Jr. won a seat on the New York City Council, becoming the first black man to serve on that body. It came as a surprise to many New Yorkers, as the press had largely ignored his candidacy. This would be remedied months later when Powell, Jr., along with Harlem real estate broker and manager of the Savoy Ballroom, Charles Buchanan, founded a weekly newspaper called the *People's Voice*. As editor in chief, Powell would use the paper to let his constituents know the issues he was raising in City Council and the focus of his out-of-town speeches.[22] His "Soapbox" column revealed his political views on national and international affairs, which always centered on racial discrimination and segregation.

What the young reverend was steadily demonstrating was his power to influence the masses above and below 125th Street. His work on New York's City Council would mark the beginning of a remarkable political career.

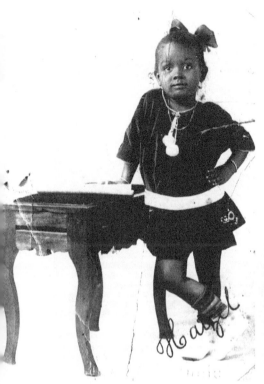

"Little Miss Hazel Scott" at the age of three or four. (Courtesy of Adam C. Powell III.)

Alma Long Scott, Hazel's mother. (Courtesy of Adam C. Powell III.)

At the age of nineteen, the "Darling of Café Society." (Photo in the author's collection, Bruno of Hollywood.)

Hazel and Adam's wedding day, August 1, 1945, with Alma standing
nearby as they leave the church in Stamford, Connecticut. (Courtesy of
AP Wide.)

The scene outside Café Society as guests gathered to attend the Powells' wedding reception. (Courtesy of Getty Images.)

Rev. Adam Powell Jr. and his glamorous wife before the pulpit of the Abyssinian Baptist Church in Harlem. (Courtesy of Adam C. Powell III.)

Hazel and Adam preparing for a night on the town. (Courtesy of Adam C. Powell III.)

Opposite: Great pianists gathered around the piano at Café Society—Count Basie, Teddy Wilson, Hazel Scott, Duke Ellington, and Mel Powell. (Courtesy of Adam C. Powell III.)

Hazel plays for American troops at the Stage Canteen in New York. (Courtesy of Adam C. Powell III.)

Congressman Powell and wife pose for a White House Christmas greeting, circa 1946. (Courtesy of Adam C. Powell III.)

Promotional ad for the *Hazel Scott Show,* circa 1950. (Photo in the author's collection.)

The Powells arrive in London, 1951. (Courtesy of Adam C. Powell III.)

In Paris, Hazel on the arm of her second husband, Ezio Bedin, with Dizzy Gillespie. (Courtesy of Adam C. Powell III.)

Hazel holds court with actress Sophia Loren while Ezio looks on. (Courtesy of Adam C. Powell III.)

Gallivanting in Cannes. With his brand new camera, "Skipper" snaps a picture of his mother, Annie Ross, Lena Horne, Lorraine Gillespie, L. B. Lucas, and Dizzy Gillespie. (Courtesy of Adam C. Powell III.)

The Paris "March on Washington." Hazel stands with James Baldwin, May Mercier, and blues artist Memphis Slim. (Courtesy of Getty Images.)

Opposite: Glamour girls Hazel Scott and Lena Horne on set in Hollywood. (Courtesy of Photofest.)

Hazel and "the Duke" share a laugh. (Courtesy of Getty Images.)

At a Paris boutique, with young "Skipper" looking on, Hazel decides on a gown to wear for her performance at Le Drap D'Or. (Courtesy of Photofest.)

Appearing less glamorous and quite serious, Hazel defends herself before the House Un-American Activities Committee, September 1950. (Courtesy of Photofest.)

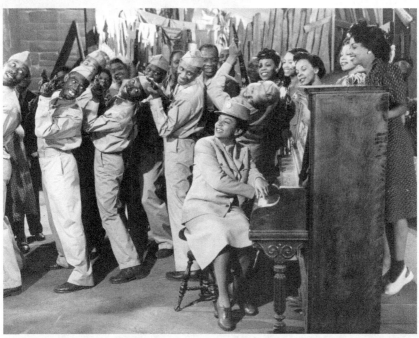

After staging a strike, Hazel appears along with the black ensemble of singers and dancers all neatly attired on the set of "The Heat's On." (Courtesy of Photofest.)

With a fresh, new look, "La Parisienne" returns to the Unted States to appear in Langston Hughes' *Tambourines for Glory* in 1960. (Courtesy of Photofest.)

Adam Clayton Powell Jr.'s funeral, April 9, 1972. Hazel is shown leaving Abyssinian Baptist Church with her son standing close behind. On the right, Rev. David Licorish. (Courtesy of Photofest.)

Billie Holiday, circa
1940s. (Courtesy of
Photofest.)

Hazel and Mary Lou
Williams seated
together at the piano
in Mary Lou's thrift
shop. January 1967.
(Courtesy of Insti-
tute of Jazz Studies,
Rutgers University.)

The great pianist Art Tatum accompanying vocalist Mildred Bailey. (Courtesy of Photofest.)

"President of the Tenor Sax," Lester Young. (Courtesy of Photofest.)

Hazel seated at the drums along with fellow band members of the Sextet of Rhythm Club of London (left to right, Albert Harris, Pete Barry, and Danny Polo); Leonard Feather stands on the right in between Pete Brown and Arthur Herbert. (Courtesy of New York Public Library Photographic Division.)

Intermezzo

"I have always been a very strong feminine creature," Hazel said, "and to subdue me a very, very strong masculine creature is required."[1]

Adam Powell was just such a creature.

A frequent stalker of Manhattan nightlife, Powell was a regular at Café Society, and he knew when Hazel was on the bill.

"Café Society was *the* supper club of New York, and Hazel Scott was its grande vedette," he said. "At the end of the long room was the black concert grand piano sticking its nose up out of the audience. All the lights would go out, Hazel would make her way to the piano, and suddenly a spotlight would catch her. For a moment the audience would gasp because it looked as if she were seated there nude—the height of the piano, the bare-shouldered dress, nothing but the golden brown shoulders and arms, the supertalented fingers."[2]

Hazel was aware of Adam Powell as well. She had seen the city councilman in action up in Harlem and had shared a podium with him at war rallies in the early 1940s. As they lent their voices in support of black troops heading overseas, Hazel found herself hanging on Powell's every word.

The first time I heard Adam Clayton Powell Jr. exhort a crowd I tingled from head to toe and realized that I was in the presence of greatness.

But it really started to happen for me when I heard him speak and saw the brilliance, the soul of the man.[3]

Although she was titillated by the many romantic overtures he made whenever they were together, Hazel was also intimidated. "He was turned on to me first and I ran. Much to my regret I have to admit that I ran from him," Hazel confessed.[4]

Neither of them was free—Adam had married Isabel Washington Powell in 1933, a former Broadway actress and now the revered minister's wife, much beloved by the congregation and the Harlem community. He had also legally adopted her son, Preston, from a previous marriage. Hazel was in a relationship as well. "The person with whom I was involved when Adam entered the picture was very much in love with me," she wrote.[5] Careful not to name names, she wrote cryptically about the young man she was dating, revealing only that her interest in him had begun to wane. Enter "shrewd old Adam."[6] Accustomed to having his way, he set out to turn Hazel's head. "He took his time. First, the gifts. Nothing elaborate: a book; a photograph; the loan of a silk scarf that I kept. His ring; his handkerchief, his favorite poetry."[7]

Soon, Adam made more demands on her time. Hazel enjoyed his company but knew he was a married man. At first, it was just dinner and drinks, a few laughs. She had not intended to leave her boyfriend and go into "another problem situation." But Adam was hard to resist.

"Adam was tall and bombastic," Hazel said. "But I was used to handsome, imposing men in my profession—that's part of the equipment and was no big deal."[8] Still, she was intrigued. Young and capricious, Hazel was flattered by Adam's pursuit of her affections. She found herself anxiously awaiting his next move. The pair began seeing each other in secret. They were often spotted snuggled up in clandestine corners of exclusive Manhattan eateries. "Our courtship was compounded of visits to Café Society, dinners at Reubens, luncheons at '21,' liberal quantities of floral perfume and hours of intense discussion of such varied topics as philosophy, politics, boogie-woogie and war," Adam Powell revealed.[9]

"We laughed a great deal and we never touched each other," Hazel confessed. "It was almost as if we knew what would happen when we finally did."[10]

As they grew closer, Adam insisted that she put a formal end to her other relationship, a bold request from someone who wasn't exactly available. "One night he reduced me to tears," Hazel recalled.[11] "He slayed me for not having officially told my former sweetheart that all was finished between us. It was my first taste of his jealousy and it was frightening."[12]

Hazel had some early reservations about getting seriously involved with Adam Powell. She knew his reputation. "I had heard he was quite a playboy, and I didn't think he was marriage material," she admitted.[13] "Basically, I'm a cynic and too honest. I don't expect more than a person can deliver, and I told him so. He said he had changed, and said, 'We're new, give us time.' But with his ego, he was not discouraged by anything I said or did. Before I knew what was happening, we were horseback riding, dining at Cherio's and so forth."[14] Unable to resist temptation, their relationship was consummated, their affair in full swing.

Adam eased Hazel's doubts by opening up to her about his work, his dreams and ambitions. Then he made it clear that he wanted her to be a part of his future.

On that night in December, he made the statement: "I'M GOING TO MARRY THAT GIRL—BUT *FIRST* I'M GOING TO CONGRESS! *NO ONE IS EVER* GOING TO CALL *ME* MR. HAZEL SCOTT![15]

CHAPTER NINE

Fervor & the Fury

In 1942, the New York state legislature, after much political wrangling, passed a long overdue congressional reapportionment bill making Harlem the city's Twenty-second Congressional District. A redrawing of political districts gave Harlem its first opportunity for representation in Congress.

Striking out early, Adam Powell Jr. wasted no time gathering support for a congressional run. Outside of Abyssinian after Sunday service, ushers petitioned parishioners as they left the church, placing small cards in every open hand, which read, "Let's go friend. Make Adam Clayton Powell the first Negro Congressman in the United States from the East."[1]

Over the next two years, he would campaign tirelessly until he became the self-proclaimed "first bad nigger in Congress."[2]

Powell announced his candidacy for Congress before a mostly black audience of twenty thousand during a freedom rally at Madison Square Garden, where he called the crowd's attention to his previous protest efforts and his work in City Council. He riled them with a vociferous speech on the work that lay ahead for the black community, the fight against racial discrimination, and the end of lynching in the South. So impassioned was his speech that the rally soon turned into a revival. With the crowd's emotions sufficiently stirred, Powell boldly declared, "I must run for the Congress of the

United States, so that we may have a national voice speaking from the national capital." He continued, "It doesn't matter what ticket or what party—my people demand a forthright, militant, anti–Uncle Tom congressman!"[3] Shouting over the cheers, he proclaimed, "My cry today and until I die is let my people go—NOW!"[4] This became his clarion call and the platform of his political campaign.

Sweeping the country with an antisegregation, antilynching message, Powell named his nationwide tour "The Conflicting Forces of the New Negro and Southernism."[5] He attended war rallies, sharing the stage with Paul Robeson and Eleanor Roosevelt. He stood shoulder to shoulder with Earl Browder of the Communist Party, gathering support from state to state. He even went to Hollywood, where he hobnobbed with celebrities, like Orson Welles, who were progressive and politically astute. He had the backing of the black entertainment community as well. Musicians Duke Ellington, Count Basie, Billie Holiday, Josh White, Mary Lou Williams, and of course, Hazel Scott made themselves available to perform whenever he needed them.

As he wound down the campaign trail, Powell made one final push in Harlem. Up and down Seventh Avenue he rode, trumpeting his campaign promises through a loudspeaker with Apollo Theater emcee Ralph Cooper on hand to give him a theatrical introduction that never failed to excite the crowd. By June of 1944, the polls showed that 92 percent of Democrats supported Powell along with 74 percent of Republicans and 83 percent of the American Labor Party.[6] Success in the primary was imminent, and a seat in Congress was certain.

Following his primary victory, Powell had little energy left to celebrate. On doctor's orders, he took a much needed break. He and his wife went to their Massachusetts summer home in Oak Bluffs on Martha's Vineyard. It was during this respite that Powell decided to tell Isabel, in his direct and unflinching manner, that she would not be joining him in Washington. He was leaving her.

Naturally, she was distraught. "I pleaded with him to make good our marriage, in view of the fact that he was sure to be elected to

Congress. He seized me solemnly by the shoulders and said it was too late," she recalled.[7]

The press caught wind of the story and immediately sought out Isabel for the details of their split. She had known about her husband's affair all along. She never named her foe, referring to Hazel only as "a nightclub performer." Hardly a fool, Isabel knew exact times, dates, and locations of their trysts. "He has visited her at the night clubs at which she performs on many occasions. He met her at the Roxy Theatre when she had an engagement there last Oct. 24. He has visited her at her home in White Plains and his association with this woman is a matter of common knowledge," Isabel told the *New York Daily News* in an article entitled "Pastor Powell Prefers Hotspot Gal."[8] Seductive photos of Hazel in low-cut gowns usually appeared alongside scathing articles outing her as "the other woman." Gossip columns were filled with tales of Hazel and Adam being together at one nightspot or another.

The two women had actually been in close proximity on more than one occasion. Isabel was aghast when she realized that her husband had taken her to Café Society to see Hazel Scott's show while he was having an affair with her. And, at Adam's personal request, Hazel had played for the funeral service of Fats Waller, which was held at Abyssinian with Isabel seated in the front row.

Few in Harlem were truly surprised. Having made their peace with Adam Powell Jr.'s lifestyle long ago, the community stood behind him now, its focus directed keenly on Congress and the progress their preacher-politician could make in Washington. If Harlem residents had anything negative to say about his behavior, his breakup with Isabel, and the extramarital affair with Hazel, they spoke of it among themselves.

Doubtless, the church's congregation was none too pleased at having their minister's personal dalliances exposed in the gossip columns. Elder members, who had long questioned his ability to uphold the dignity and grace of Abyssinian, shook their heads at the whole mess. Still, they, too, remained tight-lipped, whispering their disapproval in private.

Meanwhile, Hazel laid low. At the risk of causing more hurt and embarrassment for all concerned, she offered little information to the press about her future plans with Powell, referring to him in only the most flattering terms. Even so, this could not have been a proud moment for the girl who'd been raised in a strict household of prideful women.

When Alma first discovered that Adam Powell was pursuing a romantic relationship with her daughter, she chose not to interfere. She watched the way her daughter hemmed and hawed, chasing and being chased. Hazel remembered her mother's initial reaction: "She said, 'We don't run in this family. Either you're going to see Mr. Powell face to face and say to him, 'Sir I am not interested' or 'I am interested' or whatever it is that you are . . . or you are no daughter of mine.'"[9] Alma let Hazel know that she would stand with her no matter what her choice, but there would be no getting around the inevitable consequences.

A few weeks before Powell's inaugural ceremony in Washington, four thousand people gathered at the Golden Gate Auditorium to give him a proper sendoff. He appeared onstage, setting forth his agenda, a litany of heartfelt promises that included: "to push for fair racial practices, fight to do away with restrictive covenants and discrimination in housing, fight for the passage of a national Fair Employment Practices Commission and for the abolition of the poll tax, fight to make lynching a Federal crime, do away with segregated transportation, undergird the Thirteenth, Fourteenth and Fifteenth Amendments to the Constitution."[10] It would take a tremendous effort, but clearly he was up to the task.

On January 3, 1945, Adam Clayton Powell Jr. was sworn in as a member of the Seventy-ninth Congress. From the gallery he could feel the gaze of his proud father and the Abyssinian deacons who came down to bear witness to the historical event, and Hazel Scott, who sat beaming.

Arm in arm, Adam and Hazel walked into the White House luncheon, where she audaciously accepted the seat reserved for "Mrs. Powell." Wearing a formfitting white dress with a matching white turban and diamonds galore, Hazel dazzled the Washington set. At a party held at the Mayflower Hotel in Powell's honor, hosted by Democratic national chairman, Robert Hannegan, no one questioned their marital status and no one dared bring up the scandal, now on a low simmer back in New York.

According to Powell's biographer, Wil Haygood, the pair attended another party, this one thrown by well-to-do Washingtonians Marjorie and Belford Lawson.[11] There, Hazel was prompted to play a few numbers on their parlour grand piano, a request she rarely honored, considering it a cheapening of her talent. But this time it was all for Adam. After the impromptu performance, Adam and Hazel dashed away, leaving the crowd wide-eyed and wanting more.

Adam returned to Abyssinian in all his glory as its devoted minister and Harlem's first congressman. He strutted through the streets of Harlem, imbuing the entire neighborhood with a sense of pride and wonder. Adam Powell Jr. was the voice of the people not just in Harlem but for powerless, disenfranchised blacks all over the nation. "Keep the Faith, baby!" he'd shout from the street corner to the pulpit. And so they did, putting their faith, hope, and aspirations into the hands of the one man they believed could bring about real change.

Although most church members were aware that Hazel had accompanied Powell to his inauguration, not until she came to church for Sunday service were they forced to face the reality of their relationship. Receiving a cordial but cool welcome, Hazel understood that it would take time for the church members to adjust to her presence. But she didn't make it easy for them. She would not join auxiliary boards or other church-run organizations. "She'd speak and talk, you know, but she never became buddy-buddy with anyone, not that I could see," said Esther McCall, Powell's longtime secretary.[12]

Many church members criticized Hazel for her style of dress and her looks, and they disapproved of her profession. Some considered her nothing more than a chanteuse in a loathsome line of the work, playing secular music, and performing in nightclubs where people smoked cigarettes and drank liquor. They could only hope and pray that their minister would reconsider his relationship with such a woman, a woman he was now planning to marry. The "color-struck" crowd who favored light skin over dark made it known that their allegiance would remain with Isabel Powell, whose fair complexion and soft features they found easier on the eye, the right look for a first lady of the church and more fitting for a man of Adam Powell's stature. "Oh there was a great deal said by others about him marrying a brown-skinned woman and a nightclub performer. But Adam had married his first wife because he loved her not because she was fair, and he married me for the same reason," Hazel said.[13]

Hazel feigned indifference, projecting a devil-may-care attitude. Her insouciance shielded her from an experience that must have been extremely uncomfortable if not embarrassing. "I have never apologized to anyone for the fact that God gave me talent. I didn't feel I had to," she said. "There were those who loved me . . . and those who hated me."[14]

Whenever Adam had a spare moment, he spent it at Hazel's place upstate. "Her home in the country was just what I like, with a lake nearby where I put a rowboat for fresh-water fishing; and her mother cooked tingling, peppery West Indian dishes. I practically moved in," Powell remembered.[15] He and Alma would take long walks through the Westchester Hills and talk about his dreams and the dream he had of a life with Hazel. She recalled, "Adam had marriage in mind long before I realized how serious he was. He had discussed the whole thing with my mother but never mentioned it to me. That is, not for a long time."[16]

When the time was right, Adam took his new love to meet his father. "I knew she would make an impression on Dad, because this girl could sell herself to anyone," Powell wrote.[17] For months, he'd been telling his father all about her. "Her mind is brilliant," he would say.[18] "She is never anywhere without a book by her side, usually the heavy, challenging, demanding type. . . . She is remarkably gifted and speaks several languages fluently."[19] He got no fight from his father. After an elegant dinner in Manhattan, Powell Sr. agreed that Hazel was everything his son had made her out to be.

"We didn't even have an understanding, except for the glances that people exchange when they're in love," Hazel remembered.[20] "But he knew just how to go about it. He realized I was a mama's girl and one day, when my mother was giving a big party, he walked up to her and asked if he could marry me. Just like that. Mother took one look at me, ready to faint with joy, and said yes."[21]

After Alma gave them permission to marry, the couple had to wait a year for Adam's divorce to become final.

They obtained their marriage license on July 25, 1945, just four days after Isabel Powell received her divorce decree in Reno, Nevada.

On August 1, 1945, Hazel Scott married the Rev. Adam Clayton Powell Jr. The nuptials were held at the Bethel AME Church in Stamford, Connecticut, with both Rev. Powell Sr. and Rev. George Turner Sims Jr. presiding.

Dressed in a knee-length Chantilly lace and white satin dress with French cut lace covering her head and draped down to the hem of the dress, a radiant Hazel Scott stood at the altar with trembling hands and heart. Alma, in crème de la crème lace with a matching chapeau, stood at her daughter's side; Powell Sr. was beside his son. Charles Buchanan, Adam's business partner, acted as best man.

While the wedding was quiet and simple, the well-publicized reception, hosted by Barney Josephson at Café Society Uptown and catered by a local Harlem grocer and caterer, Bernice Gordon Jackson, was much more of a spectacle. Two thousand guests were invited, three-thousand showed up. It took twenty-five police officers to control the crowd lined up outside the club hoping to catch a glimpse of the bride and groom. The guest list was a mix of New York socialites, politicians, literary artists and musicians. Langston Hughes, Carl Van Vechten, Bill "Bojangles" Robinson, Paul Robeson, the actress Uta Hagen, the humorist Harry Hershfield, New York City mayoral candidate William O'Dwyer, and Congressman Vito Marcantonio were all in attendance along with nearly every prominent member of New York's jazz set.

Amid the music of the Gene Fields trio, well-heeled guests stood shoulder to shoulder surrounded by white gladiolas in tall crystal vases, which were placed throughout the club. The cake, standing two feet tall and beautifully decorated, was something of a sensation; those who caught a glimpse of the intricately crafted design on the top layer were surprised to discover a miniature male figurine standing at the White House door dressed in a minister's robe.

A staff photographer from *Life* magazine covered the wedding, capturing an exclusive shot of the striking couple, a glossy black and white that was featured as a two-page spread in the August 13, 1945, issue. That in itself was rare and spoke of the heightened level of celebrity Adam and Hazel, as a couple, had achieved. "They were stars, not only in the black world but the white world. That was extraordinary," commented journalist Mike Wallace, then host of the popular New York television broadcast *Nightbeat*.[22]

Some members of the press hadn't forgotten how this wedding came to be. The residue of Hazel and Adam's scandalous affair still dusted the pages of newspapers and magazines. *Time* entitled its cover story "Tabloid Dream," with an opening line that sneered, "Two of Manhattan's favorite tabloid characters got married last week. The Rev. Adam Clayton Powell Jr., 36, wing-collared pastor of Harlem's big Abyssinian Baptist Church and New York's first Negro Congressman, took as a wife (his second) round-eyed, plump Hazel Scott, 25, Bach-to-boogie pianist. Their wedding should have been a tabloid editor's dream—a cast of stars, and a comedy of errors."[23]

Adam and Hazel left the reception after all the guests had gone, collecting themselves for a moment before they took off on their honeymoon. They intentionally kept the destination private. The press reported that they had a fabulous fling at the luxurious Waldorf Astoria, but what the press didn't know was that their initial plans to get away to Vermont had been thwarted. Adam remembered the call he received the night before the wedding, writing, "I had leased a lakeside chalet in Vermont for the summer from the former Chief Justice of the Supreme Court of Vermont. The night before the wedding I received a call from him: 'My neighbors have had a meeting and have voted they will not allow a single Negro to live in any of these houses. Come ahead and I will support you, but they have the power to turn off the water . . . and to cut off other services of the community.'" This was no way to begin their life together. So

Hazel and Adam spent the night at the Waldorf. The next day Adam found a place in the quiet hamlet of Quogue on Long Island's south shore.

Finally, the newlyweds could relax, away from the scrutiny, the gossip, the excitement of it all. They spent leisurely days at the seashore, resting, relaxing, loving.

CHAPTER TEN

The Powells

They were the most sensational black couple in America. The national press followed their professional lives in feature articles; the black press published cover stories exposing their glamorous lifestyle. All over Manhattan, photographers captured images of them horseback riding, boating, and dashing in and out of their limousine. Hazel, indecisive about which fur to wear, would enter one club wearing a fox then show up at another in a mink. Adam surprised her with gifts of expensive jewelry and rare books. She serenaded him with private solos.

She called him "Daddy." He called her "Haze."[1]

As they prepared for a Broadway opening one evening, Hazel took a particularly long time to get ready. Growing impatient, Adam pretended to leave the house, thinking it would move things along. "Finally, when it appeared we would probably miss the first act entirely," said Adam, "out walked Mrs. Powell looking gorgeous in a new 'surprise' gown. She wore a tiara of white orchids. She looked divine. She glided alongside me, purred a little, then reached up and seized me by both ears. 'Kiss me Daddy,' she whispered, 'and forget we're late. I wasn't dressing for a first-night audience. This is all for you. I'd just as soon stay home now.' Well, we did."[2]

Each was fascinated by the other's particular form of genius. Said

Adam, "I remember being so moved by her playing of a Brahms concerto during a San Francisco concert that I rushed out, bought a dozen roses and bustled backstage in time to meet her coming off at the last encore. I held out the roses. 'This is for being a wonderful musician,' I mumbled. 'I think Brahms would love you too.'"[3] After his Sunday morning sermons, Hazel would rush into his church office, saying, "Darling . . . that was great!"[4]

Politically, they were of one accord. Her commitment to civil rights causes made her husband proud. "If I'm not good enough to stay in hotels in certain towns, I figure those people are not good enough to hear me play," she said.[5] Hazel believed wholeheartedly in her husband's political pursuits and had long admired his work in the community. After the gossip and scandal surrounding their marriage had simmered down, when it was no longer considered an indelicate subject, Hazel stated publicly in a feature for *Ebony* (aptly titled "Hazel's Heart Belongs to Daddy"), "We could do great things for our people together."[6] She would repeat this sentiment in many future interviews.

Financially, they were set. At that time, Hazel was making over one hundred thousand dollars a year to Adam's twenty-five thousand. "I make more money," she said, "but show business is freak business. . . . I can't wear strapless gowns and play to any audiences when I'm 80."[7] The couple combined their wealth, using Hazel's salary for investments, while living off of Adam's. They invested heavily in real estate, purchasing several multidwelling apartment buildings as income property. Eventually, they would establish their own realty company, Dorton Realty (the name taken from a combination of both their middle names).

The Powells' lifestyle included such creature comforts as maids and personal assistants, hairdressers, jewelers, and costumers for Hazel; secretaries, tailors, and haberdashers for Adam. Both traveled by chauffeur-driven limousine, and Adam often sped around in his Jaguar Mark V sports car.

Adam credited himself with expanding Hazel's life beyond music and show business. "I just took her out of her shell, forced her to go to shows and meet a lot of people. I taught her the outdoor life, made her go fishing and swimming, take trips, move around. She was the loneliest person till I got her," he said.[8] "There she was, a world-famous musician, but with no real friends or interests. Just plain work all the time."[9] Hazel agreed with him but added that Adam was "a complete idealist, always wanting to make me perfect."

Hazel enjoyed her newfound domesticity. Because of Alma's admonitions to "always protect your hands," Hazel had rarely cooked or cleaned. And, despite her Lloyds of London insurance policy, which clearly stipulated no cooking, Hazel tried her hand at the gourmet dishes and rich desserts her husband loved so much. It was a learning process, however. As great a cook as Alma was, she had never given her daughter as much as a recipe for rice and peas.

When meals were prepared, they were formal affairs. Hazel made sure to have the sterling polished, the candles lit, and freshly cut flowers on the table; Adam made sure to shave. The couple dressed for dinner.

Settled comfortably into her new life with Adam, Hazel cooed, "My marriage is the utopian platter of the century."[10]

During the spring of 1945, months before her wedding, Hazel had been working with the well-known conductor and arranger Toots Camarata (Salvador Tutti Camarata) to record several sides for Decca. Camarata had orchestrated works for several popular big bands, namely, those of Tommy Dorsey, Jimmy Dorsey, and Benny Goodman. He had studied the trumpet at Juilliard and learned the art of orchestral conducting under Cesare Sordero of the Metropolitan Opera. As a conductor, Camarata produced several important recordings with Louis Armstrong and Duke Ellington. He was also the arranger and conductor on Billie Holiday's first Decca recording session. His work with Hazel began shortly after he returned from England, where he had worked for Decca's British affiliate, conducting a classical series of albums containing the works of Puccini, Bizet, Bach, and Rachmaninoff, among others.

Together, Camarata and Hazel were able to produce recordings of American popular music showcasing Hazel's vocals with the rich compliment of his full orchestra. "Take Me in Your Arms" opens with a string arrangement that sets the stage for Hazel's rubato entrance. Her voice has a mellifluous quality that only grew richer with time. As one reviewer noted, Hazel sings "in a husky, very low and blue way. It is jazz singing of a high order."[11] Over the years, Hazel's vocals rarely received the same notice as her piano playing. She didn't necessarily have an expansive range, but it was Hazel's interpretation of lyrics, her ability to convey the emotion behind a song, that was exceptional. On "I'm Glad There's You" and "The Man I Love," her phrasing is languid and relaxed, imbuing the songs with a sense of romance and longing. "She can be a musical chameleon, but her changes are not just on the surface. Miss Scott has an unusual ability to get into her material, to find the right interpretative qualities, whether she's singing a ballad or a blues or making her piano jump," wrote New York Times critic John Wilson.[12]

When Adam met Toots Camarata, it was the first of many personal introductions to a member of his wife's world of musicians. In Ebony, Adam told the story of Hazel and Toots at the house listening to some new arrangements he'd written for her when Toots noticed him standing off to the side, listening intently and enjoying the tune. Toots looked over at Hazel and said, "He digs, doesn't he?"[13]

Adam revealed, "I've been 'digging' a lot of new people, places and experiences since our marriage. In some matters I have grown somewhat 'hep.'"[14]

Adam loved to see Hazel perform and loved the idea of being married to a famous entertainer. He kept up with her late night pace, attending jam sessions till dawn. Vividly, he recalled a night when Hazel engaged in a duet with a musician she didn't know. They were in the Fifth Avenue apartment of one of New York's "leading families," with Hazel on the piano and a mysterious man on the flute.[15] When the performance ended, Adam went over to Hazel, who "was still at the piano running dreamily through a Debussy prelude." He said, "Listen, baby. I always considered you a person of really rare proportions, but tonight's performance topped them all. Do you know who you were playing with?" She had no idea. Adam told her that she had just performed a duet with "America's Number 1 Communist," Earl Browder.[16]

Beneath all of this mutual adoration lay some grave concerns. Adam worried about the opinions of his congregation. In the early days of their marriage, he put pressure on Hazel to leave the nightclub circuit. She understood his need to please the church, but she couldn't help but think his request hypocritical. He was asking her to leave the very place where they'd met, to leave the clubs he frequented, the *very* club where she had made a name for herself. "Of course, many things had to change," Hazel confided. "I had to give up clubs. 'What? A minister's wife appearing where whiskey is sold?'"[17]

She found striking a balance between performing artist and minister's wife was often a tedious affair. On one occasion, Hazel invited a few church deacons and their wives to a Café Society set, hoping to enlighten them and change their perceptions of her profession. She thought that since they had been exposed to a "very modern preacher and a very intelligent man" they would be open-minded.[18] She would soon find that it would take more than an evening out to sway such a devout congregation, a congregation that was the life's blood of Adam Powell Jr.'s ministerial and political career.

Ultimately, Hazel acquiesced. She and Adam came to an agreement. She would leave the club circuit for the concert stage but with the understanding that the church would make no demands on her time nor interfere with her musical career.

"Presenting the New Hazel Scott," the headlines read, and "Bye-Bye Boogie." Both she and Adam went out of their way to explain her decision to the press. Hazel said she had grown tired of nightclubs. "People go to them to get drunk and show other people they're having a good time," she remarked.[19] Adam took it even farther, saying that her years at Café Society had been "tinged with a strange unhappiness." He claimed that Hazel felt "stagnated," that she wanted to "spread out and play."[20] "She enjoyed jazz, still does," he said, "but yearned for a wider repertoire and more appreciative audiences."[21]

Whether or not any of these assertions truly reflected what she was feeling at the time is unknowable. But Hazel must have realized that she was walking away from what most musicians longed for—a room of their own, a steady gig. Surely, it was a frightening proposition, one that could make or break the career she'd worked so hard to achieve.

During the 1940s, there were few, if any, nationally recognized African American concert pianists. The most prominent name in concert circles was that of the classical pianist and composer Philippa Schuyler. A child prodigy, she was only eleven years old when she began touring the country. By the time she was thirteen, she had performed her original composition for one hundred instruments, *Manhattan Nocturne,* with the New York Philharmonic Orchestra. Schuyler was something of a spectacle, a curiosity to white audiences. Her youth and extraordinary musical talent attracted crowds, but her family background garnered even greater attention. She was the biracial daughter of well-known black conservative journalist, George Schuyler, and Josephine Cogdell, a liberal white artist from Texas. The Schuylers did not like hearing the word *prodigy* applied to their daughter. They attributed her genius to her mixed race heritage, what they called "hybrid genetics." They raised her in total isolation and kept her on a diet of only raw foods (including rare meat) and daily doses of vitamin C. These bizarre stories of her home life made for titillating stories in the press, but by the time Philippa Schuyler was an adult, American audiences had lost interest in her. She eventually went overseas to continue her career.

Hazel Scott was no stranger to the concert stage, but this was the first time in her career that she had relied solely on the concert circuit for her livelihood. Leaving Café Society's nest and Barney Josephson's management was a huge step for her. So much of what she had accomplished she owed to his guidance and support. After seven years as Café Society's headliner, Hazel Scott bid the club scene farewell. She gave her good-byes over a two-week period, during which her fellow musicians, actors, friends, and fans packed the house to witness the end of her era at the nightclub.

A writer in *Ebony* observed, "Now she goes back to playing piano as she believes it should be played. She is financially set now and doesn't have to cater to the crowd with boogie. With her name as a drawing card, she should be able to succeed in becoming the first Negro pianist to make the classics pay."[22]

Hazel insisted that this new phase of her career would give her a chance to truly expand: "It made me practice and get in shape instead of coasting along with pop tunes." She regretted having to close the door on Las Vegas nightclubs, however. "My Las Vegas act was nipped in the bud, and I had just performed there," she said.[23] The lounges and nightclubs on "the Strip" paid extremely well. Not to mention that only a select few top performers had entrée to those bookings, very few blacks were among them. But what her husband had asked of her Hazel had agreed to. Nightclubs were off limits.

Hazel worked with the renowned piano teacher Richard McClanahan, whose students included some of the most important pianists of the period. "Mr. Mac," in addition to his musical education at Northwestern University, had studied in London under the tutelage of one of the masters of piano instruction, Tobias Matthay. Because solo concerts would be more physically demanding than performing several sets at a nightclub with breaks in between, Hazel's training with McClanahan focused on strengthening exercises and methods of relaxation. She made it down to his Steinway Hall studio at least twice a week.

Hazel would continue to swing the way she had always swung. Her style didn't change, but she did incorporate new elements into her show. She would play a straight classical segment, which she hadn't done since she was very young, followed by a modern segment of popular tunes by American composers. Being so closely identified with "jazzin' the classics," Hazel knew it was what audiences would be waiting to hear, so she closed all of her shows with boogie-woogie and swing improvisations of the European classics.

It was clear that she had no intention of presenting herself to the concert world as a legit classical pianist. After so many years in the business that kind of career turn would have required a total reinvention of her image and style. Instead, she built on her prior achievements, adding variety but sticking to her stock-in-trade.

The rarefied air of the concert stage was less forgiving than the club scene, and Hazel knew it. There was a certain expectation; the crowds were different, the mood more austere. She would have to answer to those critics who had long considered her a pop artist not a fine artist.

It was Hazel's custom to shrug off her critics. She would often tell the story of one performance in particular when she asked the crowd, "What would you like to hear next?" And a heckler shouted: "A piano player!" When John Hammond made it a practice to read the newspaper during her sets at Café Society, Hazel ignored him. Given his reputation among musicians for being patronizing and controlling, his aversion to Hazel's playing was more than likely based on his personal bias than his professional tastes. Hammond was known to interfere with bandleaders' choices of musicians and arrangers, using his authority as a producer to manipulate artists. He prided himself on discovering, molding, and cultivating new black talent. Someone as self-possessed and proud as Hazel, with all her Juilliard training and professional endorsements from the likes of Art Tatum and Fats Waller, didn't need or want Hammond's guidance, and very likely she let him know it.

Of course, there were those critics whom she could never please, such as James Agee, whose comments were particularly venomous: "She plays her 'classics' with a slobbering, anarchic, vindictive, rushing affectation which any mediocre elementary piano teacher would slap her silly for."[24] Agee's general contention was that black artists, by attempting "to dignify the folk by classicizing it" and illuminating the classical by "folksifying it," resulted in "a lowering or full dismissal of ethical and moral standards."[25] Along with Hazel, over the years, he vehemently criticized Paul Robeson's "Othello," Duke Ellington's "more ambitious arrangements and compositions," and "the dreadful pseudo 'cultured' dancing of Katherine Dunham and her troupe" Cab Calloway, Cootie Williams, and Louis Armstrong's "more frenzied scatting and his repeated high-notes" were also targets of Agee's vitriol.[26]

Annoyed and slightly amused by these attacks, Hazel measured her skills according to her own standards, and the opinions of her fellow musicians. She was dismissive of those who analyzed the work of musicians but had never picked up an instrument. "First I read through it without getting angry," she said. "If the critic is grossly unfair and it's only a personal attack, I just discard it. . . . But still critics can be destructive in both ways. They can be destructive if they praise you too highly and you haven't been that good. But if I'm emotionally torn up after a performance and a critic says I skimmed the surface of my material, I want to hit him in the mouth!"[27]

The success of Hazel's concert career would rely on the merging of her commercial appeal with her virtuosity. Her name alone would fill seats with an eager crowd, but only her exceptional performance of straight classics and jazz would keep them there. It was a major undertaking that could have easily undone all she had accomplished thus far.

Hazel signed with Coppicus and Schang, a division of Columbia Artists Management, whose roster of clients included Paul Robeson, Marian Anderson, Vladimir Horowitz, Leonard Bernstein, and Igor Stravinsky. The firm promptly booked Hazel on a thirty-five-week tour that would give her a national presence but take her away from her base. That was the tradeoff. If she was to play only concert halls, it would require her to be on the road most of the year. With Adam in Washington during the week, the couple would have to do some finagling of their schedules in order to make time for each other.

"HAZEL SCOTT Celebrated Star of Motion Pictures, Concerts, Radio. The Perfect Combination: Superb Pianist, Powerful Box Office," read the promo. Hazel's pay was a minimum of fifteen hundred dollars per appearance or 60 percent of the box office, whichever was greater. Her new agents were aware of her feelings about playing before segregated audiences and promised not to book her in such venues, but they didn't feel it was necessary to add the clause in her contract.

Adam decided that Hazel should kick off her concert tour on one of Washington's great stages, Constitution Hall. He deliberately ignored the fact that the world-renowned contralto Marian Anderson had been denied access just a few years earlier by the Daughters of the American Revolution (DAR), which controlled all of the hall's bookings and limited appearances to white performers only.

Shortly before the concert was to take place, Hazel's agent received a call from the hall's manager, Fred E. Hand. According to the *New York Herald Tribune,* Mr. Hand telephoned to ask if the pianist was a Negro. "When he was told that she was, the engagement date was withdrawn."[28] Hand would not discuss the DAR policy with the agent or the press.

"As a member of Congress I recoiled at the idea that a Congressman's wife, an American citizen, and a gifted artist would not be allowed to perform in a hall largely supported by tax-deductible contributions," Adam Powell protested.[29] He fired off a telegram to President Truman, whom he had not met but introduced himself by writing, "REQUEST IMMEDIATE ACTION ON YOUR PART IN THE SITUATION OF MY WIFE HAZEL SCOTT CONCERT PIANIST BEING BARRED FROM CONSTITUTION HALL BECAUSE SHE IS A NEGRO."[30] Truman answered immediately. He expressed his regret in a letter to Congressman Powell, which read, "One of the marks of a democracy is its willingness to respect and reward talent without regard to race or origin." Yet he resolved that it would be impossible for him to interfere "in the management or policy of a private enterprise such as the one in question."[31]

The DAR maintained that the "white artists" rule, adopted in 1932, was "in accordance with the prevailing custom" of segregated society in the District of Columbia.[32] While it recognized the right of citizens to request the use of Constitution Hall, it reserved the "individual right to grant or deny a request."

After discovering that Bess Truman, an honorary "daughter," had accepted an invitation to a DAR tea during the controversy, Powell quickly lashed out at the first lady. In the middle of Fifth Avenue during the Columbus Day parade in New York, he told the media, "From now on, Mrs. Truman is the *last* lady."[33]

Mrs. Truman was congenial but felt no responsibility in the matter: "In my opinion my acceptance of the hospitality is not related to the merits of the issue which has arisen. Personally, I regret that a conflict has arisen for which I am in no wise responsible. I deplore any action which denies artistic talent an opportunity to express itself because of prejudice against race origin."[34] Mrs. Truman attended the tea.

Hazel wasn't at all surprised by the DAR's denial. Washington, she believed, was just as segregated as the deep South. She considered it the height of hypocrisy that Adam could walk the halls of the Congress but was not welcome in the dining room "Reserved for Members of Congress Only." The fact that they couldn't eat at most local restaurants or stay in a local hotel made it infinitely clear to her that Washington was not nearly as progressive as it pretended to be. The congressman had his work cut out for him. Powell would be on the attack throughout his political career, calling out anyone and everyone whom he believed contributed to the problem of racial discrimination, including members of well-to-do black society who he felt didn't fight hard enough for equal rights. He called them "the black bourgeoisie . . . still wrapped in antebellum dreams of a mulatto society."[35] Prominent black religious leaders that he found lacking he lashed out at as well, calling them, "Uncle Tomming clergymen with Harvard accents."[36]

Neither Adam nor Hazel had any illusions about what Washington was or wasn't. Adam was willing to do battle. Hazel, on the other hand, threw up her hands. She made little effort to mingle in Washington's political and social circles.

She dismissed the DAR, telling a reporter from the Associated Press that she appreciated the president's condemnation of its policy but Mrs. Truman looked "as if she gives sanction" to its "white artists only" policy.[37]

Various chapters of the DAR were embarrassed and disgruntled by the controversy. The Polly Wyckoff Chapter in Leonia, New Jersey, made a statement to the press condemning the executive committee's actions: "Constitution Hall is not a local Washington city possession and should not be controlled by any 'gentlemen's agreement' made to satisfy the prejudices of local Washingtonians." Congresswoman Clare Boothe Luce threatened to resign from the organization if her chapter did not stand in protest. Public apologies, published in newspapers across the country, came from individual members, who didn't want to be associated with the DAR's actions.

Time published a letter to the editor that was a glaring example of national "separate but equal" sentiment. It asked, simply, "Is there not a statute of long standing in the city of Washington specifying that Negroes cannot hire the use of public halls designated for white people?"[38]

Hazel let Adam pursue the matter as he saw fit, but the ladies of the DAR and their "prevailing customs" had tried her patience. She left town for an engagement in Montreal. Reporters caught up with her at LaGuardia Airport in New York. She told them that she was "very angry over the incident,"[39] and made it clear that "she did not expect special favors because she is the wife of a Representative but said she is entitled to the same privileges and rights as other citizens."[40] She then turned to Adam, who had driven her to the airport, saying, "This has got to be broken down. If there is no democracy in Washington, then what did we fight the war for?"[41]

The DAR debate rattled the very foundation of Congress, erupting into a dispute of such enormous proportions that some wondered if Powell had calculated the entire thing, relying on the inevitable upheaval to make his presence known on Capitol Hill. Some even suggested that the publicity wouldn't hurt Hazel's career either. Everyone had an opinion. Congressmen took sides, and every major newspaper ran the story. But still the DAR wouldn't budge.

Powell asked his fellow congressmen from New York, "What action do you plan to take?"[42] Senator Robert F. Wagner, a Democrat from New York, replied:

> The attempt to extend race prejudice into the field of art and music is to my mind the most striking demonstration of the utter unworthiness of race prejudice in any form. The very fact that people of all races make their contribution to art and music proves how uncivilized are the barriers which now exist. It is doubly reprehensible that these barriers should be applied to the building which bears the name of Constitution Hall and therefore prides itself upon its connection with what the American Constitution stood for. I have always been ready and will con-

tinue to be ready to protest and to join others in protesting against this travesty. This discrimination does violence to the memory of the patriots who risked their all to establish our Constitution and the example of all those who fought in this war.[43]

Senator James M. Mead, a Democrat from New York, lent his support, stating in a telegram to Adam Powell, "It is indeed regrettable that such discriminatory action should be taken in the capital city of this nation which has just successfully concluded a long and costly war to stamp out a regime which was fostering just such intolerance in Europe. I have requested the management of the Constitution Hall to reconsider. Racial discrimination has no place in this nation."[44]

In the middle of all of this, another battle was brewing. When members of the Negro Capitol Press Club discovered that Hazel was scheduled to appear at the National Press Club's annual dinner for President Truman, they became outraged. They charged that her acceptance of the invitation was "inconsistent" with the "dramatic protestations" of Congressman Powell. The *Washington Post* printed their statement: "As Negro newsmen covering the Nation's Capitol we cannot help but be mindful that we are barred from membership in the National Press Club and denied the privilege of service in its dining room or at its bar."[45] They were "wondering out loud" whether this latest development was related to the DAR's denial of Hazel's concert request.[46] Perhaps this was Washington's sly way of smoothing things over with the pianist.

When Hazel discovered that black journalists were not allowed in the press galleries of the Senate or the House, she immediately sent a telegram to the National Press Club canceling her appearance on the grounds that "journalists of my race" are barred from the organization.[47] She expressed regret that she would be unable to play for the president and added that she had canceled a "profitable engagement" in Columbus, Ohio, in order to accept the invitation.[48]

With their names and images spread across national headlines, Hazel continued her concert tour without the good graces of the DAR. Her husband stayed behind and fought the proverbial good fight. In the final analysis, both houses of Congress could agree on one thing—Adam Powell Jr. was the man to watch in Washington.

The DAR never conceded in Hazel's case. It would not loosen the ban on black artists at Constitution Hall until April of 1946 when the choir of Tuskegee Institute, the all-black university founded by Booker T. Washington, was allowed (after some infighting among DAR members) to perform a concert in his honor.

Next on Hazel's tour schedule was a concert at Chicago's Orchestra Hall. Her varied program included straight classics by Chopin, Bach, Ravel, De Falla, Rachmaninoff, and Scarlatti, as well as two of her original compositions, "Passion Suite," a musical adaptation of the last days of Christ written and arranged in the spiritual tradition, and "Tales of Four Cities," a boogie-woogie journey tracing the music's influences through New Orleans, Kansas City, Chicago, and New York. Accompanied by Eugene Cedric on saxophone and cornet, Edgar Brown on double bass, and Wilmore "Slick" Jones on drums, she played to a packed house for one night only.

Unfortunately, Hazel's live concerts were never recorded. She was not fully satisfied with the way she sounded on records, but she was never able to get record labels interested in the idea of producing a live recording. Because she had so little say in the kinds of studio recordings she produced, Hazel believed that being captured in live performance would have given her greater creative freedom with "no one looking over my shoulder."[49] She thought the sound would have been truer, a better representation of her artistic voice. During this period of her concert career, information as to what she played and how she played it is solely reliant on program notes and critical reviews.

Chicago music critics were often less than kind to Hazel, calling her "New York's Dorothy Donegan." Like Hazel, Donegan—who had studied at the Chicago Conservatory of Music, Chicago Musical College, and the University of Southern California—was known for playing swing improvisations of classical works; she, too, had been mentored and inspired by Art Tatum. While she may have lacked Hazel's glamour, she made up for it with a sharp wit and an infectious performance style. Donegan had a habit of performing pianistic stunts onstage, playing with one hand behind her back or doing mock impersonations of other pianists. She'd even get up and dance to her own playing. Still, her virtuosity was never questioned. As the first black jazz pianist to concertize at Orchestra Hall, Dorothy Donegan's career did not live up to her remarkable talent. Some critics suggested that her onstage antics undermined her brilliance, her madcap personality upstaging her finely tuned skills. Donegan recorded numerous albums and spent most of her career performing in nightclubs across the country as well as on the jazz festival circuit in the United States and abroad. Talent aside, her inability to achieve mass appeal is evidence of just how difficult it was to forge a major career path in the male-dominated world of jazz.

Although her talent was certainly on par with Hazel's, Donegan never received the same kind of promotion or publicity. Despite the similarities of their styles, comparisons between the two women were rarely, if ever, made. In fact, most women pianists of that period were judged by how well they measured up to Mary Lou Williams, who was considered the best and most authentic among them. Only in Chicago was Hazel subjected to the critics' preference for Donegan, where typical headlines read "Hazel Scott's Bop outshines her Bach," and reviewers labeled her overall performance as mediocre, wild, and undisciplined.[50]

Pleasing critics was one thing; pleasing audiences was another. Claudia Cassidy of the *Chicago Tribune* remarked on the reaction to Hazel Scott, observing that Orchestra Hall's capacity crowd was "so devoted it sometimes verged on the devout."[51] When she began her boogie-woogie stride, the audience was "almost dancing in the aisles."[52]

From Chicago, Hazel returned to New York to perform a recital at Carnegie Hall. In the advertisements for the show, her transition from sex kitten to concert artist was most apparent. The "former nightclub pianist" appeared in more conservative dress—blouses with high collars, tailored jackets and cardigans. Her image, though still glamorous, was now less provocative.

Accompanied by her trio—Eugene Cedric, Slick Jones, and Edgar Brown—Hazel fared much better among the New York critics, who were, of course, more familiar with the artist and her repertoire. Her Carnegie Hall concert began with the more sublime "Passion Suite" then moved into the classical works of Scarlatti, Chopin, and Rachmaninoff. To complete the classical segment, her trio joined her in an improvisational performance of Grieg's incidental music from *Peer Gynt*. From the songbooks of Jerome Kern and George Gershwin, she played and sang a number of popular tunes, then she moved into her swinging renditions of Bach, Liszt, and Chopin. While it was considered a complete, well-conceptualized show, critics would give Hazel an average grade on her straight classical work. Francis Perkins of the *New York Herald Tribune* wrote, "She is considerably less at home in straight concert music. Her fingers flew swiftly, but she seemed to have little idea of the expressive purport of these works."[53] Of her contemporary works, another critic wrote, "She plays better than any of the other pianists prominently identified with this type of music. She brings to it a certain style and a true piano technique and tone that enable her fully to realize its peculiar rhythmic, melodic and harmonic characteristics."[54] Hazel closed the show on a high note with her swinging "Tale of Four Cities."

Overall the concerts were sellout successes. And while her reviews were not all raves, they were favorable enough to garner a steady stream of concert bookings. After Hazel's concert date at Detroit's Masonic Auditorium, the *Detroit Times* was exuberant: "In Chopin numbers she displayed impeccable technique, weaving the gossamer melodies with delicacy and brilliance. . . . There wasn't a still foot in the audience."[55] The *Cleveland News* wrote simply that Hazel "wowed 'em at Music Hall."[56]

She enjoyed the warm reception of her fans. Playing in a new city before a different crowd every night was exhilarating; the amount of focus it demanded she found stimulating. But Hazel missed Adam, Alma, and home. She would make frequent trips to see Adam in Washington when her schedule allowed, but before she could get settled it would be time to go again. She touched base with Alma in White Plains between rehearsals and her studies with McClanahan. Then she was back on the road.

Around October, in the middle of her tour, Hazel discovered that she was pregnant. When she told Adam, he was thrilled and immediately shared the happy news with his congregation. "About June, there will be another big noise here beside me," he exclaimed.[57]

Ed Sullivan (who had not yet become a famous television host) broke the news in his entertainment column in the *New York Daily News*. Thereafter, Hazel raved about her pregnancy in all of her press statements.

Amid all of the excitement, trouble loomed. Throughout 1945, Adam Powell Sr.'s health was in decline. After suffering a massive stroke, he was no longer able to make it up the stairs of his home and had to be moved to a ground floor apartment on Convent Avenue. During his recuperation, he would spend the majority of his time upstate at Adam and Hazel's. Then, just as Powell Sr.'s needs had been taken care of, Alma began experiencing her own health problems. After a hospital visit, doctors diagnosed her with viral pneumonia. Initially, they believed that with the proper medication and some rest her lungs would clear. But Alma's health deteriorated rapidly.

On December 14, 1945, Alma Scott died at St. Agnes Hospital. She was forty-six years old.

For Hazel, the devastation was beyond description. After depending on her mother her entire life, how was she to navigate a new marriage and a pregnancy without her? The emotional flight, from elation over her pregnancy to this incredible loss, was nearly unbearable. Adam rushed to her side, as did her mother's best friend, Mabel Howard.

Alma Long Scott's obituary appeared in several major publications, including the New York dailies and *Time* magazine. All of them mentioned her accomplishments as a musician and her dedication to her daughter's musical career.

Hazel would speak adoringly of her mother, rarely doing an interview without some mention of Alma's name. Throughout her life, she referred to her as the "biggest single influence in my life."[58]

The family was in mourning, but with the holidays upon them they had perfunctory duties to fulfill. There were holiday church functions, gifts to buy, and Christmas cards to be mailed to a long list of politicians, constituents, congregants, family members, and friends.

The holiday card featured a smiling photo of the couple wrapped in each other's arms. In Hazel's handwriting, the inscription read:

> That the unity which won this war may win the peace; that this peace shall be one of good will between all men of all races, nations and faiths—This be our heartfelt wish.
> Hazel and Adam Powell[59]

Quietly, the Powells spent their holiday at home. There was little celebration, only time to gather together, collect themselves, and heal.

In 1946, Hazel forced herself to go back to the studio. She had signed a new contract with Signature Records. *Hazel Scott: A Piano Recital,* her first album with the label, was an offering of popular music, a few boogie-woogie numbers, and rare recordings of her concert piano. Given her condition, Hazel was surprisingly focused, having come into the studio and played her original composition, "A Rainy Night in G," with no rehearsal and no retakes. Unlike so many other black American jazz artists whose roots were in the South and whose aesthetic sensibilities were naturally attuned to blues and gospel music, Hazel made a conscious effort to incorporate the blues into her style. This original composition, while it meets all of the requirements of a twelve-bar blues, does demonstrate why a fellow musician once told her, "You play the blues like a lady." "A Rainy Night in G" sounds a bit pristine and not quite as swinging as some of her other arrangements.

Nevertheless, Hazel is right at home on "How High the Moon." After the rubato intro, filled with lush chords and running passages, she adds syncopation and harmonic progressions to make the popular song her own. In contrast, she plays the Dietz and Schwartz tune "I Guess I'll Have to Change My Plans" legato, an instrumental interpretation invoking the lyrical sentiment of the melancholy tune. She is joined by the Toots Camarata Orchestra on a swinging version of "I've Got the World on a String" and "On the Sunny Side of the Street," where she adds bright, lively vocals after a big brass intro.

Her solo piano can be heard on three of her favorites by Chopin. *Fantasie Impromptu,* considered one of Chopin's most challenging compositions, and the pastoral "Nocturne in B-flat Minor," which she plays straight with little embellishment and no improvisation. Only on the "Valse in C-sharp Minor" does Hazel play around with the rhythmic structure and contrasting minor to major tonalities; she adds bass notes in several measures, and the waltz swings for awhile before she returns to Chopin's original ideas. Among the other classics she performs are "Toccato," by the Italian composer Pietro Domenico Paradies, and Scarlatti's "Sonata in C Minor." Hazel's original composition, "Idyll," is a free-form melody, played in a minor key, in which she uses diminished and augmented chords to create a languorous blue feeling. Recordings of "Ich vil Sich Shpilen" (I Want to Play for You) and another original piece, "Butterfly Kick," Hazel produced with Camarata, but neither of those sides were released with this collection.

A Piano Recital sold more than seventy-five thousand copies, placing Hazel Scott among the industry's most popular solo artists. Considering the times, her accomplishments in the music industry were noteworthy. A young black woman pianist with crossover appeal, sellout concerts, and record-breaking album sales was rare indeed.

Artistically, Hazel may have wanted to stretch out, to venture beyond her "Bach to Boogie-Woogie" repertoire, but, given her popularity, she chose to continue performing in the style that fans, concert organizers, and record companies expected from her. Even so, the new, innovative sound of bebop that was happening uptown and in the 52nd street nightclubs fascinated her. For years, she had been a fan of and friend to musicians Dizzy Gillespie, Charlie Parker, and Bud Powell, catching their shows in Harlem at Minton's Playhouse. Although it was her command of the classics that they admired, Hazel marveled at their ingenuity.[60]

While she would begin to incorporate some bebop elements into her music in later years, Hazel stuck with her "Bach to Boogie-Woogie" repertoire. There were other pianists on the scene who may have incorporated one or two "jazzed" versions of classics into their performances, such as Art Tatum and Dorothy Donegan, but Hazel's name was synonymous with the style. Considered a novelty act by some, she viewed it as the chance to show off her full range, to fuse her affinity for the classics with her passion for jazz. Yet to assume that Hazel continued "swinging the classics" for purely artistic reasons or entertainment value alone would be to assume that she had plenty of options. In a male-dominated industry that offered little in the way of respect and recognition for women, Hazel could hardly turn her back on the opportunities she was afforded. Although she was working hard for every single booking, Hazel knew she was in a more coveted position than many of her contemporaries. Now, much more than a youthful indulgence, "swinging the classics" was a living.

For the 1946 congressional election, Republicans chose Grant Reynolds, a former army chaplain, war veteran, and graduate of New York University, to oppose Adam Powell Jr. Like Powell, he was smart and handsome, a powerful speaker capable of galvanizing the black vote. When New York governor Tom Dewey heard Reynolds speak at his Madison Square Garden rally in 1944, the Republicans were sure they had found their man. With his charisma, his resume and his political agenda, he could give Powell a real fight. People in Harlem called the election "the battle of the giants."[61]

Powell's absenteeism was Reynold's first point of attack. Powell had missed fifteen of thirty-two roll call votes, prompting Reynolds to call him "Part-time Powell."[62] The conservative black paper *New York Age* and the *Amsterdam News* threw their support to Reynolds, while the *People's Voice* remained Powell's major organ. Reynolds attacked Powell's position on segregation as outlined in his book *Marching Blacks* (published earlier that year by Dial Press), which attacked southern racism and called for blacks living in the South to make a mass exodus north. Matters became personal when he brought up Powell's rumored infidelities, his womanizing, his partying and drinking. His divorce from Isabel and the embarrassment it caused his congregation were also brought to the fore. "[T]he people of the 22nd district are sick and tired of buffoonery and showmanship in politics," Reynolds proclaimed. As the campaign progressed, the Reynolds camp grew optimistic. Dramatic and hyperbolic stories about his chances of actually beating Powell began to spread through the community. Still, Powell Jr. never broke a sweat. It didn't matter that Reynolds had the support of high-profile blacks such as the boxer Joe Louis and author Zora Neale Hurston. Powell knew his own strengths and the emotional hold he had on Harlem. He also had Hazel, whose West Indian roots influenced the turnout of Caribbean blacks.

On the day of the election, Harlem voters remembered the man who took on Blumstein's on 125th Street, who challenged Consolidated Edison, the phone company, and the Transit Authority. They had marched side by side with Reverend Powell; they had stood on their stoops and listened to him preach on street corners. They had picketed, shouted, rallied, and cried together. That November Adam Powell beat Grant Reynolds by a two-to-one margin.

Following his win, Powell sold his interest in the *People's Voice*. The grapevine had it that he needed to distance himself from the paper, as the journal was gaining the reputation as a mouthpiece of the Communist Party. Powell issued a statement explaining that his schedule was too full to carry out his editorial duties. Between his responsibilities in Washington and at the Abyssinian Baptist Church, he could no longer fulfill the duties of editor and chairman of the Powell-Buchanan Publishing Company.

Soon Powell would be able to add another duty to his list of responsibilities. On the morning of July 17, 1946, Hazel gave birth to a baby boy, eight pounds, seven ounces, at Sydenham Hospital in Harlem. He was given the name of his father and grandfather. Adam Clayton Powell III (nicknamed "Skipper"); he "had Hazel's looks, my early curly blond hair, and bones that said he would one day be bigger than his father," Adam observed. Mabel Howard was named as young Adam's godmother.[63]

"My greatest thrill was the first time I saw Skipper," Hazel beamed. "I remember looking at him and thinking, 'My goodness, it's really true.'"[64]

Hazel returned to work about six months after the baby was born. She had concerts scheduled in San Francisco, Seattle, and Richmond, Virginia. Dates were also lined up months in advance with symphony orchestras in Toronto, Milwaukee, Philadelphia, and Los Angeles. Adam raved about his wife's success, declaring, "She is the first Negro instrumentalist to hit the big time in the concert world."[65]

But her arduous itinerary came to a sudden stop one night before her show at the Roxy in New York. On the way to the theater, Adam began experiencing chest pains. The limousine driver changed course and rushed to the nearest hospital.

Adam, only thirty-nine years old, had suffered a heart attack. He was hospitalized for several days, after which he was instructed to take time off work.

Congress granted him an indefinite leave of absence. After so many years of relentless campaigning, politicking, and preaching, Adam Powell was able to get some much needed rest. Although the circumstances weren't ideal and Adam's health issues were indeed serious, he and Hazel were glad to have this rare respite with their son.

Hazel kept her husband sufficiently entertained in and out of the house. She loved his applause most of all. "At home, Adam used to turn on the Capehart stereo and say, 'Go on and dance.'" And there in the living room, with a great big audience of one, she would dance for hours. She was a self-confessed "frustrated dancer" all of her life. One night at the Latin Quarter, a popular nightclub owned by Louis Walters (father of journalist Barbara Walters), Hazel made her "living room show" public. This time she performed a cabaret act that included her playing piano and singing, then dancing several numbers as the band played on. Scant details are available as to the exact tunes she performed or the choreography (whether it was her own or someone else's). Still, much was made in the press about her appearance and her surprising dance debut. Hazel appeared in a black, beaded, strapless gown, ankle-length with a thigh-high split up the middle. She wore fishnet stockings and open-toed shoes, red lipstick, long lashes, and "cat-eye" makeup. Just as Abyssinian members were adjusting to Hazel's presence in the church and her career outside of it, "all the old rumors were hashed up" once they got wind of her Latin Quarter number.[66] When Adam came backstage after the first show, agents, managers, and producers were all gathered around, waiting for his reaction to his wife's performance. Everyone expected him to be angry. His response caught them off guard: "I'm not surprised at all. She's been doing this for me for years. The only thing I find wrong with the show is that you don't get to the dancing soon enough."[67]

In the early part of 1948, Hazel's schedule turned hectic again. She went back into the recording studio to begin work on her next album. She had recently signed a new deal, this time with Columbia Records. Aptly titled *Great Scott!,* the album showed off Hazel's swing piano and pristine vocals on eight of her most requested songs. "Dancing on the Ceiling" and "Nightmare Blues," Hazel's voice is the highlight as she sings in the legit style of the period, soft and melodious. Sissle and Blake's "Love Will Find a Way" and "Love Me or Leave Me" are approached in much the same manner. On the instrumentals, she swings harder, pulling out all of her pianistic flair, particularly on "Emaline," "Mary Lou," and her own infectious "Brown Bee Boogie."

The whimsical, upbeat selections made the record a hit among fans and most critics. However, some reserved their praise. One reviewer in the *Chicago Daily Tribune* wrote that "without exception the vocal sides are entirely inadequate. 'Brown Bee Boogie' is one of the best instrumental sides, but it shows an overanxiety to be inventive."[68]

In stark contrast to all that swing, in the summer of 1948, Hazel was asked to perform a concert with the New York Philharmonic Orchestra at Lewisohn Stadium. The six-thousand-seat facility, located on the campus of the City College of New York, was designed for both athletic events and theatrical performances. Hazel's much-publicized concert was filled to capacity, including the infield, which seated thousands more. According to program notes, with Walter Hendl conducting, they opened with Beethoven's "First Concerto" and continued with other contemporary American orchestral works, including Aaron Copland's *El Salon Mexico,* a tone poem based on Mexican folk music; the overture from Gian Carlo Menotti's opera

Amelia Goes to the Ball; William Schuman's *Sideshow;* and the overture to *Roman Carnival* by the French composer Hector Berlioz. Critics were impressed overall with Hazel's command of the classical
works. But once again it was her popular renditions of songs like
"The Way You Look Tonight," "Body and Soul," "Tea for Two," and
her own standard blues tune, "A Rainy Night in G" that were received most enthusiastically. "Miss Scott was so much more in character and at ease in her elaborations on Kern, Youmans and such.
Undoubtedly her concourse with music of Beethoven and Mozart
has had a good deal to do with the fluency and specific virtuosity of
her jazz style. But her 'serious' efforts are still far from the finish she
has achieved in her more familiar role," said the *New York Times.*[69]
Hazel ended the show in grand style, playing the piano with only
rhythm accompaniment, Jimmy Crawford on drums and Lloyd Trot-
man on bass.

As the New Year rolled around, Hazel performed an original suite,
Caribbean Fete, before a sold-out Carnegie Hall crowd. She had been
quietly working on the composition for several months. Set against
the colorful backdrop of Trinidad's Carnival celebration, each of the
suite's four movements are based on the traditional tunes performed
during the last three days of the pre-Lenten season festivities. She
played "Dame Lorraine," a lively melody typically performed in the
Sunday night parade of mummers in Trinidad. It was followed by
"Castellan," a tune written in the tradition of the Spanish waltz, and
"Paseo-Careso," a standard calypso. Without pausing between the
third and fourth movements, Hazel played "Ash Wednesday," mark-
ing the end of the fete. Although no live recording of her performance of this music exists, it is safe to assume that Hazel chose to
play these traditional Caribbean tunes in a nontraditional way,
adding swing elements whenever she had the chance.
    In the second part of the concert, Hazel played straight classical
piano. She chose the Prelude and Fugue in C-sharp Minor from
Bach's *Well Tempered Clavier,* as well as "Rhapsody in C Major" by
Dohnanyi; Mendelssohn's "Rondo Capriccioso in E Major," opus 14;
and Bach's "Jesu, Joy of Man's Desiring," arranged by Myra Hess. She

ended the classical segment with Chopin's "Sonata in B-flat Minor," opus 35. The pop segment included songs by Rodgers and Hart, Irving Berlin, and Vincent Youmans. She brought the night to the close with her trademark "swinging the classics" repertoire. This time she swung Beethoven's "Für Elise," Dinicu-Heifetz's "Hora Staccato," and finally what she called "The Three B's" (Blues, Boogie-Woogie, and Bop).

In 1949, when their son was about three years old, Adam and Hazel decided that the White Plains house no longer suited their needs. So they purchased an impressive home on two acres of land in the Fleetwood section of Mount Vernon, New York. It was a beautiful estate, well staffed with all of the amenities to which they had grown accustomed—ten rooms, four baths and two servants.

Adam's love for the open air, fishing, and sailing lured them to Westhampton, Long Island, in search of a summer retreat. The beach house was in a fairly isolated area on Dune Road with the nearest neighbor a quarter of a mile away. (That neighbor happened to be Charles Addams, the famed cartoonist for the *New Yorker.*) With his pipe in one hand and a scotch-on-the-rocks in the other, Adam spent long afternoons fishing, leaving it to Hazel to prepare the catch. "I can't believe I'm cleaning fish!" she protested.[70] Hazel had developed into a fantastic cook, able to put her spin on any dish, be it West Indian, southern, French or Italian. Cooking became one of her favorite pastimes in addition to reading.

In the spring of 1949, Adam surprised Hazel with a Steinway grand piano, which he had installed in their new beach house. A rare model D, the piano was believed to have once been owned by Josef Hofmann, the great Polish American pianist and composer. Because of Hofmann's exceptionally small hands, Steinway had customized the keyboard, making the keys narrower to accommodate him.

With both of them back in full swing, Adam and Hazel agreed that they would make sure to be home on the weekends. When Hazel was on the road and Adam was in Washington, the housekeeper cared for their son. Says Adam III, "They decided to try to have as normal a life as possible. He would be in Washington during the week at least January through May, and she'd be traveling a lot, but on Saturday and Sunday we were going to be a family. And so wherever they were, the deal was they would have to get back to New York by Friday night."[71]

"Saturday is what we call our family day," Hazel said.[72] "We make it a point to be at home. The help usually has that day off, anyway. We take Skipper to the show and sit through millions of cartoons. After coming out of the show, with tired eyes and a headache probably, I make it to the house and cook. Adam, who fancies himself quite a cook, is always a pain in the neck, running in and out of the kitchen, peeking in pots."[73]

In the evening, while Adam put the finishing touches on his sermon, Hazel and young Adam would spend hours together reading and watching television. These cozy family evenings were a big change from their days of cocktail parties, club hopping, and opening nights. Adam reflected, "My life with Hazel has been chockfull of the kind of experiences that would excite the Average American Husband—warm, golden brown hot cakes on a winter morning, lazy summer afternoons on our Long Island beach; beer and crackers and cheese on our terrace, relaxing evenings at the neighborhood movie house and in the living room before the fire with Rachmaninoff's *Second Piano Concerto* coming out of the phonograph."[74]

The Powells were an enigma to America. Never had there been a more celebrated black couple, a more high-profile black family. From all outside appearances, their lives were idyllic. But behind the closed doors of their wealthy estate they had their share of problems.

Much later in life Hazel would confess to her son that in the first year of her marriage to Adam Powell she wanted out.

The marriage that they both described as glorious could also be quite volatile. "We fought bitterly but loved each other deeply," Hazel admitted.[75] The constant pressure of their demanding careers, the public persona they had to keep up, and the everyday issues common to all newly married couples complicated their relationship.

Hazel's life had undergone such a dramatic change that she often found it difficult to navigate. All at once, she dealt with the death of her mother, a new marriage, a new baby, and a new direction in her career. Throughout her life, Hazel had relied on Alma's guidance. With her mother gone, Adam became her sole source of emotional support.

Overwhelmed and filled with self-doubt, Hazel repressed her emotions for the sake of her marriage and family, burying them so deep that it would be years before they were unearthed, rising to the surface in the most unexpected and uncontrollable way.

CHAPTER ELEVEN

Black and *Red*

During the late 1940s, postwar America found itself grappling with major social and political issues that left the country divided. Democracy was worthy of battle overseas, but at home it remained an elusive ideal for many of America's citizens.

On a trip to Panama in 1949, Adam Powell, accompanied by his wife and son, addressed the Panamanian National Assembly regarding the building of the canal, and in particular about the working conditions and treatment of the workers. This subject eventually led to a discourse on the poor state of race relations in the United States. "We are living today in one world, and whether we be Jew or Gentile, Protestant or Catholic, black or white, Americans or Panamanians, we are all equals in today's society. Unfortunately, there are some people of my nation who are ignorant. They think that they are better than anyone else. I wish to assure you that those people do not represent the majority thinking of the American public."[1]

As unemployment, overcrowding in urban areas, and poverty plagued northern cities and southern blacks became more resistant to "Jim Crow" segregation, racial tensions across the country escalated. Following a string of successful concerts in South America, Hazel returned to the United States and the widespread hostility and discrimination of which her husband spoke.

Touring Canada, where she presumed she'd have no problems,

Hazel was forced off a train. It was reported in the black press, but details surrounding the incident were vague. Apparently, blacks were not allowed to travel on this particular railroad line. With ticket in hand, Hazel had been asked to exit the train. She went straight to her husband with the news. Although Adam threatened to make noise about it in Congress, telling Assistant Secretary of State Edward Miller, "If this happens again, I intend to air it with a full speech on the floor before the House," this did not ease Hazel's frustration nor did it prevent similar incidents from happening.

Arriving in Austin for a scheduled appearance at the University of Texas in the Gregory Gymnasium, Hazel was surprised to find all seventy-five hundred seats entirely segregated, divided by a red carpet down the middle of the aisle. Without hesitation, she turned around and left the theater, canceling the show. Her agents had failed to make her standing request for an integrated audience known to the concert organizers. "Why would anyone come to hear me, a Negro, and refuse to sit beside someone just like me?" she commented in *Time*.[2] Hazel made no apologies before leaving town. She dared the school officials to sue her.

After his mother returned to New York, Adam III overheard his parents discussing the matter. "One Saturday morning, I heard my father saying, 'Oh don't tell the boy.' And she said, 'Well, he should know that his mother was escorted out of Austin, Texas by the Texas Rangers last night.'"[3]

Months later, on her way to Spokane, Washington, Hazel's train was stuck in a drift for three days due to heavy snowstorms across the western plains. Traveling nonstop, she had become ill. "I had a raging fever. I was sleeping in my fur coat," Hazel said.[4] All of the passengers headed to Spokane were placed on a bus. At the first rest stop, in Pasco, Washington, she and her traveling companion, Eunice Wolf, went into the diner and tried to order. The young waitress told them that they didn't serve "colored." Hazel was accustomed to this kind of treatment in the South, where restaurants boasted signs that read "No Dogs or Negroes Allowed" or simply "Whites Only." But never had she experienced anything like this so far north. Tired, shocked, and outraged, Hazel looked at Eunice in disbelief: "If you go any further north, you'll be in Canada! This is the state of Washington."[5] At Hazel's insistence, the two women went in search of a police station. When she explained to the desk sergeant what had taken place, he responded, "Are you going to get out of here or am I going to have to run you in for disturbing the peace?"[6]

Later that night they arrived in Spokane. Roy Goodman, a friend who was a concert booking agent, and his wife met them at their hotel. Hazel told him, "I want the following things in the following order: a hot bath, a hot drink and a lawyer."[7]

Hazel contacted her husband in Washington, D.C., and told him the whole story. The Powells filed a lawsuit for fifty thousand dollars in damages against the diner owners, Harry and Blanche Utz. Attorney Willard J. Roe was hired to represent them. The complaint alleged that Hazel was denied service "without any reason whatsoever except that she was a Negro."[8] Soon it became an incident of national interest, covered not only by local Washington state newspapers but the New York press as well. Powell took it to the floor of the House, pointing to his wife's experience as evidence of the pressing need for national civil rights legislation.

At the Federal Courthouse in Spokane, Mr. and Mrs. Utz and the waitress who had refused service, Hilma Victor, claimed that it was Hazel's behavior, not her race, that caused the problem. Ms. Victor suggested that Hazel was "sarcastic, haughty, and demanding."[9] (Given the situation, she was probably all three.) According to the waitress, Hazel had become loud, threatened to "tear her apart," and then walked up and down the aisles asking the other patrons if they'd heard her say that she would not be served. The judge asked for an explicit explanation of the restaurant's policies, which forced Ms. Victor to admit that she had been trained by the owners not to serve "colored people." Black customers were only allowed to order food to go.

Hazel's touring schedule prevented her from attending the trial, but her testimony was read aloud by her attorney while the all-white jury listened. Then a surprise witness was called to testify. A man named Hollis D. Cowell claimed to have been seated in the chair right next to Hazel at the diner. He testified that Hazel Scott had "conducted herself in a lady-like manner and did not shout or tap people on the shoulder, use profanity, or threaten to tear apart the waitress."[10]

After two days of deliberation, the jury decided that the restaurant's actions were a violation of Hazel's civil rights as outlined in the Constitution and the laws of the state of Washington. Having won a small settlement of $250.00, a victorious Hazel exclaimed, "I sued and I won, and I gave all of the money to the NAACP!"[11]

Considering the racial hostility Hazel was experiencing on her tour, it was perhaps ironic that the year 1950 also presented her with an unprecedented opportunity.

Hazel had been a familiar name and face for years all across the country, appearing on the ever-popular Ed Sullivan television show *Toast of the Town* (later named "The Ed Sullivan Show") and making regular appearances on the radio. When the DuMont network—owned by DuMont Laboratories, a maker of television sets—was looking to expand into television broadcasting, it presented Hazel with the idea of hosting her own show.

For a financially strapped startup like DuMont to compete with giants such as NBC and CBS, it had to be innovative in its operations and programming. Unlike most networks, which had a single sponsor for each show, DuMont was one of the first to sell advertising to multiple sponsors, allowing television producers to have greater freedom and creative control over their programs. During its short-lived existence, DuMont produced some of television's most memorable comedy and variety shows, including *Cavalcade of Stars* with Jackie Gleason, the *Morey Amsterdam Show,* the *Arthur Murray Party,* and the popular children's sci-fi series, *Captain Video and His Video Rangers.*

DuMont offered Hazel a standard fifteen-minute show that would run locally on its New York affiliate, WABD, every Friday night. It would be the first television show to feature a black woman as the star host performing solo without sketch comedy or a variety of guests.[12] Recognizing the significance of the opportunity, Hazel gladly accepted the offer.

Whether the network was trying make a social statement by hiring Hazel Scott or simply saw it as a shrewd business move is difficult to ascertain. Whatever the intent, both Hazel and DuMont were making television history.

The Hazel Scott Show debuted on July 3, 1950. Each broadcast opened with her playing "Tea for Two," her theme song, as the camera panned over a cityscape before focusing in on the set, which was designed to resemble a penthouse terrace.[13] Always costumed in gorgeous gowns, diamonds, and neatly coifed hair, Hazel sat at the piano, announcing directly into the camera in a husky, honey-toned voice, "Hello, I'm Hazel Scott."

The black film historian Donald Bogle's description of the show presents a vivid picture: "There sat the shimmering Scott at her piano, like an empress on her throne, presenting at every turn a vision of a woman of experience and sophistication."[14]

She played a mix of standards, classics, and spirituals, performing the vocals occasionally as well. The network readied itself for the audience's reaction. Interestingly, white viewers did not object to Hazel's image, which contradicted the prevailing image of black women on television at that time. Although American viewers had grown accustomed to certain kinds of characterizations—the subservient Negro maid or the nervous, giggling incompetent—they appeared willing to tune in to the elegant pianist, whose confidence and beauty were an unexpected addition to her wonderful playing.

The Hazel Scott Show delivered better than projected Hooper ratings.[15] Its sponsor, Sitroux tissues, delighted with the result, sought out other sponsors to come onboard. Within weeks, the network expanded the show from a local broadcast to a national one that aired not once but three evenings a week.

It was director Barry Shear's first television series. Many years later Adam III was told by a CBS cameraman who had worked on the show that Shear, who had been inspired by the Salvador Dali dream sequence in the Hitchcock film *Spellbound*, experimented on Hazel's show with different camera angles and "wild, crazy shots" where the camera had to be turned on its side in order to capture various diagonals.[16] Even such visual and conceptual daring met no objections from network executives. Among critics the show was a hit. A review in *Variety* stated, "Hazel Scott has a neat little show in this modest package. Most engaging element in the air is the Scott personality, which is dignified, yet relaxed and versatile."[17]

It must have been a thrilling moment for Hazel. Her own show provided her a platform on which to project all she had to offer—her virtuosity, intelligence, and sophistication. She was also able to come off the road and work from New York. Surely, she looked forward to all of the great gains such national exposure was sure to bring. But before things were to get better they would become infinitely worse.

As the 1950s progressed and the Soviet Union continued to rise as a world power, suspicion, fear, and paranoia over the dangers of communism began to run rampant in America. Senator Joseph McCarthy, an opportunist with boundless ambition, had been in search of a political issue that would make his name known. He found it in the Cold War.

The fuel for McCarthy's "red scare" was incessant finger pointing: conservatives accused the Truman administration's adherence to New Deal politics communistic; business leaders considered strikes by union workers communistic; and the two media capitals, Hollywood and New York, were accused of attempting to subvert American citizens via television, film, and radio. The American public quickly got caught up in the hysteria.

In 1947, McCarthy's House Un-American Activities Committee (HUAC), whose prime objective was to investigate subversives, took unprecedented action against communism and its sympathizers. With a pronouncement by Congressman Richard Nixon that it was time for action not words, HUAC began full-fledged investigations of individual citizens, union leaders, and members of the entertainment community.

Not surprisingly, Café Society made the government's hit list. Musicians and comedians who performed at the club, the artists who painted the club's murals, and even some regular customers fell under suspicion. Agents from the FBI had been lurking around both club locations for years; the staff was closely watched, stalked, and repeatedly questioned.

Hazel found out from a fellow musician that her name appeared in *Red Channels,* a small tract published by the right-wing journal, *Counterattack.* Considered the semi-official guide to suspected communists, its listings updated weekly. Among the many communist organizations she was said to belong to or support were the Artist Front to Win the War, the Musicians' Congress Committee, and the Civil Rights Congress.[18] And, perhaps most damning, she had performed (along with many other black musicians associated with Café Society) for the Citizens Non-partisan Committee to Elect Benjamin Davis, Jr. A member of the Communist Party, Davis had been Adam Powell Jr.'s choice in 1943 to fill his vacant seat on New York's City Council, a post Davis had gone on to win.

Hazel's ties to Café Society made her a suspect, but her outspokenness on civil rights issues made her a target. While she had never been a card-carrying member of the Communist Party, like many black activists who took on the fight for racial justice, Hazel did not and would not denounce the party's efforts on behalf of the struggle. Additionally, in the early days of the Communist Party of the United States, the organization had attracted many West Indian Americans, including Hazel, due to its opposition to colonialism.

In a documentary film on the subject, *Scandalize My Name,* Adam Powell III commented, "Throughout the 1940s, something that could be used against my mother and others was the assertion that the causes that they embraced were also causes that the Communist Party embraced. When my mother was confronted with this, she said, 'I'm not going to relax my effort to get the rights for people of color merely because the Communist Party embraces that effort.' And she rejected as totally false any attempt to claim that she was a communist or communist sympathizer because of her work with civil rights."[19] She was also accused of playing for Soviet troops, which Hazel believed was completely legitimate considering that the Soviet Union was an ally of the United States in 1943: "She thought it was no small irony that she was accused of being unpatriotic for something which five years earlier was considered the height of patriotism."[20]

Despite his involvement with the *People's Voice*, his association with Earl Browder (who by now had been expelled from the Communist Party), and his early campaign endorsements from the Communist Party, the communist tag evaded Congressman Adam Clayton Powell Jr. He made his opinion known on the floor of the House, stating, "I make no brief for Communism. However, I must defend the right of any individual to maintain whatever particular view he holds until such a view is declared illegal by an act of Congress."[21] He further suggested, "Those of you who are so afraid of Red scares should have the guts to make Communism illegal. Until then it is legal."[22]

Hazel's first instinct was to fight. She and Adam discussed her situation at length, and soon realized that Hazel's listing in *Red Channels* and *Counterattack* might have had less to do with her work at Café Society than it did with her husband's work in Washington. It seemed all too possible that Powell's enemies would try to get to him through Hazel. Whatever the explanation, she refused to remain silent. She told Adam that she wanted to appear before HUAC. Since she hadn't been summoned, he could see no real benefit in her appearing voluntarily. It could easily make matters worse. Past trials had made it clear that HUAC members had little patience with suspected communists' attempts to defend themselves. Powell knew it would be difficult to sway them. Only if you were in total agreement with them, or appeared contrite, would an accused subversive be cleared.

It was a volatile combination of pride, fear, and rage that sent Hazel down this destructive path. She couldn't bear to sit still, awaiting an unknown outcome. "Stubbornness is one of my faults," she admitted.[23] "If I believe that I am in the right, I will die before I allow myself to be dissuaded. No one has ever been able to make me swerve from a decision once I have made up my mind. It has never been my practice to choose the popular course. When others lie as naturally as they breathe, I become frustrated and angry."[24] Hazel submitted her request for an appearance before the House Un-American Activities Committee, and it was granted.

That there was tremendous risk involved was a given, but Hazel also understood that remaining silent could be equally as damaging, if it was interpreted as an admission of guilt. Hazel was impervious to all warnings. "Many people advised her not to do it. But she said 'This is a matter where my name has been taken and used improperly,'" Adam III recalled.[25] "She was particularly vulnerable because of the fact that her livelihood depended on acceptance not only by the public, who were buying the tickets and turning on her radio show and television show, but also by the networks and advertisers."[26]

On September 22, 1950, Hazel Scott, dressed conservatively in a classic black suit and very little makeup, took a seat before John S. Wood and the other HUAC members, her prepared statement in hand. Before the start of the session, Congressman Wood made it clear that her voluntary appearance was not customary but had been granted as an act of generosity on the committee's part out of respect for their colleague, her husband.

After a formal swearing in, she asked if she could read "just a few highlights" aloud from her prepared statement. The full statement was extremely lengthy; she wanted it included in the committee's records and printed as if it had been read in full.

With permission to proceed, Hazel expressed her outrage. She condemned *Red Channels* and *Counterattack,* challenging their methods, their listings, and their very existence. She explained that most of the listings next to her name were false. *Red Channels* had found at least nine organizations with communist ties that Hazel had been involved with as a performer. "One of these listings was for an appearance, by direction of my employer, which was perfectly proper at the time," she said. Others she claimed she'd "never heard of before." She repeatedly tried to make it known that as a performer you worked for hire and rarely knew the political affiliations of the organizers or organizations you played for.[27]

When asked how she ended up playing at a fund-raiser for the communist-backed city councilman Benjamin Davis, she answered:

I don't recall exactly how this appearance came about, but I believe it was by direction of Mr. Barney Josephson, my then employer and manager, who often lent my name and time to affairs without consulting me.[28]

Congressman Francis E. Walter of Pennsylvania asked, "Did the publishers of this pamphlet ever contact you in order to verify any of these statements?"[29] Hazel replied, "In no way. It was brought to my attention I was in the book. I never heard from them by wire, phone call, or anything."[30] Throughout her testimony she would reiterate to the committee that the compilations of names, dates, and associations listed in *Red Channels* were made without verification. "*Counterattack's* failure to consult me before including my name in *Red Channels*," Hazel continued, "establishes a presumption of their insincerity regarding 'the protection of innocents and genuine liberals.' Unless they have reasons for this, that fact alone damns them and calls for the cessation of their malicious activities."[31]

When entangled in a war of words with Congressman Burr Harrison, Hazel remained firm. He asked, "What I am getting at is whether the listing is false or the information is false?"[32] The prickly gentleman from Virginia continued to quibble, asking for clarification of the difference between the words *listing* and *information.* Hazel went along with the charade, stating, "The information is false and the listing is unjustified."[33]

Back and forth they went. Harrison retorted, "I don't agree with you that it is a false listing,"[34] to which Hazel replied flippantly, "If you were in danger of losing your job because of this you would agree with me."[35]

She continued:

> May I ask you a question? If any committee, an official committee, lists me as having two heads, does that make me have two heads, and does that give *Red Channels* a right to publish I have two heads?[36]

Agitated, Harrison defended the publication. "They make no bones of the fact that they do not evaluate the listings,"[37] Hazel fired back "They simply prepare a blacklist."[38]

In a final attempt to state her case, she asked committee members to consider what purpose it served to label American authors, composers, painters, and entertainers of stage, screen, and radio "Red": "Are we ready to say, in effect, that the Communists have taken over the whole country except for a few self-appointed patriotic virgins, such as the gentlemen of *Counterattack?*"[39]

Hazel concluded:

I, for one, Mr. Chairman, am not ready to hand over America's entertainment industry to Moscow. A few cunningly contrived lies, some false statements, an impressively long list, such as *Red Channels,* and the years of preparation, sacrifice, and devotion are killed. Instead of a loyal troupe of patriotic, energetic citizens, ready to give their all for America, you will demoralize them and end up with a dejected, wronged group whose creative value has been destroyed.[40]

Now that you gentlemen have heard me so patiently, may I end with one request, and that is that your committee protect those Americans who have honestly, wholesomely, and unselfishly tried to perfect this country and make the guarantees in our Constitution live. The actors, musicians, artists, composers, and all of the men and women of the arts are eager and anxious to help to serve. Our country needs us more today than ever before. We should not be written off by the vicious slanders of little and petty men. We are one of your most effective and irreplaceable instruments in the grim struggle ahead. We will be much more useful to America if we do not enter this battle covered with the mud of slander and the filth of scandal. Thank you.[41]

Hazel Scott's complete statement, filed with HUAC, contains pages and pages of explanations about all of the organizations she had performed for, charitable organizations and churches where she donated her time and money; her religious background and church affiliations; and names, dates, and locations that may have been misconstrued by the committee. None of it helped her case. The damage was already done. She was given the benefit of being heard, but she was never given the benefit of the doubt.

Her name appeared across headlines in the national press— "Hazel Scott Assails Listings of Artists as Red Supporters" and "Hazel

Scott Denies Knowing Any Links with Communism" read the *Washington Post. Time* listed her in a column entitled "The Accused." None of this sat well with the sponsors of her television show. Squeamish, they pulled out. One week after her HUAC appearance, the *Hazel Scott Show* was canceled.

Undoubtedly, she received the support of her fellow musicians and friends in private, but little else was written about her stand against McCarthyism aside from the facts of the trial. Considering the times, it is quite likely that no one wanted to speak too loudly in her defense.

McCarthyism eclipsed the careers of many former Café Society performers. Leon Josephson was the first of its casualties. In 1947, he refused to testify, calling on his Fifth Amendment rights. He was found guilty of contempt and ended up serving a ten-month prison sentence.

The former Café Society comedian Zero Mostel had made no secret of his liberalism; he incorporated fierce political comedy into his act, including a character named "Polltax T. Pellagra" who openly mocked red baiters. When the choreographer Jerome Robbins named him as a known communist during his HUAC trial, Mostel was immediately subpoenaed.

Mostel tried to diffuse the contemptuous atmosphere during his trial with his fierce wit. When asked who his employer was, he answered: "Nineteenth Century Fox." Refusing to name names and denying ties to communism, Mostel was banned in Hollywood and locked out of many lucrative nightclub jobs. His career would not regain momentum until the late 1950s. Madeline Lee Gilford, wife of the comedian and former Café Society emcee Jack Gilford, was also named by Jerome Robbins. Years of social and political activism placed both husband and wife on the blacklist.

Folk and blues singer Josh White, who was one of Café Society's headliners, was hit from all sides, suffering through numerous government interrogations and HUAC trials, harassment from J. Edgar Hoover and the FBI, as well as the censure of the black community. During his HUAC trial, he denounced communism but in doing so made some allusions to Paul Robeson's participation in communist affairs. His statement rambled from America's responsibility toward its own citizens to the cruel facts of racism and injustice. Throughout, he emphasized his love for his country. His words were heartfelt but deeply confused. His fellow musicians believed he was simply pandering to the committee, while anticommunists resented what they perceived as his liberal sympathies. As White's biographer, Elijah Ward, observed, "The unfortunate fact was that Josh was trying to take the middle ground in a battle that had none."[42]

In the aftermath of her hearing, Hazel was accused of "naming names" by referring to Barney Josephson in her testimony. Her single mention of him as "her employer" would destroy their decade-long relationship. Aside from Café Society's well-documented ties to the Communist Party, Barney Josephson was never summoned by HUAC. Yet, his affiliation with leftist artists and causes eventually put him out of business. The press conspired against him. Westbrook Pegler, a syndicated columnist for the Hearst newspaper corporation, wrote an article about Barney's brother, Leon, implying that he was not only a communist but a drug addict. At the end of the article, he added, "And there is much to be said about his brother Barney."[43] That was all it took. Soon attendance at Café Society Uptown club dropped off. Stars were afraid to perform there for fear of damage to their reputations. Within a year's time, both clubs uptown and downtown, were closed.

Father Peter O'Brien, Mary Lou Williams's manager, recalled that decades later, after Josephson had recovered financially and opened another popular nightclub, the Cookery, he still hadn't forgotten what Hazel's testimony did to him. "He started crying and Mary was there, the three of us standing in The Cookery, he burst into tears. 'Why did Hazel do that to me Mary? Why did Hazel do that?' Why did Hazel do that to me after all I did for her?' And then he turned to me still blubbering saying, 'I should have done for Mary what I did for Hazel.'"[44]

After her HUAC hearing, Hazel said very little publicly about its outcome. If she discussed the fallout with Barney Josephson at all, she did so in private.

Although she'd taken her stand, Hazel would struggle to keep her career afloat. For the next several years, she would find that concert bookings, while they didn't dry up completely, were harder to come by. Unwilling to play for audiences that weren't integrated and unable, because of her agreement with Adam, to perform in nightclubs, her opportunities were limited. Like so many other black artists and performers before her, Hazel Scott would soon seek work and solace across the Atlantic.

CHAPTER TWELVE

Notes of Discord

Summers overseas became something of a family ritual beginning in 1951 when Hazel scheduled a concert tour with engagements stretching clear across the continent. Onboard the *Ile de France,* the Scotts were off to explore Europe. It was a working vacation for her, a sightseeing tour for young Adam, and a semiofficial trip for her husband. Throughout the tour, Adam acted as his wife's quasi-business manager and a kind of congressman-at-large. On their daily excursions, Powell fraternized with international political leaders and visited U.S. military bases, while Hazel entertained the multitudes. With nanny in tow, the foursome turned heads from ship to shore, their every move recounted in the American press.

Powell, unmoved by criticism on Capitol Hill that he was away from his office much too often, was proud. He took great pleasure in showing off his talented and beautiful wife and their young son. They carried themselves with an air of royalty. They were invited to the homes of dignitaries, took in the nightlife, and attended Sunday morning church services in a host of cities. Hazel's time for traipsing through quaint towns and villages was limited, however, to a few hours a day before rehearsals for the evening's performance. The tour was expansive, with dates scheduled in London and Birmingham, Glasgow and Stockholm, Paris and the south of France, as well as Greece, Israel, and several cities in Scandinavia.

HAZEL SCOTT

All of her concerts were heavily publicized, so there was a sense of excitement and anticipation in the air upon her arrival in each locale. Hazel prepared to dazzle the international crowd with her signature style—the gorgeous off the shoulder gowns and sparkling jewels, the infectious mix of jazz and classics, and the occasional pop standard sung in the native language of whatever city she was in.

She and Adam set themselves up in grand fashion, throwing cocktail parties in a swank Mayfair apartment they had rented for their stay in London. Adam dealt directly with his wife's agents and handled the finances. Sparing no expense, he saw to it that their lifestyle overseas matched their glamorous reputations. There was plenty of food and liquor, great music, and good times. Party guests were mostly from the jazz world, singers and musicians performing overseas; Dizzy Gillespie, Duke Ellington, and members of their bands passed through, along with a few American actors and socialites.

Hazel's first show was at the London Palladium. It was her first appearance at the 2,200-seat theater, which was, at the time, one of the city's largest venues, known for booking the biggest names in the business such as Sammy Davis Jr., Ella Fitzgerald, Judy Garland, and Frank Sinatra. Londoners had been flocking to the Palladium for decades to see British comedic acts and variety shows. Now they came to see the performer billed as "Star of motion pictures, concerts and radio . . . one of the piano's most provocative exponents."[1]

Hazel received such a fantastic response at the Palladium that word-of-mouth alone led to sellout crowds at her future engagements. Although English audiences were tantalized by her vivacious performance style, Hazel found them polite almost to a fault. It was their custom to hold their applause until the very last chord was played, and even in the nightclubs there was no finger popping or shouts of praise between numbers. Instead, they responded to her jazz selections with reverence and to her swinging the European classics with interest and reserved enthusiasm. She was surprised but flattered by their deep respect for the music. She often joked, "Listening to jazz in Europe is like to going to church."[2]

One afternoon before her show in Glasgow, hundreds of Scottish fans gathered in the courtyard of the luxury hotel where the Powells were staying. What an incredible display of affection, everyone thought. Adam III remembered, "I must have been five or six. . . . I remember looking over the stone railing of this incredible suite at this huge square. My mother's hairdresser, L. B. Lucas, went out on the balcony to acknowledge the masses and let them know 'She'll be out shortly!' It was full of people. And all of these people are looking up, and they're waving."[3] As it turned out, Princess Elizabeth (not yet the queen) was staying in the room right above them. It was *her* crowd, not Hazel's. "And there was this black woman from America, waving and shouting, 'She'll be out shortly!' "[4]

Days later, as the Powells made their way to Sweden, Hazel received an unexpected request via the American Embassy. Princess Elizabeth was hosting an event in Baghdad and wanted Hazel to perform an impromptu concert. Flattered by the offer, Hazel had no intention of turning it down. Her performance for the princess was touted in an English-language Baghdad paper, but Hazel couldn't stick around to receive her accolades. She returned to Stockholm immediately to fulfill her concert obligations there.

Weeks later the entire crew headed to the Middle East.

Opening night in Jerusalem was hosted by the American ambassador to Israel with an audience full of international dignitaries. "The Powells were entertained several times by the Ambassador," reported the *Herald Tribune*. "Hazel Scott Scores in 10-Concert Israel Tour," read the headline. The Israeli press reported her tour as a huge box office success with a response so enthusiastic that she could have added ten more shows. The family was welcomed by Prime Minister Ben-Gurion, who made a rare appearance at the farewell concert at Hazel's personal request.

In a feature story for the *New York Daily News,* entitled "Adam According to Hazel," she reflected on their trip to the Middle East, sharing some of the more personal details of their time there. One incident in particular she found particularly amusing. At Mandelbaum Gate, the former checkpoint between the Israeli and Jordanian sections of Jerusalem, Hazel and Adam were accosted by guards, and told to get out of the car. "Adam stood up, boiling," Hazel said. "I could see he was about to blow his top and declare this an international incident. He was even madder when I burst out laughing. One of the guards had pushed a pad and pencil in my hand. All they wanted was an autograph."[5]

Adam later claimed to be accustomed to incidents like these, where Hazel's celebrity overshadowed his own. "We share each other's glory," he told a reporter, "and find it great fun to be identified in terms of the other. I'm as frequently referred to as 'Hazel Scott's husband' as she is as 'Congressman Powell's wife.'"[6]

But there were many occasions when Adam found himself the 'odd man out' in his wife's world of musicians. Once, backstage at a Paris nightclub, "Adam—who is always neat and dapper . . . was faultlessly attired in a tuxedo. One of the musicians, who didn't know Adam eyed him suspiciously, then blurted out: 'Hey, man, you gonna MC'?"[7]

Adam Powell typically laughed off these kinds of misunderstandings. And Hazel would thank him for being a good sport. But there were times when he didn't find it funny and she didn't feel like smoothing things over.

With two such titanic personalities, there were bound to be clashes. Slight shifts in the spotlight's focus could easily create an undercurrent of tension—competitive jealousy, ego, and pride crashing beneath the surface.

Crisscrossing the globe at such a rapid pace, the magnitude of Hazel's accomplishments was sometimes lost on her. She was among an extremely small cadre of solo musicians who could claim a place on the world stage. Yet the warm receptions, the appreciative crowds, the parties, and the performances were all happening in a blur. With each leg of the tour, she was becoming more and more exhausted. She'd expend her last bit of energy on her son to make sure every part of his European holiday was special. She would also accompany her husband to political and military gatherings, which commanded from her a performance of an entirely different sort. Having mastered the necessary moves, she transitioned from Hazel

Scott to Mrs. Adam Clayton Powell with her usual grace. But this, too, was draining.

Hazel came to miss the old Café Society days when she had her own room and the crowd was her crowd, where there was less to prove. Back then she could bank on her name and reputation alone. And when the night was over she said her good-byes to familiar faces and names she knew and went home to sleep in her own bed. As a concert pianist, the old showbiz adage always applied—she was only as good as her last performance, in a perpetual state of proving herself to a new and different audience, in different venues and different cities, night after night. And always with the hope, not the guarantee, of being invited back.

From Israel, the family traveled to Greece. And from Greece they landed in France. By this time, the thrill of the whirlwind tour had lost its thrust. Fatigue was setting in.

In Paris, Hazel went into the studio to make a recording for the Decca label with sidemen Georges Hadjo on bass and drummer Gerard "Dave" Pochonet, whom she had worked with previously on club dates in Paris during her first trip in 1951. He had played for Hazel's run at the Salle Gaveau all those years ago, and the two had remained friends. A Paris native, Pochonet had also performed with many prominent American jazz artists, including Mary Lou Williams, Buck Clayton, Lucky Thompson, and Don Byas.

After completing the self-titled record, which included the popular jazz standard "Body and Soul," W. C. Handy's "St. Louis Blues," "The One I Love Belongs to Somebody Else," "Tea for Two," and an original composition, "How Blue Can You Get?" Hazel began a weeklong engagement at Salle Gaveau, where she perfected her command of French by incorporating more vocals into her program. Singing George Gershwin and Cole Porter tunes in the native tongue endeared her even more to French audiences.

Of all the cities she toured, Paris was her favorite. She loved the city, its laid back atmosphere, and the way French fans dug the music. There she could be carefree, unburdened and unrestrained.

But the joys of Paris were soon overshadowed by a tricky piece of business that had its roots across the Atlantic, reminding both Hazel and her husband that no matter how far away the problems of home were hot on their trail.

While in Paris, the Powells had the option of staying in one of two hotels run by the U.S. Army and U.S. Air Force. Congressmen were allowed to stay at either location for a small fee below the standard rate. Within days of checking in, Hazel and Adam suspected that they were being watched. Adam III remembers, "I heard my parents talking about how the FBI was listening to them and tapping their phones. And my mother would always get very upset." Hazel would shout out into the air, "All right, we're going to bed now. You can turn off the tape recorder!"[8] Their suspicions were confirmed one night when young Adam noticed an open door in the hotel hallway. Curious, he peeked in. Microphones had been rigged up in the ceiling, directed toward Adam and Hazel's room next door. "In case you're wondering," Hazel shouted, "we'll be out until ten tonight!"[9]

Hazel was furious. When Adam asked the FBI to explain why they were under surveillance, he was told that it was for his own protection. But Powell's trips overseas made some members of Congress very uncomfortable. They felt threatened by the rapport he had with international leaders and the freedom with which he used his political position. His investigations of U.S. military bases, which provided the ammunition needed in his push for desegregation of the American armed forces, were also a growing concern among staunch segregationists in Congress.

The summer passed. They had been overseas for several months. Powell, in fact, was due back in Congress but chose to continue his European vacation. Hazel, however, had grown weary. Yet, expert as she was at putting on the happy public face, no one could have recognized just how emotionally drained she was. But when the ready smile and hearty laugh disappeared the side of her that was short-tempered and high-strung emerged.

"A person needs to go off somewhere and be alone so that his body can catch up with his soul," she said. "Before I got married, I did have some private life. But I find being a public figure and being married to a public figure makes privacy a luxury."[10]

The weight of a demanding career and a high-profile marriage had begun to overwhelm her. What she longed for was some time away from the spectacle of the stage and public life. Perhaps, if she had gotten it, Hazel's international tour would not have come to such a cataclysmic end.

In the autumn of 1951, everything fell apart. One evening before a show in Paris, she couldn't go on. Her moods were swinging madly from uncontrollable crying to angry outbursts to numb silence. Her manager and assistant scrambled to calm her, but nothing worked. While it is difficult to speculate on what single event or series of events triggered her emotional unraveling, it is clear that Hazel's state was desperate and serious. Adam realized right away that it was something more than a case of exhaustion. He rushed her to the American Hospital in Paris, where doctors diagnosed Hazel as having experienced a nervous breakdown. The family flew back to the States immediately via a U.S. Air Force jet. Her remaining engagements were canceled.[11] Few details were made available to press. A small blurb ran in *Jet,* which read, "Gravely Ill, Hazel Scott Flown Home from Paris," reporting only that she had suffered a breakdown, she was unresponsive to treatment, and her condition was considered "serious."[12]

Back home in Mount Vernon, Hazel received expert medical attention. She was given a psychiatric evaluation and prescribed sedatives and electroconvulsive shock therapy, but her emotional state remained unstable. Adam organized members of his staff to keep track of her, day and night, while he was in Washington. The household staff looked after young Adam.

Even with exceptional medical care and round-the-clock attention, Hazel felt very much alone. The loneliness and isolation she had felt as a child began to creep in. It was not her style to worry others with her problems, so very few friends knew the gravity of her condition. Briefly in her journal she makes small mention of fellow artists Judy Garland, Yul Brynner, and Erroll Flynn as friends who understood her plight. Little else is revealed about her exact state of mind. There was no clear diagnosis of her condition beyond the frighteningly vague label "nervous breakdown." While concert dates were continually canceled and her social calendar cleared, the circumstances surrounding Hazel's illness were kept quiet. The family did not discuss her mental health in the media. Very few details about the episode appear in her personal journal. What is known for certain is that when rest and time off from work failed to make her feel better, Hazel began to self-medicate, using alcohol and prescription drugs to calm her nerves. She had been an occasional smoker, but now she was up to two packs of Chesterfields a day. She had been a social drinker, but now her drinking had escalated to an extreme. Her weight fluctuated; she ballooned to a size much larger than she had ever been. Depleted, she had no energy to sort out her feelings. She remained in seclusion, left to sort out the complex mass of emotions that had rendered her confused, agitated, and depressed.

By the year's end, consumed by feelings of hopelessness, Hazel had lost her desire to live. Death, she reasoned, would bring relief. While the exact details of her actions remain a mystery, she is believed to have taken a handful of pills in an attempt to take her own life.

Suicide was the farthest thing from her mind when she was onstage, playing to admiring fans, feeling the heat and glare of the footlights, and hearing the rapturous applause; when her husband came through the door surprising her with sparkling gifts of rubies and emeralds; when her little boy greeted her with a mischievous smile and a warm hug. How Hazel had arrived in such an unbearably dark place, in such utter despair, was beyond even her own comprehension.

Adam's schedule was full and tight, as it had always been. He went from one appointment to the next with little time in between. When he was in New York, he had church board meetings, two sermons on Sunday mornings, and speaking engagements on Sunday afternoons. He met with his constituents at the local Democratic club, meetings that usually went long into the night. Then he headed back to Washington. He was in the middle of his own re-election campaign and traveling throughout the country on behalf of Democratic presidential nominee Adlai Stevenson when he was told about his wife's attempt to take her life. He rushed to her side.

Hazel was hospitalized for several weeks, during which Adam made certain that she received the best possible care. He used his influence to ensure that she was left undisturbed by the press, which was anxious to obtain the details of her situation. Her illness would remain a private family matter. No one, not even Abyssinian's members, was given full disclosure. In press accounts regarding the cancellation of her concerts, the reasons given were "due to illness" or "due to influenza."

Recuperation was not swift, but it was steady. Slowly, over the course of several months, Hazel took an encouraging turn for the better.

Her son was a vital part of her recovery. Returning to the kinds of simple domestic activities she used to enjoy—cooking, knitting (which she claimed had always helped keep her fingers nimble for piano playing), decorating, and gardening—was also salutary. Weekend mornings, Hazel played football with her son and the neighborhood kids. "She wasn't supposed to do anything that could possibly endanger her hands. She could go on a sailboat, but she wasn't supposed to handle the lines, which of course she did. She used to say if it was fun she probably couldn't do it," Adam III remembered.[13]

Hazel referred to her son as a "very self-sufficient little gentleman."[14] He was her touchstone. Young Adam was enrolled in the prestigious Riverdale Country School in the Bronx. He was smart and well mannered. Recalling the period when she was in rehearsal for her appearance at the Latin Quarter, she said, "He whistles at me. When I come home from rehearsals in black leotards with a coat thrown over them, he lets out a long low wolf whistle."[15] Dining at Sardi's one evening, young Adam and his mother made a charming couple, capturing the attention of the other guests. Hazel recalled with pride, "They were delighted by the way Skipper pulled out my chair for me and in general acted like a gentleman."[16]

Adam III recalled those Saturday mornings when Louis Marshall, his mother's accountant, would come to the house with papers for her to sign or to address other financial matters. Marshall had a habit of bringing fresh bagels and cream cheese, smoked salmon, tomatoes, and onions, which made his visits a real treat for Adam but less of one for his mother, who never cared much for handling finances. For as long as she could remember she always had someone else to deal with money matters—her mother, her husband, an agent or manager. When Marshall arrived, she typically braced herself for the worst. Because of her income, she was carrying a heavy tax burden. After Marshall gave her the news of how much she owed, Adam III recalled, "She'd always respond by saying, 'I'm never going to work this hard again for the rest of my life. I'm just working for Uncle Sam. I'm going to start taking more time off. I want to travel and enjoy myself.'"[17]

In May of 1952, Hazel Scott returned to Carnegie Hall to perform with the New York Philharmonic–Symphony Orchestra in an evening of music by Gershwin. With Charles Paul conducting, the program began with two classical works, "An American in Paris" and "Concerto in F." Following a selection of Gershwin melodies, soprano June McMechen and baritone Todd Duncan took the stage, singing "It Ain't Necessarily So," "Summertime," "I Got Plenty o' Nuttin'," and "Bess, You Is My Woman Now" from the *Porgy and Bess Suite*. The evening ended with Abba Bogin on piano, playing "Rhapsody in Blue."

This performance not only signified Hazel's return to the concert stage after overcoming a serious illness, but in many ways it was a victory over HUAC and its ruinous accusations.

Months later, Hazel went to California to record for the first time with Capitol Records. The label, founded by Johnny Mercer in 1942, was the first major West Coast competitor in the recording industry. During the 1950s, the roster included some of the biggest names in the business, including Frank Sinatra, Judy Garland, and Dean Martin. In a Hollywood studio, Hazel teamed up with bassist Red Callender and drummer Lee Young. *Hazel's Scott Late Show* was an homage to great American composers—Richard Rodgers and Lorenz Hart, Jerome Kern and Harold Arlen, George Gershwin, and Cole Porter. The instrumental album included tunes that had become part of the American songbook. Interestingly, Hazel did not perform vocals on this record. Whether or not this was her decision or the record company's is difficult to know. Had she chosen to sing, she would have been competing with the recordings of jazz women who were now giving these nostalgic tunes a thorough makeover, particularly Sarah Vaughan, Ella Fitzgerald, and Dinah Washington. The "ladies who sang with the band" were now center stage soloists, taking all kinds of artistic leaps; their phrasing was inventive, their interpretations more improvisational. Nevertheless, Hazel hardly disappoints. She is right at home playing richly textured, swinging renditions of familiar songs such as "The Way You Look Tonight," "I Get a Kick Out of You," and "That Old Black Magic." It was nearly two years since she had been in the recording studio. Although the commercial sales of *Late Show* fell below the label's expectations, Hazel was simply happy to be back.

On June 12, 1953, several months after his son had won reelection to Congress, Rev. Adam Clayton Powell Sr. passed away at the age of eighty-eight. He was buried in Flushing Cemetery in Queens, in the family plot, next to his first wife Mattie and their daughter Blanche. Self-made man, visonary and pioneer, Adam Powell Sr.'s unyielding commitment to his family, his church and his race had made him one of the most loved and respected leaders of his era.

A couple months after his passing, Hazel booked a tour in Germany. Accompanied by her husband and son, she entertained troops at U.S. Air Force bases with her "Bach to Boogie" repertoire. It was a timely trip for Adam, a cathartic, deeply personal journey through the country that had held so much fascination for his father.

At the personal invitation of Haiti's president, Paul E. Magliore, the family started off the new year of 1954 in Port-au-Prince, traveling on the Panamanian liner *Cristobal* to attend the 150th anniversary of Haiti's independence. An international guest list of politicians, journalists, artists, and activists gathered in recognition of the eighteenth-century slave revolt that led to an organized revolution against the French colonial government. Under the leadership of Toussaint l'Ouverture (and later Henri Christophe and Jean Jacques Dessalines), Haiti became the first black republic on January 1, 1804.

An ardent anticolonialist, Hazel felt a natural kinship with Haiti and its people. She had, for years, kept abreast of the political scene in Trinidad, especially its struggle to break free of British rule. Walking the streets of Port-au-Prince likely caused her to think about independence in her native Port of Spain. When Trinidad finally became an independent nation some years later, Adam III remembers his mother screaming through the house, "We're free! We're free!"[18]

There was great excitement at the presence of the black congressman among Haitian officials and much interest from the American press in Powell's reactions to the island country's state of affairs. When the Powells were formally introduced to President Magloire, Hazel spoke in French, Adam in English. The president smiled at Hazel, then teased, "Your husband is not an educated man?"[19] Despite the ribbing, Powell commended the president on his leadership, telling Magloire that he had affected a "20th Century renaissance" by improving the country's infrastructure.[20] He added that he would like the United States to invest in Haiti to help the country start out on a firm financial footing.

A staff photographer for *Ebony* captured shots of the family touring the Iron Market, spearfishing in the bay of La Gonave, and dining at lavish parties. Hazel, dressed in festive floral dresses and silk head wraps, shopped for perfumes to add to her reportedly four-thousand-dollar collection of 150 bottles. The family attended services at the Roman Catholic church and even ventured to a voodoo ritual in a temple at Croix Des Bouquets, thirty miles outside Port-au-Prince.

At the elegant state dinner and ball held in the presidential palace, Hazel gave an impromptu performance personally requested by the president. Accompanied by native drummers, Hazel played several swinging jazz numbers, then sang in French and Creole. Marian Anderson topped the evening with an a cappella performance of the Haitian national anthem.

On the final day of the trip, Adam Powell was photographed placing a wreath of roses at the monument of Toussaint l'Ouverture, sculpted by Harlem Renaissance artist Richmond Barthé. Following the five-day celebration, father and son stayed on while Hazel flew to Florida to perform at a concert in Miami.

Her departure would be the first of many future separations.

Restless, in 1955 Hazel decided to travel to Paris, a trip her husband not only approved of but encouraged. Whether or not this vacation apart was related to troubles at home is unclear, but it is clear that during this period Hazel and Adam's marriage began to fall apart. Little things that were once endearing had become annoyances, sparking arguments, loud fights, and stony silences. Hazel's tendency to write music in the middle of the night was interrupting Adam's sleep, particularly on Saturday nights, when he had to preach the next morning. Frustrated, Hazel would argue, "Well, Adam, God is giving me this inspiration and what do you want me to do—tell Him to come back some other time?"[21] Instead of loving each other's company on those treasured weekends, they looked for reasons to be apart.

With Hazel in Paris for weeks on end and Adam dividing his time between New York and Washington, their time apart gave "birth to thousands of fantastic rumors."[22] Hazel found herself constantly on the defensive, trying to keep their marital problems private. She told the reporters just enough to keep them at bay: "We're America's strangest family. Nobody understands us, but we understand each other."[23] In a 1956 article written for *Ebony,* entitled "I Found God in Show Business," by Hazel Scott Powell, she attempted to dispel the rumors about their lifestyle as well as make a point about her dedication to her faith, family, and career. She appeared on the cover in a strapless gold lamé gown with a thigh-high split (looking very much the showgirl not the pianist). She wrote, "So many people have asked me, are Adam and I going to break up. All those newspaper stories: POWELLS DENY SPLIT. Fantastic. I've decided that I'm not going to say anything else about it and let them write what they want to write. These stories always start out: 'Sources close to the Powells say . . .' But there are no 'sources close to the Powells.' We have few close friends and we never discuss our private life with anyone."[24]

She explained that their time apart was normal for them. She tried to remain lighthearted about the incessant interrogation. In a vain attempt to calm gossip's flames, she declared, "For a married couple, he's a wonderful bachelor, living alone in Washington; and

I'm a wonderful old maid, trampling around the country all by my-self."[25] But no matter how cleverly she turned phrases to throw off the media, the truth was that Hazel and Adam's marriage was nearly over.

Among the many things Hazel kept private were her suspicions that Adam had been engaging in extramarital affairs for years. His absences were one thing, his disappearances quite another. Often-times, when Hazel thought Adam was in Washington, she'd find out from a friend that he was spotted in a Manhattan nightclub or restaurant. His philandering became fairly common knowledge once the gossip columnists caught wind of his indiscretions.

Hazel fumed. Things always erupted when she broached the sub-ject of his whereabouts. Their fights, sometimes fueled by alcohol, escalated. She was angry and hurt, of course, but Hazel was also was embarrassed. Suffering through the incessant gossip, suddenly she found herself in a situation disconcertingly reminiscent of what she had gone through when she first met Adam Powell Jr.

Hazel's retreats to Paris often coincided with domestic disputes. At one point, Adam even suggested an "open marriage." He wanted the freedom to spend time with different women but wished to maintain the veneer of a married man. "But what happens to Casanova's wife, while she's out?"[26] Hazel asked. "She should be above reproach. Why? Casanova can become the Creature from the Black Lagoon when it comes to his own wife. A man can roll in the dirt and get up and be Dr. or Mr. So-and-so. Let a woman try it. It's the old boys-will-be-boys double standard."[27] She was anything but satisfied with the arrangement. "I couldn't face a marriage of conve-nience" she said, "especially if it was at my inconvenience."[28]

Upon her arrival in Paris, Hazel decided to forgo hotel living and found an apartment on the Left Bank, just across the Seine, with Notre Dame in broad view. Mabel Howard joined her on the ex-tended retreat. Around that same time, Billie Holiday was on tour in Europe. And Mary Lou Williams had been living in London and Paris. These three women—Mabel, Billie, and Mary—were mother, sister, and friend. In their presence, Hazel found healing. Away from Adam and the stress of their marriage, Hazel went soul-searching. It had never been her habit to blame others for her disappointments. Her tendency was the other extreme. She could be very hard on herself. Wishing to be cleansed of all the things in her life that were destructive, she turned to prayer for answers. She made several decisions during that trip that she hoped would bring about the personal transformation she was after. First, she wanted to become a practicing Catholic again. A return to her faith would bring clarity and peace of mind. And, to firm this religious commitment, she decided to give up alcohol. Even though she had never been a heavy drinker, she considered it a vice. She wanted nothing to do with anything that would impair her judgment, so vital now that she felt her life changing course. Interestingly, it was Adam who would write with pride in his memoir of his wife's spiritual quest: "[T]here took place in her life one of the greatest acts of faith I have ever seen. One morning, accompanied by Mabel, Hazel went to Notre Dame, got down on her knees in front of the altar, and vowed she would not move until God gave her strength. She stayed there until her knees actually became bloody. When she finally did rise to her feet, she had the power and strength and the faith never again to touch or desire a drop of alcohol. She became an exceptionally religious person."[29]

By midyear in 1955, Adam Powell and several Abyssinian church members were under federal investigation. A Senate Banking Committee had been investigating financial irregularities at the Federal Housing Administration (FHA). At a hearing, David Kent, the developer of an interracial FHA-insured housing complex in Queens, New York, admitted that he had lent Powell three thousand dollars in return for the use of his office at Abyssinian Baptist Church to sign up potential tenants.[30] Allegedly, Powell had used the money to purchase a Nash Healy sports car. As was often the case, Powell had solicited this unwanted attention by blurting out in the press the details of his extravagant lifestyle, telling reporters that he could make it from Mount Vernon to Washington, D.C., in "four hours or less" in his two-seater sports car. But the FHA was more interested in knowing whether Powell had used his political influence to assist

Kent in obtaining an FHA loan for his building. Also at issue was the fact that Powell had repaid less than 10 percent of the loan. During his hearing, the savvy congressman turned the attention away from himself and preached an end to "Jim Crowism" in the housing market and a need for more affordable housing in New York. Powell's argument won over the court. He was cleared of the allegations.[31]

But when three members of Abyssinian Baptist Church became involved in a tax scandal, Adam Powell's personal business affairs came under scrutiny once more.

Hattie Dodson, Acy Lennon, and Joe Ford had worked free of charge as income tax preparers, providing tax service to Abyssinian church members. Apparently, the Internal Revenue Service (IRS) had been watching. The preparers' signatures on all those returns made the government look twice at each of their individual tax documents. Dodson, Powell's secretary and church business manager, was indicted on thirty-four counts of tax evasion, charged with evading $5,000 in taxes from 1948 to 1952, reporting only a partial church salary of $5,200 per year, then filing a separate return under her maiden name and using a different address that listed a $3,100 salary she received for additional church work. She and her husband at the time, Howard Dodson, were also accused of listing fictitious dependents—two boys and a girl.[32] In May 1956, Hattie Dodson, the petite and pristine high-standing member of the church whose dedication to Adam Powell Jr. was so absolute that many believed she was in love with him, would be convicted on nine counts and sentenced to seven months in jail. She also took the blame for the charges against her husband, who was cleared of all wrongdoing. Acy Lennon was convicted and sentenced for filing his own fraudulent return. Joe Ford, who originated the idea of providing a tax service to members, was able to talk his way out of the charges and never served jail time. As a result of these indictments, U.S. Attorney Paul W. Williams launched a thorough investigation of the Powells' joint tax returns.[33]

Powell's political enemies, who wanted nothing more than to see him ousted from his seat in Congress, anxiously awaited the outcome of the IRS investigation. It would be years before an indictment was made, at which time Hazel would find herself caught up in the maelstrom.

With the lofty goal of establishing a maverick record label where musicians would have control over what they produced and would be unencumbered by the outside pressures often associated with large commercial record companies, bassist Charles Mingus and drummer Max Roach established Debut Records in 1952. Although the company lasted only five years, its output was impressive, producing the debut recordings of trumpeter Thad Jones and pianist Paul Bley as well as the music of Hank Mobley, Mal Waldron, Oscar Pettiford, and Kenny Dorham. The label's most memorable recordings, *Jazz at Massey Hall, Volumes 1, 2, and 3,* were taken from a Massey Hall concert recorded live in Toronto in May of 1953. Now considered an epochal collaboration of jazz giants, volumes 1 and 3 featured "The Quintet" with Charles Mingus, Charlie Parker, Dizzy Gillespie, Bud Powell, and Max Roach (it was the final recording of Parker and Gillespie playing together); Volume 2 featured the Bud Powell Trio with Mingus on bass and Roach on drums.

Two years later, in January of 1955, Hazel joined Mingus and Roach for her seminal work, *Relaxed Piano Moods,* which marked her first real departure from the style and sound that had made her famous.

It was a propitious, if unexpected, collaboration for all three musicians. Together they created one of Hazel Scott's most significant recordings as a jazz pianist. Although the exact circumstances under which they came together are not known, their timing was apparently perfect. Mingus's biographer Brian Priestly suggests that the signing of a commercially successful artist such as Hazel Scott might have been evidence of the label's financial woes. Whatever the case, it's clear that each had something to be gained by working with the other.

Relaxed Piano Moods reveals a gentler, more reflective, Hazel Scott; the arrangements are less aggressive than her early "swinging the classics" recordings. Each ballad, "Lament" and "Like Someone In Love" and her original composition, "Peace of Mind," is languid and beautiful, where she allows herself the time and freedom to explore her artistic range. There are no fast runs or thundering trills here, only thoughtful, conscientious renderings of compositions she obviously loved. Her delivery is passionate, demonstrating a true desire to communicate a different side of herself to audiences. The songs that swing, Ellington's "The Jeep Is Jumpin" and Hazel's own "Git Up from There," reflect Hazel's seasoned skills, her fast hands and confident stride. Gershwin's "A Foggy Day" and Rodgers and Hart's "Mountain Greenery" are played midtempo and highlight the prodigious gifts of her rhythm section. (Alternate takes of "Lament" and "Git Up from There" were also included on the album.)

Relaxed Piano Moods stunned Hazel's critics. They could find little fault in the performance. As Murray Horwitz observed, given Hazel's stature in the business, such a daring move was not one she necessarily had to make. "For a woman of her stature to take musicians of such incredible strength and . . . I mean in the case of Mingus, you know, the adjective *saturnine* comes to mind. She didn't just get just anybody to back her up because she was the star. She got Max Roach and Charles Mingus."[34]

In the weeks following their work in Debut's studios, Hazel and Mingus decided to continue their collaboration, forming a trio along with drummer Rudy Nichols. The Hazel Scott Trio made several concert and television appearances, including one in mid-January at Toronto's Massey Hall. Accompanied by the Toronto Symphony Orchestra, Hazel played straight classics during the first segment, conducted by Paul Scherman. According to reviews, her performance of Schumann's "Concerto in A Minor" was a standout. "She gave it a sound reading, technically proficient and characterized by good tone," one critic wrote.[35] In the second half, Hazel was joined by Mingus and Nichols in a series of instrumental jazz numbers played straight with Hazel adding vocals on "Teach Me Tonight" and "Lullaby of Birdland." Overall, the crowd was enthusiastic and the critics satisfied, all concluding that the combination of Hazel Scott's "pianobatics," Mingus's inventiveness, and Nichols's ability "to rise above the monotony of setting the beat," added life to the concert hall.[36]

At a March of Dimes telethon that same year, the trio could be seen performing a swinging rendition of "A Foggy Day." Hazel plays and provides the vocals, singing the Gershwin tune in English, and using her lower register to add texture to the upbeat arrangement. Then, in stark contrast, she sings the jazz standard "Autumn Leaves" (or "Le Feuilles Mortes") in French where the language change affects her articulation and placement, giving her voice a more dramatic quality. Throughout their performance, the great chemistry between Hazel and Mingus is apparent; his bass was the perfect complement to her love of rapid tempos and complex chord changes.

Under much different, much sadder circumstances, Hazel would again share the stage with Mingus that spring. On April 2, 1955, to the dismay of the adoring jazz world, Charlie Parker died of pneumonia, a death hastened by years of drug and alcohol abuse. Hazel, along with other luminaries of the jazz world—Thelonius Monk, Dizzy Gillespie, Lester Young, Charles Mingus, Mary Lou Williams, Sarah Vaughan, Dinah Washington, Barry Ulanov, Stan Getz, Erroll Garner, Oscar Peterson, Pearl Bailey, and Sammy Davis Jr.—performed in a memorial concert at Carnegie Hall.

Hazel was already a star at Café Society when she met Charlie "Bird" Parker in the early 1940s. At the time, Bird was just hitting the New York club scene. Awed by his playing, Hazel was a regular in the crowd at his jam sessions uptown. Unbeknownst to her, Parker was aware of her work as well, recording a live overdub of himself playing tenor sax to her 1942 Decca recording of "Embraceable You." This rare performance was part of a group of private recordings done in hotel rooms, unearthed and released in recent years. According to Parker's biographer, Carl Woideck, "This is the first document of Parker playing what would become a staple in his mature period repertoire. Scott played the song in F concert (G on the tenor), as altoist Parker often later did (although transposed to D on the alto). . . . [T]he novelty aside, this is a very successful performance." Hazel was never aware of their "duet."[37]

Months later Hazel would also mourn the loss of her friend and mentor Art Tatum, who died of kidney failure on November 5, 1956, at the age of forty-seven. Not only had he been a formative influence on her development as a pianist, but his death also severed yet another link to the early days of her career.

Despite the string of losses, Hazel's revived recording career maintained its momentum. In 1956, she made 'Round Midnight, a recording of exquisite piano solos without vocals, only the rhythm accompaniment of Jimmy Crawford on drums, Sandy Block on bass, and Everette Barksdale on unamplified guitar. On Thelonious Monk's classic "'Round Midnight," her use of space, block chords, and running figures accent the sublime melody without accelerating the tempo. Interestingly, the new, more soft and mellow approach she employs actually reveals her command of the European classics just as much, if not more than her swing versions of classical compositions. Perhaps this is simply a matter of tempo, the grazioso treatment giving the ear a chance to absorb the beauty and texture of her piano. There are times on "'Round Midnight," as well as on other ballads such as "(In the) Wee Small Hours of the Morning" and "It's Easy to Remember," when Hazel's chordal voicings are more akin to Chopin than the bebop master Monk. Victor Young's "Love Is the Thing," Leonard Bernstein's "Lucky to Be Me," and Frank Loesser's "Warm All Over" add to the warm jazz mood of the recording. From the selection of the songs (mostly ballads)—"Just Imagine," "Maybe," "Love Is the Thing," "Ev'ry Time," "For You, For Me, Forevermore," "It's You or No One," "I Wish I Didn't Love You So," and "Warm All Over"—to each emotionally expressive arrangement, 'Round Midnight delivers one of the most inspiring performances of Hazel's recording career. It would also be one of the last recordings she'd make in America for some years to come.

Later in 1956, her agents booked her in Las Vegas, thinking perhaps that the desert air and change of atmosphere would do her good. Although she arrived there with a heavy heart and many things other than music on her mind, she was blazing a trail. Hazel was one of the first black performers to play the Vegas Strip along with Sammy Davis Jr. and Nat King Cole. She enjoyed the large sums of money Vegas offered, but she worked hard to earn it, often playing multiple shows, back-to-back, every night. Adam III recalled, "It was an extreme amount of work. She would lose lots of weight. They had her playing four shows in one room, then three shows in the lounge. One night she told me, 'I just heard the best news. The doctor told me I look thin, I should have a shake.'"[38]

Hazel and her son would also take intermittent trips to Los Angeles to visit Mabel Howard, who had relocated to the West Coast. "She bought a three or four bedroom house on Glycell Street. We would go at least once a year to visit her. Mabel was always very much in the picture." Since Alma's death, Mabel had been there to help Hazel in times of crisis. Now, since it appeared that Hazel and Adam's marital problems were not on the mend, Hazel found herself calling on Mabel's support more frequently.

In 1957, Hazel booked an engagement at the Olympia Theater in Paris. "So I had a talk with my husband," she said.[39] The couple had reached an impasse. They decided that they would both be happier living apart. Hazel confessed, "I went there originally for three weeks to rest and play an engagement. I was not too happy with the work situation here and I was not happy personally. Adam said, 'If you're not happy here why don't you stay over there a while and work.'"[40]

Neither of them would confirm their separation publicly. When questioned by the press, they were evasive. For several years, no one was really clear on the status of their marriage.

Many years later Hazel would admit, "I was in the middle of an unhappy marriage. I'm an independent person. Every year I'd go overseas, and just as it was getting interesting I'd have to come back—it would be up to me to make some gesture to save the marriage."[41]

During the eleven years of the Powells' marriage, church members had come to embrace Hazel, or "Mrs. P.," as she was called. Now not even they knew what to make of the rumors spreading through Harlem.

Adam and Hazel made arrangements for their son to spend equal time with each of them while continuing his schooling at Riverdale. In his characteristically direct way, Adam gave his ten-year-old son the news. "My father told me 'Your mother's not coming back. If you want, you can go spend Christmas with her, or you can work out whatever you want.'"[42]

Looking back, Adam believes his mother's unhappiness was rooted in the relationship's beginnings. He concluded, "The resolution of this tangle, all very much in the public eye and all very much in the eyes of his congregation, never quite came together, and her early misgivings were the seeds that grew to contribute to the destruction of her marriage, and almost of her life."[43]

A few months later Hazel traveled to Brazil for an engagement. Her son met her in Rio, and from there they traveled to São Paolo. Adam recalled that she had packed for only three weeks of work at the Copacabana Palace, but every time she prepared to leave the country there were additional demands for her to perform. They wound up spending the entire summer in Brazil. A tutor was arranged for Adam so he could continue his studies. When the tour was over, mother and son flew to Paris to set up house together.

CHAPTER THIRTEEN

La Paix de Paris?

Home for Hazel was no longer tied to a romantic ideal of suburban bliss. Home would be where she was happiest. At thirty-seven, she began anew, surrounding herself with the company of friends, old and new, fashioning the lifestyle of a newly single woman. "My Paris is not the city of champagne and caviar," she said.[1] "My Paris is a pot full of red beans and rice and an apartment full of old friends and glasses tinkling and the rich, happy sound of people laughing from the heart."[2] In November of 1957, she moved into a luxurious top-floor apartment at 80 rue Miromesnil in the fashionable Eighth Arrondisement. She had left many of her belongings behind in New York, with the exception of her gowns and jewels, which she needed for her performances, and her precious Steinway, which she had shipped overseas. Adam III remembered the apartment well, recalling the way the piano took up most of the living room. And beneath the massive instrument is where Hazel would find him; he was fascinated with the vibrations it created and would often lie on the floor directly under the piano when she played. Hanging on the wall near the piano was a large black and white hand-tinted portrait of Alma. According to Adam, whenever Hazel engaged in any kind of offensive behavior, she'd look at her mother's portrait and say, "I know you wouldn't approve of that, would you?"[3]

Eleven-year-old Adam had his own room with a bookcase bed,

filled with all the things he liked, plenty of books and international maps. He was enrolled in the American School of Paris. They added to the family a Siamese cat, Brigitte (named for Bardot), and a German boxer named Sacha. Hazel reassured Adam about their new living arrangement. She explained that his father would always be in the picture. "Now, we're still going to be best of friends. And I'll still yell at him on the phone."[4]

To carry on her work, Hazel signed with the booking agency Tavel et Marouani. Happily, she returned to the nightclub circuit, playing such chic nightspots as Le Drap D'Or and Salle Gaveau. She now had the opportunity to appear regularly at the Olympia and the Alhambra Theatre, two of the largest concert halls in France. The resort club circuit on the French Riviera in Cannes and Monte Carlo was also a source of steady work. "During this period I entertained at clubs all over the Continent and in North Africa and the Near East. Between engagements, I relaxed and absorbed the healthy, restful atmosphere of Paris," Hazel said.[5]

That autumn Hazel was cast in the lead role of a French stage version of the Philip Yordan play *Anna Lucasta*. It had been made into a film in 1949, starring Paulette Goddard and John Ireland, then again in 1959 with Eartha Kitt and Sammy Davis Jr. Hazel's acceptance of the role made the American press even more curious about her marriage to Adam Powell Jr. If she had committed to a two-year theater run, surely that was an indication that their marriage was over. "Nobody understands Adam and me except us," Hazel told the *Amsterdam News* in an article with the headline "Hazel (Scott) Says She 'Digs' Adam."[6] When asked about divorce rumors and the state of their marriage, she responded pointedly, "Honey, it couldn't be better than the relationship we have now."[7] She refused to explain it further. Then, adding to the reporter's confusion, she revealed that their Mount Vernon home would be put up for rent "to anyone who wants to rent it and that Adam would be living in his Harlem parsonage."[8] Hazel ended the interview by saying that she and Adam "dig each other the most."[9]

Weeks after her arrival in Paris, rehearsals for *Anna Lucasta* began, and Hazel was exhilarated. She would finally have the chance to test her acting chops, something she had longed to do. She felt that she had the maturity and life experience now to give layered, multi-dimensional portrayals. But before she could dive into the role, production was suddenly stopped. A legal battle over copyright issues ensued, ultimately preventing the producers from staging the show. Hazel was crestfallen. Steady work had kept her mind off her personal problems, but now, for a time, things slowed down considerably. On top of everything else, Hazel discovered that she needed an operation to remove painful fibroid tumors. The surgery would keep her out of commission for several weeks.

As the years progressed, Hazel's career overseas would be an erratic enterprise. Gaining a firm footing on the Paris club scene would prove challenging, the concert stage even more so. She had the fresh start she wanted, but in many ways she was actually starting over.

Hazel began to think twice about her decision to relocate. Fearing the worst, she went to see Billie Holiday at the Mars Club one evening for some much needed inspiration. Once again Billie was able to snap her back to reality. "While wondering where I was going and what I was doing, I began to cry," Hazel remembered.[10] "Billie stopped me, gripped my arm and dragged me to a back room and slammed the door. 'The next time you begin to feel like this,' she said, 'just remember that you've got Skipper and Lady only has a little Chihuahua and Lady's making it. And another thing: Never let them see you cry.'"[11] It was timely advice, but it would take a while for Hazel to develop the skill.

Just as she was settling into her new life, her estranged husband showed up in Paris unannounced. From out of the dust of bitter arguments, vicious fights, and innumerable infidelities, Adam Powell appeared with ideas of reconciliation heavy on his mind. At first, Hazel resisted. But, with Paris as a charming backdrop, Adam continued to woo her. He wined and dined her, held her hand on long walks along the Seine, listened while she spoke, and made passionate apologies, convincing Hazel that their marriage was worth saving. After listening to his contrite pleas, she gave in. The familiar touch, the long glances from the man she had once loved deeply, had gotten the best of her. Before she knew it, they were having loving discussions about having a second child.

But it was not to be.

Instead of reconciliation and a new baby, their time together took an awful turn. Powell's visit conjured up painful reminders of the issues that had torn them apart in the first place. After the luster of his early words and gestures dulled, Hazel and Adam fought new fights and opened old wounds, bleeding years of frustration and disappointment. Confronted with everything she was trying to put behind her, it was more than she could handle. Hazel's emotional state skidded back into instability. This time it became more obvious that her husband was and had always been a trigger for the uncontrollable mood swings and violent outbursts she experienced. "Adam knew how to push all her buttons," said a close personal friend, Betsey Crawford.

Whether it was a real attempt at suicide or a maneuver intended to get Adam's attention, Hazel, for the second time in her life, took an overdose of pills.[12] On her way to the hospital, paramedics had difficulty resuscitating her and believed she was a lost cause. Emergency room doctors worked on Hazel for some time before they saw signs of life. Miraculously, she came around. She was admitted into the intensive care unit and watched around the clock. She would find out later that she had been listed as "dead on arrival."

Mabel Howard came to Paris and stayed until Hazel recuperated. Billie Holiday made regular visits. And Lester Young came by every day; Hazel never forgot the two of them sitting for hours listening to Sinatra's album *Only the Lonely*.[13]

In the months ahead, Hazel sorted out her feelings and vowed never to allow herself to sink so low again. Although she did not reveal any specifics about why she made this second attempt or how she went about it, Hazel was open about the end result and what she had learned from the experience. Eventually, she would write a personal account called "The Truth about Me," which *Ebony* published in its entirety in the fall of 1960. She wrote:

I learned a lot in Paris about people and about myself. One does not look into the face of death, as I have, and come away worrying about pettiness and cattiness and gossip and conforming. It seems that every time I am near death, someone or something is asking me over and over, "How stupid can you get? How many changes will you need before you find out what's important?" This last time, when I spent a month or so in bed, I got the message. I am not likely ever to forget it. Love is important. Love.[14]

Hazel knew without a doubt that her marriage to Adam Powell Jr. was over. The emotional turmoil that characterized so many of their years together would no longer define or threaten her life.

In January of 1958, Hazel's talent agent, Isabelle Kloukowsky, submitted her for a film, *Le Desordre et la Nuit* (Disorder of the Night), directed by Gilles Grangier and starring one of France's premier film actors, Jean Gabin, and German actress Nadja Tiller. Hazel won the small supporting role as a dancer named "Valentine Horse." It was the first time she allowed herself to play a character other than herself. Shot in black and white, the story follows a Paris police inspector ("Vallois") who falls in love with an addict (Lucky). Together they bust the ring that supplies her drugs.

On set, Hazel remembered her old days in Hollywood, reflecting on how long it had been since she'd worked on a film. She saw little difference in the way things were done in France. The director shouted "coupé" instead of "cut," but the hours were just as long. Having to speak all of her lines in French made things more challenging. "I had to think in the language as I acted," Hazel said.[15] Adam III recalled his mother's first day of filming. She swung open the apartment door and walked in shouting, "YOUR MOTHER does not speak French." (According to Adam, whenever she began a sentence with "Your Mother" he knew there was trouble.) "YOUR MOTHER was informed today that she does not speak French. They're giving me a French coach!"[16] Even though it was more of a question of her accent than fluency, Hazel bristled at having to take instruction in a language she thought she had mastered.

After the first day of shooting, Hazel came home from the Boulogne studio exhausted. The chauffeur dropped her off at home and on her doorstep was a copy of the European edition of the *New York Herald Tribune*. Hazel glanced at the paper and "went rigid with shock."[17] The headline reported that the president of Columbia Pictures, Harry Cohn, had died. Hazel called Jean Gabin that instant. She explained the whole story about Cohn, swearing that she would never make another movie until the day he died. And there she was working on her first film in years on the very day he passed away.

It would become one of her favorite stories to tell, so full of drama and intrigue. In some small way, Hazel felt vindicated by Cohn's death. No longer would his threats of career destruction haunt her.

Une Balle dans le Canon (A Bullet in the Gun Barrel), directed by Michel Deville and Charles Gerard, was Hazel's second French film, starring Brigitte Bardot's younger sister, Mijanou. The story followed a few ex-servicemen as they masterminded a robbery. Although it was a forgettable film and her role was small, Hazel was beginning to think she might have a serious second career as an actress.

When *Paris Blues*, a feature film starring Sidney Poitier and Paul Newman, was set to be shot in Paris, Hazel read for the female lead. Director Martin Ritt liked her audition and considered casting her, but ultimately the role of "Connie Lampson" went to a more established actress, the exceptionally talented Diahann Carroll, whose work on stage and screen made her the more viable choice. Hazel's image as a pianist and vocalist was hard to shed. "Once you've played the priest, you can never play the gangster," she'd say.[18] "She really wanted the part and thought that she could do it," Adam III remembered.[19] "But she thought that people would be 'distracted' by her music. She said, 'Everybody just wants me to come on and sing. And I can do so much more than that.'"[20]

In 1958, Hazel returned to her music after securing a record deal with Polydor Records. She produced an album of solo piano and French vocals called *Hazel Scott: Joue et Chante* (Hazel Scott Plays and Sings). "Venez donc chez moi" (Come to My Place) and "Avril à Paris" (April in Paris), she plays up-tempo with bright chords and lively vocals. "L'homme que j'aime," (The Man I Love) is a tune she had performed numerous times on previous recordings and quite often in her live performances, always approaching Gershwin's works with a great deal of affection and reverence. But in French, Hazel's vocal delivery takes on a different luster. She is deliberately sensual, dramatic even, using the sultry tone of her voice to imbue each lyric with great depths of emotion. She saves her most passionate rendering for "Reponds-moi," (Answer Me), the English version of the tune made popular by Nat King Cole in 1954. *Joue et Chante* reflects the artist at her most content.

The jazz critic Leonard Feather, in an article for the *Los Angeles Times,* observed, "Not surprisingly, the ambiance of France in the '50s was just her bag. When she was not playing or listening in a jazz boite, studying cooking at the Cordon Bleu, or working as an actress, she could often be found entertaining lavishly in her apartment, which rapidly took on the aura of a salon."[21]

Unencumbered by the expectations of others, Hazel felt, perhaps for the very first time, truly free. She loved the fact that in France she was treated like "an ordinary citizen" with some semblance of privacy.[22] "This is exactly what I have always wanted here," she confessed.[23] She spoke in almost poetic terms of her life abroad: "My Paris is like the very first time you realize you're in love, like the very first time you're kissed."[24]

Hazel had finally achieved a balance between work and play. She lived "like a Neopolitan fisherman!"[25] She'd work a few gigs, take a break until the money ran out, then return to work. Her apartment became a gathering place for artists, who talked long into the night about "the world, people, and the arts."[26] In the living room, there would be half a dozen musicians from the Ellington and Basie bands. Art Blakey and Horace Silver, Joe Williams, Buck Clayton and Lucky Thompson swung by often. She remembered, "And there, stretched out on a couch because he hurt his back at the studio that day. . . is Anthony Quinn. You keep going, and in the kitchen is Quincy Jones tasting what I have in the pot."[27] Around this time, Hazel and Quincy Jones had a brief fling, which grew into a lifelong friendship.

179

The expatriate author James Baldwin, Dizzy Gillespie, and Mary Lou Williams were regulars at Hazel's place, stopping by for some of her West Indian cooking, good conversation, and fine wine. She hosted Kenyan students from the Sorbonne, who were infatuated with her talent and intelligence. Billie Holiday called her "Queen of the Mau Maus" because of their constant presence at her apartment.[28] Hazel loved the constant company and her apartment's revolving door. Her Paris flat had become like her childhood home in Harlem with her mother—"a mecca for musicians."[29]

That was the up side of her life in France. However, those early years abroad also came with some pain. Hazel endured several great losses. Some of her dearest friends would pass away, all from the devastating effects of alcohol and drug abuse.

In the early part of March 1959, Lester Young was on tour in Europe, and he stopped in Paris to do a studio recording. Everyone on the jazz circuit knew that Young was drinking himself to death. By the time he arrived at Hazel's, he was barely eating, only consuming huge amounts of liquor. He looked old and worn out; years of alcohol abuse had aged him badly. He was listless and weak. It was obvious to Hazel that Young was dying. After abbreviating his tour due to illness, he left Paris, telling Hazel, "Don't worry, Lady Haze. It's not you, it's me. I gotta split. Pres doesn't want to wear out his welcome." He returned to New York on March 15, 1959. A few hours later, the forty-nine-year-old saxophonist died.[30] "Lester, who is (not was) such a beautiful individual. . . . It pains me to remember that he went from my apartment to an airplane which took him to America and death," Hazel said.[31]

Billie Holiday had been on tour in Europe since the end of 1958. During this time, she and Hazel spent a lot of time together. Like Lester, Billie was in poor health. Her drug addiction had broken her down. When Billie left Paris, she returned to New York, road weary and seriously ill. On May 31, 1959, she was admitted to Metropolitan Hospital with a deteriorating liver and a bad heart. While hospitalized, Billie was arrested and handcuffed to her hospital bed for alleged drug possession.

Adam III remembered, "She was at our house, at the apartment in Paris, just before leaving to fly back to New York, and I remember telling her, 'Oh, please stay.' And I took this photograph of her, which came out perfect with the two pinpoint lights that were in the room. And my mother kept it, especially since she knew it was one of the last pictures taken of her."[32]

Two months later, on July 17, 1959—the same day as Adam's thirteenth birthday—Billie Holiday died from cirrhosis of the liver at the age of forty-four. Hazel remembered her dear friend this way:

> I remember her one night, toward the end, singing a bitter blues, trying to say everything, trying to explain everything within the confines of twelve bars. She had been robbed, again, and she was blue. Sitting there in the Mars club in Paris, listening to this woman who represents (not represented) so many years of my life, sitting there remembering how she used to protect me and curse me and run me home when I was 15 and working on 52nd street in New York, I was overcome by all the tragedy, all the greatness and all the beauty of her life.[33]

Despite the distance, the American press remained interested in Hazel's personal life in Paris. *The National Enquirer*'s Paris Bureau wrote after spotting her on the arm of an artist, "Coffee colored pianist Hazel Scott is acting oh so ooo-la-la during these spring nights with a fair skinned Left Bank artist who specializes in nudes. . . . Hazel and the artist are really suffering from April in Paris."[34] They didn't have to know her companions by name to know that Hazel was behaving like an unmarried woman. Their real interest was, of course, the status of her relationship with Adam Powell Jr. When prying into her affairs, they questioned her about Adam's involvement with other women in the States, which she generally ignored. "I owe the public my best on the stage and a certain moral fibre and character when I appear in public. But after that, as long as I am a lady, what I do is my business and my God's," she told them.[35]

In the summer of 1959, Hazel was playing the Casina delle Rose, an open-air theater in Rome, when she met an Italian Swiss performer, Ezio Bedin. Young, handsome, and charming, Bedin was a comedian who had the ability to mimic hundreds of sounds—the opening of doors, sirens, electric razors, birds, and blowtorches. His solo shows were a crowd-pleasing spectacle. At the Casina delle Rose, Bedin shared the bill with Hazel. He recalled, "One night after the show, I asked Hazel Scott if she would like to go to a nightclub, La Rupe Tarpea. She thought for a moment. And then she said: Yes!"[36] Soon after their impromptu date, Hazel traveled from Rome to Oran, Algeria, for a concert. But before leaving she gave Bedin her Paris address and number.

When they reunited in Paris, a romance blossomed. Bedin was fascinated by Hazel's glamour and sophistication, her lifestyle and the people she knew. He vividly remembered the good times they shared. Sketches of memories he still treasures—her lively apartment always filled with actors and musicians, members of the Comédie-Française, and French actors Jean-Marc Thibault and Roger Pierre; singing with Quincy Jones in his studio, where Hazel taught him "Inchworm, inchworm measuring the marigolds"; and a party in the Paris apartment of the *Life* staff photographer Loomis Dean, where actor Anthony Perkins and Ukranian filmmaker Anatole Litvak talked shop while Sophia Loren prepared her specialty, "spaghetti Carbonari a la Ponti"—spaghetti with bacon, julienned ham, raw eggs, and Parmesan cheese. As a couple, Hazel and Ezio hung out regularly at the Blue Note, commingling with her famous musician friends. "Sometimes we went to a small restaurant, Haynes, and ate soul food, black-eyed peas, fried chicken."[37] (Now considered a national landmark, Haynes was the first black American restaurant to open in Paris.)

Ezio and Hazel vacationed in Barcelona and Naples and performed together throughout France, Turkey, and Spain, enjoying the VIP status and exclusive accommodations that Hazel's name and connections got them. Ezio accompanied her to engagements in Monte Carlo and Deauville. When she appeared on TV España in Barcelona, he stood proudly in the background. And for her birthday, they celebrated at Tito's in Palma de Mallorca, Spain. Ezio was enchanted by it all. Eventually, he moved into Hazel's Paris apartment. Later the couple would maintain a second residence in his native Switzerland.

In March of 1960 the IRS's investigation into Adam Powell Jr.'s taxes finally came to trial, exposing the explicit details of the couple's extravagant lifestyle and very specific financial information about Hazel's professional engagements. Although Hazel had been hounded by the press about her involvement in the tax case, she remained evasive. Once, while performing in Lisbon, questions from reporters about the case and her estranged husband interrupted her good time. "My mind's a blank," she told the reporter. "I know nothing about this. Do you want to talk about my playing, my work? I'm an artist."[38]

But the ongoing investigation of the Powells' tax returns was not going away. Now regretting having relinquished so much control over her business affairs to Adam, Hazel flew to the States to testify in the case.

The indictment charged that Powell's 1951 and 1952 tax returns for himself and Hazel had defrauded the government of over $3,000. They had paid only $1,690 on their total combined earnings of $158,500. The government's case sought to prove that the deductions claimed had been paid for with government funds that Powell had received for congressional business trips abroad. Hazel was absolved of any wrongdoing after it was determined that she didn't sign or prepare her own returns. She didn't have to testify after all. Adam Powell Jr., on the other hand, was facing a $10,000 fine and up to five years in prison if convicted.

His appearances at the Foley Square courthouse in lower Manhattan were a steady source of entertainment for onlookers. "Despite the gravity of the charges," reported *Time*, "Powell's flock remained true. A dozen Negro ministers, dressed in clerical garb, were among the 150 Harlem supporters who hovered outside the packed courtroom. Some prayed in hallways."[39] The press also made mention of the droves of beautiful women, finely dressed, who were seated in the courtroom whenever Powell's proceedings took place. Powell, described as the handsome, "carefully tailored" pastor and politician and "alltime prince of New York's big (900,000) Negro community," appeared nervous.[40]

Throughout the investigation, Adam Powell insisted that this was the work of his Republican enemies. He told reporters at the *New York Times* that there were those who aimed to discredit him because he was in line for the chairmanship of the powerful House Education and Labor Committee. He added that his backing of President Eisenhower in the 1956 presidential election (he participated in a "Democrats for Eisenhower" campaign that had a record number of black Americans voting the Republican ticket and sent Eisenhower to a huge victory over Stevenson) drew the ire of his enemies in Washington and New York's Tammany Hall. All of these things, Powell believed, had conspired against him and placed him in this messy business with the IRS.

In an article cleverly titled "The Powell Amendments," *Time* reported that U.S. District Attorney Paul W. Williams had found a long list of discrepancies on Powell's returns, including: non-deductible expenses as insurance premiums, theater tickets, phone bills, jewelry and furs, a liquor bill amounting to five thousand dollars a year, personal dinners at 21 and Sardi's, television sets, and two boats.

Hazel's agents had been asked to provide statements of her earnings from her European tours. Harry Foster, the head of the British theatrical agency that booked her on her two-month tour of the British Isles, reported that Hazel netted $16,720 during the tour but that she did not handle her own financial affairs. "We were asked by Miss Scott to discuss whatever business matters we had with her husband," the agent said.[41] Helmer Enwall, a Swedish concert manager who handled the Scandinavian leg of her tour, was also called to court. He stated that all of Hazel's payments were turned over to Adam Powell. Both agents were disgruntled about having to testify. They weren't too pleased about the fifteen dollar a day witness fee either, which was not nearly enough to cover their international travel.

Hazel's hairdresser, Nina "L. B." Lucas, was called and questioned about her salary and expenses, all of which were paid by Hazel during the tours overseas. Lucas stated that she was paid a salary of fifty dollars per week plus expenses. Also under investigation was a deduction for Hazel's gowns totaling forty-five hundred dollars. Lucas testified that Hazel usually carried fifteen gowns with her and two or three new gowns were designed before each tour. The elderly Harlem hairdresser, appearing frail and obviously in poor health, was finally excused when it appeared that she was disoriented and unable to proceed.[42]

The *Washington Post* ran the headline "Court Told of Powell's Parties." When Pearl Swangin, Hazel's friend and longtime assistant, was questioned about specific details of Hazel's tour expenses, Adam Powell's attorney called for a mistrial. Edward Bennett Williams contended that these expenses were not at issue. State Department witness John Reddington testified that he had been assigned to meet the Powells and Pearl Swangin at the ship upon their arrival in London. He recounted his duties as having to rent a luxurious Mayfair apartment for them for six weeks, arranging for liquor for two parties where they entertained actors Shirley MacLaine and Jose Ferrer, bandleader Artie Shaw, and the cast of a London theatrical production. He confirmed that Adam Powell was in London on semiofficial business to attend a World Parliament government meeting.[43]

Powell remained "a cool cat" according to his attorney.[44] By the time all of the testimony was in, Adam Powell and Edward Williams had transformed the case into an indictment of the U.S. government. They insisted that the entire case was a misuse of taxpayers' dollars. Attorney Williams twisted the defense in such a way that when all was said and done the government owed Powell money! Judge Frederick van Pelt Bryan threw out two counts against Powell, citing a lack of sufficient evidence. The remaining count, alleging that he had filed false returns in 1951 for Hazel Scott, went to a jury. After twenty-four hours of deliberation, the jury was deadlocked with a final vote ten to two for acquittal, leaving the judge no other choice but to discharge the verdict.

All ended well with the tax trial, but Hazel and Adam were engaged in another personal battle. Over the course of the trial, the two of them picked up where they'd left off, fighting nonstop. Their bitter exchanges led to Hazel's final decision to divorce Adam Powell Jr. As soon as one legal battle ended, another began.

In the fall of 1960, Hazel traveled to Juarez, Mexico, and filed for divorce. She solicited attorneys Vincent J. Malone and Angelo Maurino to represent her.

News of the divorce reached the local papers in Harlem. It was mistakenly reported that an agreement had been reached between the couple. Hazel immediately retorted, "That could not have come from either my attorneys or any one close to me."[45] She was explicit in her feelings about what she would and would not reveal in the press, enumerating her wishes as: "1. I have asked for a divorce from Adam Powell. 2. My reasons for doing so are my own affair. 3. I have asked for no financial settlement from him, no alimony for myself— nothing. I have asked only that he support our son and that he pay the costs of this divorce."[46]

Around this time, it was common knowledge that Adam Powell was intimately involved with Yvette Diago, whom he'd met while on political business in San Juan, Puerto Rico, at the invitation of Governor Luis Muñoz Marin. Not long afterward, Diago came to Washington and joined Powell's staff.

Insinuations were made in the media that Hazel's request for a divorce was instigated by Powell's new love affair. She immediately quashed the accusations. "Whether Mr. Powell intends to remarry or not is a matter of complete indifference to me," she said.[47] She insisted that her primary concern was finalizing the divorce and obtaining child support. Again, Hazel tried to resist being overly emotional. But her statements to the press were venomous. Because Powell was slow in fulfilling her requests, Hazel lashed out, claiming that she had no way of paying the legal fees for the divorce. She also claimed that Powell was obviously reluctant to support his son financially. She called the whole situation "ridiculous." Adam was busy wrapping up a twenty-six-city tour for the 1960 Democratic presidential election. In response to Hazel's allegations, his publicist issued a formal statement: "Adam Powell loves his son Skipper, and is paying all of his costs for tuition and board at the exclusive Riverdale School . . . a sum which runs into the thousands of dollars. He also has the highest respect for Skipper's mother, Hazel, and only regrets that others have persuaded her to issue this statement at this time."[48]

Back and forth, the bickering continued for several weeks. By the year's end, Hazel received her divorce decree along with full custody of their son. Adam Powell and Hazel Scott went their separate ways for good.

With new and interesting projects on the horizon, Hazel moved on. She stayed in the States for several months to perform. Her first stop was Harlem, where she appeared on the Apollo stage in an "Afro-Jazz Revue" along with the "Philly Joe" Jones Quintet and the Herbie Mann Sextette featuring percussionist Olatunji. Her homecoming was a welcome event for Harlemites. She had been missed, and despite the problems she'd had with Adam, Harlem continued to think of her as one of their own. Fans saw little difference between the Hazel who used to play in jam sessions up at Minton's and the Hazel who had spent years abroad. That consistency earned her credibility in the community. After her Apollo appearance, *Variety* wrote, "Miss Scott is a welcome-back heroine on stage. . . . Still looking like an ingénue despite a veteran background, Miss Scott turns in a strictly professional job with both vocalistics and pianistics. Gal has charm and poise along with expert delivery and stage know-how. Her songs pack wallop in terms of audience reception; she can do no wrong in this obviously partisan location." The review ended with the observation that "the 'soul sister' (Miss Scott) has come home."[49]

In July of 1960, Hazel was approached by the Theater Guild and her old friend Langston Hughes to read for the lead in his new play with music, *Tambourines to Glory*. Exclaiming that she gave new meaning to his lines, Hughes offered her the role immediately. A Broadway-bound workshop of the piece got under way at the Westport Playhouse in Connecticut featuring Hazel Scott and comedian Nipsey Russell.

At the start of rehearsals, Hazel approached the work with a great deal of focus. But as rehearsals continued she became distracted, losing interest in the sometimes arduous process that went into mounting a new play—script rewrites, repeated changes in stage blocking, lighting, movement. Hughes's poems, which were set to music and transposed into gospel tunes by Jobe Huntley, were fine-tuned and rehearsed repeatedly. On top of all that, Hazel was not thrilled with the intimate scenes she had to share with Nipsey Russell. She would come home and tell her son, whom she believed was old enough to know about such things, "You know what he does every night? He puts his tongue in my mouth!"[50]

Hazel made it through the Westport run. But when it was time to move the show to Broadway she didn't make the cut. The *Pittsburgh Courier* wrote: "Hazel Scott will be dropped from the lead role in the much-talked about 'Tambourines to Glory' play, because she did a bit too much laughing at the 'wrong time.'. . . Talk is that the producers will announce a new lead very shortly."[51]

Two months after obtaining her divorce, Hazel married Ezio Bedin in a quiet ceremony at Manhattan's Saint Francis Xavier Roman Catholic Church. Mary Lou Williams was her matron of honor. Fr. Anthony Woods, Mary Lou's spiritual advisor, presided over the ceremony.

Just a few weeks earlier, Adam Powell had celebrated his election victory and a new marriage of his own. A few months after the couple's honeymoon in Puerto Rico, Yvette Diago, the new Mrs. Powell, gave birth to a son, Adam Clayton Powell IV.

In many ways, Hazel and Ezio Bedin made a peculiar match. There was a fifteen-year age difference between them—she was forty and he was twenty-five. Raised in Ticino, Switzerland, Bedin spoke very little English. He and Hazel spoke to each other mostly in French. Although she'd had no intention of marrying again, Hazel had a teenage son to think about. She wasn't altogether comfortable with him seeing her romantically involved with a man who wasn't her husband. But this admission wouldn't come until later. At the time, she gushed about her new man, saying that she had found someone who loved and appreciated her and the feeling was mutual.

Jet ran a cover story about the newlyweds entitled "Hazel and Husband's New Act." In the interview, Hazel outlined their plans to be booked on tour together. And, without going into detail about their interracial marriage, Hazel commented, "It doesn't matter where we are as long as we're together. Of course, we aren't planning to settle in Alabama or Mississippi."[52]

The Bedins didn't leave the States right away. They bought a new place at 245 East 17th Street in Manhattan and maintained their two residences in Paris and Switzerland. The press got ahead of itself, publishing reports of "Hazel Scott's Return Home" and her plan to recapture "the fame that once skyrocketed her to the top."[53]

After fulfilling a longstanding engagement at Mister Kelly's in Chicago, Hazel went to Washington to perform for several political events for John F. Kennedy's electoral campaign. But when all the galas were over Hazel was faced with the harsh realities of the New York music scene. Work was dreadfully slow for jazz artists.

She was contemplating her next move when U.S. Attorney Morton S. Robson called her in for an interview in connection with her ex-husband's tax case. During the hour and a half of interrogation, she was careful not to say anything that would damage Powell's standing in Congress or implicate herself. Soon after that meeting, the *New York Times* reported that a tax lien had been filed against her real estate holdings, including the Mount Vernon house and the newly purchased property on 17th Street, for unpaid federal income taxes, not for the years questioned in the Powell tax case but for the years between 1949 and 1955.[54] There would be no trial. Instead, Hazel was hit with a tax bill for eleven thousand dollars, a sum she was in no position to pay. Bedin later recalled that Dizzy Gillespie and his wife Lorraine gave them a thousand dollars to get out of town. Ezio and Hazel flew back to Paris immediately.[55]

CHAPTER FOURTEEN

Saint Mary Lou

"In Paris nowadays, it is rather more difficult for an American Negro to become a really successful entertainer than it is rumored to have been some thirty years ago," observed author James Baldwin. "For one thing, champagne has ceased to be drunk out of slippers, and the frivolously colored thousand-franc note is neither as elastic nor as freely spent as it was in the 1920's."[1] Baldwin described himself and other black expatriates living in Paris in the 1950s and 1960s as "the new lost generation."[2]

Indeed, "lost" is precisely how Hazel had begun to feel. Throughout the 1960s, she would have difficulty finding steady work. Since her bohemian lifestyle in Paris never lent itself to saving, she often found herself financially strapped. "It's not cheap to live in Paris any more, and I don't earn fabulous sums, like in Las Vegas," she said.[3] Money soon became a major worry. Her Paris agent, Felix Marouani, worked hard to put together a string of engagements for her, but things were slow. The concert halls were booked months in advance, and the pay at nightclubs wasn't substantial.

Financial stresses, along with the usual tensions of a new marriage, played their part to rip at the romance of the Bedins, which was shaky from the start. "Sometimes our marriage . . . [was] sweet then sour. Different ages, different colors . . . problems. Few engagements!," Bedin confessed.[4]

To make matters worse, Hazel, while hanging out at the Blue Note one night, decided to join a musician friend's set, playing not the piano but the drums! She broke her little finger on her right hand in the process. "The tendon contracted and she was no longer able to play chords that for decades she had played with ease," her son said. The fact that her Lloyds of London insurance policy had lapsed only added to Hazel's misfortunes. The broken "pinky" put her out of commission for weeks.

Although she constantly resisted the idea, convincing herself that only under the proper circumstances—a lucrative contract and the promise of steady work—would she return to the States, she'd soon realize that going home was her only chance for survival.

As the civil rights movement gained momentum in the States, the urge to join the fight tugged at her. The huge expanse between Paris and the front lines did not lessen Hazel's fighting spirit. She stayed abreast of the American news, watching news telecasts regularly and reading all the papers. "I've looked at that television screen and seen these people who are quietly kneeling and praying and singing 'We Shall Overcome.' They're not preaching violence. They are not preaching racial hate. And they are being attacked," she commented in an interview for John Bainbridge's book on expatriates, *Another Way of Living*.[5] She was torn. Given all her years of fighting for civil rights, a real movement now existed that she could lend her voice to, and there she was, far from home. Hazel described her status as a black expatriate as "painful." It was a very isolating experience. She had very few people to talk to on the subject. Her husband had very little knowledge of her struggles in America. And French friends could hardly understand why anyone would want to return to a place where they were not wanted. Other American expatriates were her only outlet.

Adam Powell III, having no intention of following the career paths of his parents—neither show business nor the clergy held his interest—was now an undergraduate at the Massachusetts Institute of Technology. He told his mother, "While living in Europe . . . you've gotten used to coming out with exactly what you feel like saying, exactly when you feel like saying it, and devil take the last fellow over the fence. . . . I think, Mops"—he rarely called her Mom—"that the best thing for you, actually, would be to stay in Europe and, you know, fight the battle from over there, because you don't have the weapons that we need any more." To this Hazel responded, "He was telling me in a very sweet and extremely sort of tactful way, 'Darling, this is a new generation.'"[6]

When James Baldwin, photographer Richard Avedon, and actor Bill Marshall approached Hazel with the idea of organizing a protest march in France, she joined the effort. This would give them all a sense of purpose and participation. They gathered at her apartment and planned a public demonstration before the American Embassy in Paris to coincide with the 1963 March on Washington for Freedom and Jobs led by Rev. Dr. Martin Luther King, A. Philip Randolph, and Bayard Rustin. One week before the march, on August 21, 1963, Hazel, Baldwin, Avedon, Marshall, Memphis Slim, "Mezz" Mezzrow, and a host of other American artists and musicians marched before the American Embassy in Paris, presenting Ambassador Cecil Lyon with a petition in support of the historic march.

James Baldwin, unable to stand on the sidelines, returned to the States intermittently to lend his voice to the cause. But other black American expatriates, like Hazel, remained abroad during that tumultuous period of protest and civil unrest, watching repeated televised accounts of marches and picket lines and riots breaking out in Chicago and Detriot, Watts and Newark, seeing the attacks of vicious dogs and water hoses sprayed across the backs of protestors. And, while they were undoubtedly moved by Dr. King's uplifting words and Odetta's songs of protest, touched by the tenacity of Fannie Lou Hamer and Rosa Parks, and emotionally shattered by the cries of the embattled and the massacred, each of them would individually, and in their own way, have to defend their absence to those who believed they had walked away from the fight.

During the summer of 1963, Bedin had a two-week engagement with the great French singer Edith Piaf in Marseilles. "The last day Madame Piaf she asked me if I was free to go with her in the Theatre

Olympia and Bobino," he remembered.[7] He turned down the offer, opting to go to Israel with Hazel instead, where she was booked for two months with the Israel Philharmonic Orchestra. "The same year Piaf died!" Bedin said.[8] Putting Hazel's career before his own naturally led to feelings of resentment. Hazel, too, was beginning to have regrets about their relationship. Just months into it, the marriage began to fall apart.

In his premarital counseling sessions with the couple, Father Woods had warned Hazel that marriage so soon after her divorce was not a good idea. He also questioned whether Ezio, at just twenty-five years old, was emotionally prepared for such a life-altering commitment. He tried to dissuade them, but neither listened.

Later that year, after a huge fight, Bedin left. He spent four months working in Australia, at which point the couple unofficially and unceremoniously separated. A Mexican divorce was soon to follow.

Bedin believes that he was too young to marry Hazel, but he found the woman and lifestyle irresistible. "I learned a lot! Today I am glad that I had this experience!" he said.[9] After the marriage was over, he would later confess to a friend, "Hazel is a Maserati, and I can only handle a Fiat!"[10]

Hazel admitted that because she had a growing son she wanted to "do the right thing" by getting married. "Right away, the relationship soured. Ezio was talented and kind but was insecure about following the great man," she said.[11] "People called him Mr. Scott. I saw him being destroyed. It cost me a lot emotionally."[12]

Hazel vented her frustration over her failed second marriage and other matters of personal importance in letters to her friend Mary Lou Williams, who was now back in New York. Confiding the most intimate details of her life, Hazel sought Mary Lou's listening ear and spiritual counsel. The letters became a form of prayer and confession. She would begin each one with an endearing salutation—"Darling," "Dear Sister," or "Dearest Mary." And she signed them all "Love always, your sister Hazel." The postscript typically acknowledged her friends, Lorraine and Dizzy Gillespie: "P.S. Love to Lo and Diz." Jumping from topic to topic, Hazel wrote candidly about everything that was on her mind.

The familiar refrain in all of her letters was that work was slow but she was determined to press on. "Sure I've been having a rough time!" she wrote. "So who has it easy in this world?"[13]

Beyond her two marriages, Hazel kept her romantic life private. After the breakup of her second marriage, she started up a romance with a well-known American entertainer, Dick Haymes. "She was crazy about him," recalled her friend Betsey Crawford. Haymes had a solid career as a vocalist at one time, performing with the big bands of Benny Goodman and Tommy Dorsey. As a Hollywood leading man, he starred in *One Touch of Venus* with Ava Gardner, *On the Town* with Mickey Rooney, and *State Fair* with Jeanne Crain. He was known to be a sweet and quiet man, but Haymes had personal problems. An alcoholic, he had been married five times (once to actress Rita Hayworth). By the time Hazel began dating him, his career was well past its peak. No longer a commodity in Hollywood, Haymes was in debt and had gone to Europe to find work.

Perhaps it was their similar state of affairs that drew them to one another; it was certainly what tore them apart. With them both in financial straits and coming out of bad relationships, their romance fizzled after several months.

When the press clamored for information about her love life, Hazel was contrary. "Generally speaking, men amuse, entertain and delight me. I don't take them seriously. I haven't got the time. I've got a living to make and a child to raise. If I were a wealthy woman I would take time out to make a study of them and see what makes them tick but I don't have the time."[14] She would reveal little else about other lovers, adhering to her mother's old advice, "A lady never tells."

Proud, Hazel didn't want anyone to know that she was floundering in Paris. Her career couldn't seem to get any traction. "Honey, I don't want the world to know I'm financially embarrassed! There is no crime involved but *you know* the world and how people think!!!," she wrote in a letter to Mary Lou.

But with each gig, new hope sprung. Hazel performed at the 1965 Cannes Film Festival, providing her with a break from the city and some much needed cash. She kept her expenses down by staying at the home of a friend. Merv Griffin caught her concert and decided to tape her for his television show on NBC, singing and playing solo on the waterfront without accompaniment. Guitarist Mundell Lowe would fill in the accompaniment once they returned to New York. The segment ran on the *Merv Griffin Show* some weeks later.

It had come to this. Hazel Scott, who was once one of the most sought after entertainers in the industry, who negotiated demanding contracts and pulled in six figures a year, found herself scrambling for work, relying on the good intentions of producers and club owners, and waiting on promises to be delivered. She was now thankful for whatever work she could get.

Hazel often received small monetary gifts from Mary Lou. Even in these lean years, whatever Mary Lou had she shared it. She was one of the few who knew of Hazel's money problems, and without waiting for Hazel to ask, she would drop a few dollars in the mail. These small gestures of kindness meant the world to Hazel. She knew Mary Lou truly understood, and that made her situation less frightening, less lonely.

The subject of returning to the States came up often in Hazel's letters to Mary Lou. She worried that her popularity was waning on both sides of the Atlantic. In one postscript, she wrote, "Over here the work is slow—it would be better if I could come back for a while. Increase my value. You know how it is—people only appreciate the hard to get!!"[15] Considering how famous Hazel once was, how wealthy and in demand, to show up in the States as anything less than that was another source of frustration. She simply could not go back begging. She had been hearing firsthand accounts from jazz musician friends about the scene at home, which for many of them had become quite bleak. Jazz musicians were feeling stuck in the States, having to continually come up with creative outlets for their music while the industry changed directions and audiences developed a taste for other music. Still, Hazel exclaimed, "What have I got to sell! Nothing—but what God gave me—talent baby! No credit goes to me!"[16]

Meanwhile, her debts were mounting. Aside from her day-to-day expenses, Hazel received word from the U.S. government that her tax bill was overdue. "My bill came June 10th and I cried all day. Eleven thousand (about) dollars for the years 1949 through 1955 . . . plus the lawyers and accountants who were hired for me—plus other debts—plus, plus, plus!" she wrote.[17] Because salaries were lower in Europe, Hazel had no idea how she could ever earn enough money to pay the tax bill working overseas. Promises of work back in the States were often tossed about, but they rarely materialized. And Hazel refused to return without steady work, a long-term contract that could guarantee a decent living. Until then, Paris would remain her home.

When she returned from her concert engagement in Cannes, Hazel came home to an insect-ridden apartment and a disconnected gas line. "Keep this to yourself," she told Mary Lou, "but my gas has been cut off—for the moment. All I have to do is hope and pray that something unusual happens at the end of this month so that I can hold on till the next gig."[18] Even when she landed nightclub work in countries outside of France, her contracts were not up to par. She often complained, "They don't pay the fare and the price is nowhere for the gig, but who can refuse work?"[19]

Long periods of unemployment rendered Hazel depressed and desperate. Living hand-to-mouth was taking its toll. And there seemed to be no relief in sight. There were days when she had nothing more than a few dollars in her pocket. Normally, she did everything she could to hide the fact of her poor circumstances, but one night, while out with a group of musicians, she got into an argument over four dollars. Someone had borrowed it from her, and she wanted it back. The fight took place in front of other musicians. When drummer Arthur Taylor interjected, asking, "What are you doing NEEDING two mille?" she cussed him out, too. "It was necessary for me to tell him that when I ask *him* for 'bread' then and only *then* he can consider himself free to cast reflexions and look at me with scorn!"[20]

Frequent calls from her son and Mabel brightened Hazel's spirits. Neither of them had any idea how badly she was suffering. At least she didn't have to worry about Adam III's college tuition; his father covered those expenses, and he had secured a summer job working for CBS-TV. "Skip tells me his dad has broken with his Puerto Rican wife and sent Pearl down to get the baby. It seems he has been constantly accompanied by another one of his secretaries, Connie Huff!! Poor Adam. Marriage no. 3 down the drain!"[21] But her concern for Powell's personal affairs had long passed, especially now that she had more pressing matters to worry about. Even though he was wealthy and may have been inclined to help, Hazel had absolutely no intention of going to her ex-husband for assistance.

In the meantime, she managed the best she could, relying on her wits to make ends meet. She gratefully accepted whatever money Mary Lou sent. And Lorraine Gillespie, who had some knowledge of Hazel's predicament, would occassionally put a little cash in a card wishing her well.

> Dearest Mary,
> You are what you are praying to become. A saint. One day, and please remember that I used to cut your picture out of the paper and had an Apollo poster of yours stuck up in my room on the wall; you will be recognized as exactly that.[22]

Mary Lou gave freely and without strings. She never asked for it back because she never considered it a loan. She never wanted Hazel or any of the other musicians she helped to feel beholden to her. The money she sent was considered a "grant." The significance of this gesture was not lost on Hazel. "Thank you for the use of the word," Hazel wrote. "It indicates my darling, that you really understand."[23]

Hazel spent hours listening to new music. As Leonard Feather observed, "She never lost contact with the jazz scene. She is ready with a firm evaluation of any pianist you can name."[24] In a *Los Angeles Times* interview with Feather, she remarked on a number of fine pianists whose work she admired. "Bill Evans is beautiful—a poet. Bobby Timmons—an unsung hero. McCoy Tyner is just beautiful, Joe Zawinul—wow, he's real greasy!"[25]

But it was Mary Lou Williams's music that kept Hazel sane. "Black Christ of the Andes," she found particularly inspiring—"'A Fungus A Mungus'—WOW! 'Dirge Blues' breaks my heart," she wrote.[26] The album included Mary Lou's interpretation of the four-teenth-century devotional prayer "Anima Christi" (Soul of Christ), which happened to be one of Hazel's favorite prayers, one she prayed daily. Commonly described as a jazz waltz with gospel influences, "Anima Christi" features the vocals of Jimmy Mitchell and Grant Green's guitar.

As her circumstances forced her to look deep within, Hazel wrestled with God, Catholicism, and the meaning of it all. She prayed:

Soul of Christ, sanctify me
Body of Christ, save me
Blood of Christ, inebriate me
Water from Christ's side, wash me
Passion of Christ, strengthen me
O good Jesus, hear me
Within Thy wounds hide me
Suffer me not to be separated from Thee
From the malicious enemy defend me
In the hour of my death call me
And bid me come unto Thee
That I may praise Thee with Thy saints
and with Thy angels
Forever and ever
Amen

When she was able to pull her attention away from her daily financial concerns, Hazel sat down at the piano and played. Desperately needing to be productive, she worked on new compositions and began writing her memoirs. She prayed for "strength, health and above all TIME—plus the facilities to set things down."[27]

In early 1966, Hazel booked a concert engagement in Israel. But again there were contractual problems that caused a long delay in her getting paid. In letters to Mary Lou, she expressed her frustration at having to fulfill requests to "jazz the classics." It was a maneuver she had outgrown. Mary Lou could only respond by stating the obvious, that it was what the people wanted and she'd have to give it to them.[28] Sounding totally exhausted, Hazel confided to Mary Lou, "My life is one long series of fighting to stay alive. Period."[29]

Hazel had spent some time with pianist and vocalist Nina Simone, who gave her a contact in London for possible work but also tried to persuade her to consider moving back to the States. She told Hazel plainly, that she wasn't getting the respect she deserved in France. Ironically, just a few years later Nina Simone—following her active participation in the civil rights movement—would herself become an expatriate, taking up residence first in Barbados, then Liberia and Switzerland before finally settling in the south of France, where she remained until her death.

Before Hazel had time to give her next move any serious consideration, she was waylaid by illness. One day, she collapsed in her kitchen. Her doctor administered a series of tests, but was unable to determine the exact cause of the problem. Initially, he thought it was leukemia, then later ruled it out. Hazel was weak and lethargic, with no appetite and no physical strength. She hadn't worked in over three months and had no money. In a letter to Mary Lou, she gave a litany of reasons as to why she needed to get well and get back to work as soon as possible—her phone bill was past due and would be cut off soon; her bank account was overdrawn and the bank was calling; the prescriptions the doctor gave her were necessary but expensive; and the rent was due.

Ashamed but desperate, Hazel finally reached out for help. Beulah Bryant, a blues singer, came to visit her one day and was shocked by her appearance. Wan and frail, Hazel tried to explain her situation, but Beulah went on a rampage. She said she was going to call Adam Powell Jr. and tell him what poor condition she was in. That was the last thing Hazel wanted, but Bryant insisted. On Hazel's behalf, she planned to tell him "if he had ever been a friend of mine to prove it now. Only thing is—I don't believe he ever was a friend of mine," Hazel confided to Mary Lou.[30] Then she wrote, "Have to stop, baby. I'm whipped."[31]

Hazel's illness lingered for over a month. She hadn't gotten her strength back when she was hit with the news that Beulah Bryant had gone to the press with a full, detailed story of Hazel's life in

Paris. Hazel was livid. She had told Bryant only limited details about her physical condition and nearly nothing about her finances. So she wondered where Bryant had gotten her information. Hazel looked to Mary Lou. In a letter dated April 20, 1966, she wrote:

> Dearest Mary:
>
> I want you to understand me well baby! Do you realize that I had no idea what was in the papers? Do you realize that I had no idea that Beulah Bryant had sent letters to everybody under the sun—people I know and people I don't—saying that I was destitute and that they were trying to raise money to send me back there??[32]

Bryant had gone to the *Amsterdam News, Jet,* the *New York Daily News,* the Actor's Fund, and the Negro Actor's Guild. She was a member of Abyssinian Baptist Church and took it upon herself to circulate the story among the congregation as well.

> Mary, you know very well that pride is something I have learned to do without—but *dear God* what is wrong with that woman??[33]

Beulah Bryant had done the unspeakable as far as Hazel was concerned. Friends were contacting her regularly, telling her about yet another news article. A rumor spread that Hazel was dying of leukemia. In each story, Bryant comes off as helping a friend in need while Hazel is portrayed as a pitiful waif wasting away in Paris.

Weeks later *Jet's* Paris bureau followed up on the story. When the editor began asking Hazel to confirm very personal details that he should not have known, she knew her trust had been betrayed. First, he asked if it were true that Mary Lou Williams had sent her $650 for medicine and treatment. "Now I wonder WHERE he got that kind of information?" she asked in a missive to Mary Lou.[34]

> First of all, Mary, I must ask you again if you realize what all this scandal is doing to me and to my son who is in school. I hope you realize how this hurts him??[35]

It hurt Hazel deeply to think that Mary Lou might have participated in any way in fueling the rumors. "Are you talking to those
newspaper people Mary?" Hazel asked. "I have asked you to help put
an end to the ridiculous newspaper stories. I wrote you air mail special and asked that you please see that the rumors about leukemia
(God forbid!) are untrue."

Joe Glaser, the ubiquitous agent to the biggest names in the music business, sent Hazel a long cable offering her a ticket home. She
had worked with Glaser in the past but was not a signed client. Hazel
told the *Los Angeles Times*, "It wasn't that I needed it, but knowing
he wanted to do it made me feel so good."[36] But to Mary Lou, she
wrote:

> Mary! I refuse to be "Exhibit A" in the Rogues Gallery, or any
> freak side-show. Please don't think that I am being proud and
> foolish. It is just that I am the way I am and it is too late for me
> to learn new tricks.[37]

The letter went on for many pages, all handwritten and filled
with exclamation points, underscores, and capital letters for emphasis. Hazel was seething. And, although she didn't know precisely
how Mary Lou had contributed to the madness, hers was the only relationship that she felt was worth fighting for. When Hazel discovered that Mary Lou had been organizing a benefit on her behalf in
New York, she implored:

> PLEASE. DON'T RAISE ANY MONEY FOR ME. PLEASE!!
> How often must I write the same thing?[38]

Desperately defensive, Hazel claimed she didn't need anything
from anybody. She had just completed an extended engagement for
a decent amount of money, but it was far from the high-paying gig
she made it out to be, just one day's work at an outdoor venue. Still,
the idea that people would gather to drop money in a collection
plate on her behalf, for Hazel, was infinitely worse than what she
was going through. Nothing in her upbringing or her life experience

would allow her to accept such charity. What she needed was "work, work and more work." She appealed to Mary Lou as a musician, telling her that if the world believed she was sick and destitute it would do irreparable damage to her reputation and career. No one would hire her.

In some respects, Hazel had Mary Lou to thank for instigating the chain of events that would lead her home. Despite her intransigence, Hazel was no longer in any condition, financial, physical or otherwise, to maintain a healthy lifestyle abroad. Home beckoned.

Hazel told her side of the story to *Jet*. Journalist Charles L. Saunders began by writing, "When pianist-singer Hazel Scott is angry, really angry, she can let you know it in English, French, Italian, Schwyzerdutsch or (since her recent trip to Tel Aviv) right passable Hebrew. Nowadays she's exploding in French, and even the bearded lexicographers at L'Académie Française couldn't catalog the words she's tossing around. It's all because of what she calls "that $&*#%&* leukemia rumor" that's cropped up in newspaper columns across the U.S."[39]

Doctors had finally determined that Hazel had contracted mononucleosis.

Hazel explained that it all began when she blacked out during a concert in Tel Aviv, then again in Barcelona while doing a TV show. She thought she was just overexerting herself until it happened again while she was at home cooking, at which point she sought medical attention. "Look, if there's anything I don't need yet it's a Benefit for Hazel Scott. I'm no Mrs. Vanderbilt or Lady Astor, but I'm not exactly poor either. Not only did that kind of stuff embarrass me, but I've got a 19-year-old son at Massachusetts Institute of Technology. How do you think he felt about it?"[40]

With his father living in self-exile in the Bahamas, embroiled in a corruption scandal and engaged in the fight of his career—the battle to save not only his seat in Congress but his political legacy—and his mother unwell in Paris, Adam III needed at least one of his parents in the States.

He sent his godmother, Mabel Howard, over to the rue Miromesnil with a simple but clear message: "Your son wants you home."

CHAPTER FIFTEEN

Rondo

"Hazel Scott Comes Home to the 'Action'" exclaimed *Ebony*. "Hazel Dorothy Scott Powell Bedin has, in the span of what might be considered a short lifetime, been many things: child prodigy, darling of café society, concert artist, civil rights pioneer, the wife of a famous and powerful man, mother, divorcee, expatriate."[1] Hazel returned to the United States the only way she knew how, in grand fashion, looking very much like her old self. She appeared svelte and at her sexy best on the cover of the magazine. In the interview she revealed that she had undergone a complete and thorough rejuvenation regimen. Under a physician's care, Hazel was placed on a high-protein diet to get her strength back and given regular massage therapy and rigorous physical training that resulted in her shedding over fifty pounds. It must have come as a shock to those who'd read the reports of her illness and expected to see an aged, broken down version of the pianist they once knew. Considering all that she had gone through, Hazel appeared surprisingly young and refreshed.

There were many stories circulating about why she came back. No matter how many times she explained that her son wanted her home, many assumed that she must have come back to join the struggle or what *Ebony* writer Louie Marshall called her "old love for a good fight."[2]

Having suffered the assassinations of Malcolm X, Medgar Evers, and President John F. Kennedy, and a few short years later Martin Luther King Jr. and Robert Kennedy, the civil rights movement raged on. There was more work to be done, and the black press wanted to know where Hazel Scott fit into that equation. "I have to stay here now," she said. "It's not just a question of career; it's more than that. It's a question of what's happening here. I see this creeping horror, and what happened in the cities last summer is not what I am talking about."[3] Riots in urban cities across the country, as far as Hazel was concerned, were overt displays of anger spilling out into the streets. The broader issue, the "creeping horror," was the unbridled hostility between the races that now showed itself openly in the attitudes of ordinary citizens. After living overseas nearly ten years, it was unfathomable to her that Ku Klux Klan activity, brutal lynchings, cross burnings, and other forms of barbarism were still taking place in America.

Hazel questioned the goals of the movement, asking rhetorically, "It boils down to this: What are we going to finally do? Are we just going to say that blood must run in the streets? Whose blood, and why? Before black people and white people are killed in the streets, I want to know what they are dying for."[4]

When confronted with accusations of having abandoned the fight, Hazel didn't speak of her time abroad in blissful terms. Nor did she apologize for needing a break from American's race problem. She did not claim that France was without racism, though she did point out that racially motivated incidents overseas were the exception not the rule. "I'm not going to say that France is paradise, but I will say this: You can live anywhere you've got the money to live. You can go anywhere you've got the money to go and whomever you marry or date is your business."[5]

She was openly attacked, not only in the press but by the public, for her expatriation. On one occasion, a hotel waiter in New York confronted her, stating, "I once thought you were the greatest but you have fallen in my estimation because you left America where the fight is."[6] Such accusations, Hazel said, came from "uninformed people."[7] Feeling misunderstood and underappreciated, she spoke out in her own defense, saying that she had been fighting "the fight" long before it became a movement. In nearly every press interview on the subject, she cited her years on the road, her insistence on performing before integrated audiences, and her experiences traveling in the Jim Crow South, unable to stay in a hotel and having to find a black family in every town that would allow her to spend the night. "In order to avoid being arrested in the South, I wouldn't use the "Colored" entrance, and I wouldn't use the "White" entrance. I used the Yellow Cab entrance."[8]

Hazel was highly critical of anyone who suggested she had not done her part. She blasted members of the younger generation, whom she felt too often dressed for protest with their natural afros and dashikis. "The instant African is a drag," she said.[9] "I have a deep and abiding resentment for the so-called 'new Negro' because I think he has been a little late in arriving." Furious at having been labeled everything from a radical to a communist, a black Joan of Arc to an apologist for her race, Hazel retaliated: "I am not about to sit still, now, and let anybody tell me that nothing was done until these 'new Negroes' started letting their hair grow long. Let's not go in the other direction and become reverse snobs."[10]

But a war of words with a younger generation that had little knowledge of the burden she had borne in the 1940s and 1950s did little to further the civil rights cause. Besides, her contribution hardly needed defending. She wrote a piece in her journal entitled, "To Young Black People," where she suggests that they respect the path that had been paved for them by those who came before. "The road along which you move today was carved out of life by the bare hands of your ancestors," she wrote.[11] Insisting that they set only the highest standards for themselves, she asked, "Since we have been categorized as 'inferior,' why should we be angered when the opportunity presents itself to make liars of them all?"[12] It reads like an assignment giving "students" of the movement specific instructions on how to proceed. "Those who are for the right must take heart. There is no need to falter, there is no place for self-doubt. There is no room for the slow to decide. There is not time for dissension among the leadership—*every* clan must march."[13]

Accused of mismanagement of his committee budget, misappropria-
tion of funds, taking personal trips with public funds, flagrant absenteeism, and a series of other corruption charges, in January of
1967 Adam Clayton Powell Jr. was stripped of his position as chairman of the Education and Labor Committee by the House Democratic Caucus. While a thorough investigation by the Judiciary Committee was conducted, the House of Representatives voted 307 to 116
to deny him his congressional seat until the investigation was complete, leaving Harlem without its congressman for a period of nearly
two years. "Privately politicians will admit that other Congressmen
have been guilty of putting relatives on the payroll, globe-hopping
at public expense and spending more time at home than in Washington. But nobody does all these things at once and so blatantly,"
commented the *New York Daily News*.[14]

Throughout the 1960s, Powell had also been involved in a libel
suit stemming from a television appearance in March of 1960, where
he accused police officers in Harlem of being in the pockets of gamblers, drug dealers, and pimps. He also accused a Harlem resident, Esther James, of being a "bag woman" for the police. Powell would ultimately pay out a five-figure settlement to Mrs. James, but in the
interim he decided to steer clear of New York, his constituents, and
his church.

On the floor of the House, he spoke out against his enemies, calling Harlem's cops "the dregs of the police force." Powell claimed
that he was being victimized by New York's "lily-white bench and
underworld-controlled judges," adding that the police force and the
criminals were working together to prevent him from cleaning up
Harlem.

The outcries of New York senators Robert Kennedy and Jacob Jav-
its, as well as Powell's Harlem constituents and devoted Abyssinian
church members, could not sway the House Democratic Caucus to
reconsider its decision.

Adam Powell's political career had suffered blows before, but
now it was evident that his power was waning as well as his energy.
Fleeing the turmoil, he returned to the Bahamian island of Bimini.

Meanwhile, Hazel Scott's life remained strangely intertwined with Adam Powell's. With the congressman's corruption scandal one of the biggest news stories in the country, Hazel was approached by her ex-husband's enemies, who were hoping to extract vital information they could use against him. In several televised interviews, she flatly refused to speak ill of him and expressed her disgust and outrage at their tactics. No matter what they had been through personally, Hazel stated unequivocally, "Adam is a good man. He's done great things for his people." That was her final word. In an interview with *Jet,* she stated bluntly, "I will discuss my return to the United States, music, musicians, performers, styles, fashions, foods—anything except—Adam Clayton Powell and politics. I've made my position clear on how I felt about what they've done to him."[15] As a result, she gained even more fans in the black community, especially among Abyssinian church members, by refusing to join ranks with those who wanted to disgrace the congressman. "I remember a lot of people at church saying, 'Oh, Mrs. P. is really standing up,'" Adam III said.

It was a trying time for their son as well. Adam III was away in college at MIT but could hardly forget the days of his father's trial. "At noon, I would catch the Eastern Airlines shuttle to Washington, and be there in the house gallery for the hearings of my father. Then I would catch the 5:00 pm or the 6:00 pm up to New York to catch my mother's first show."[16]

In 1967, around the same time Congressman Powell's political troubles were brewing, Hazel, on her way back to New York from a concert in Montreal, phoned her son. "YOUR MOTHER is at Kennedy airport," she announced.[17] Immediately, Adam knew there was trouble. "YOUR MOTHER is being told by the immigration people that she needs a sponsor." Adam assumed she'd forgotten her passport. "YOUR MOTHER is being told she is not an American citizen."[18] Hazel was not allowed entry back into the country. After completing "a routine check," immigration officials informed her that they had reviewed the 1924 microfilm of papers her mother had filled out on the ship from Trinidad and, because a box was left unchecked, Hazel Scott was not officially a citizen of the United States.

Adam rushed down to the airport and spoke directly with the immigration officer, who admitted that all of this was rather unusual. He agreed to allow Hazel entry but warned that unless the matter was cleared up she would not be allowed to the leave the country again. "Please have it done within thirty days," he said, "because this is obviously on somebody's desk."[19] That single statement made it more than apparent to Hazel and her son that this sudden bureaucratic confusion was likely tied to the ongoing investigation of Adam Powell Jr.

After following up on the matter with the U.S. Immigration and Nationalization Service, Adam III decided to go to the Trinidad and Tobago Consulate. Because Hazel was born when the island was still under British rule, she was born a British citizen, which entitled her to a British passport.

Hazel's final word on the matter: "If I'm not a citizen, I want all my taxes back."[20]

She used the British passport from that point on whenever she needed to travel outside the United States. In the past, this kind of event would have sent her into a rage, but she'd seen too much to be surprised by what she perceived as a deliberate act of vengeance by the U.S. government. She summed up her feelings in an interview with a newspaper reporter.

> I don't know about politics. I'm not following that anymore. You might say I'm to the left of some radicals, but I'm conservative in many ways. My politics is strange. I haven't kept my faith in this country—I've kept my love for it.[21]

With the nation now moving to the beat of rhythm and blues, the Motown sound, and the British bands, Hazel wondered if there was still a place for her. Even jazz music had taken on a sound that she hardly recognized. "I have no argument with those who want to play 'free' or avant-garde jazz. I say 'bless them' and they don't have to worry about competition from me."[22]

At this point in her long career, Hazel had dispensed with "jazzing the classics" altogether. Now, she was comfortable admitting, "It was childish; then it became a novelty." Now, she had reached a new level of maturity, and her music had greater depth. "I don't play what I don't like," Hazel said. "My playing and singing have improved. My chief fault as a young performer was total arrogance. I have more experience; more feeling."[23]

She created a new repertoire of straight jazz, ballads, torch songs, and some popular music. The only tune she played from her earlier period was the Tatum-inspired "Tea for Two," where she'd often slip a few bars of Debussy's *Clair de Lune* into the arrangement.

Admiration for her early work would surface over time in the work of other artists, among them the choreographer George Balanchine, who is said to have been inspired by Hazel's swing interpretations of classical compositions to create *Concerto Barocco,* now considered one of his greatest works. The piece draws parallels, through dance, between the contrasting cadences of baroque music and boogie-woogie.[24]

Hazel worked hard to get her career back on track in the States. She was very uncertain about the New York club scene. So much had changed. She signed with managers Andrew Stroud and Buddy Clarke, who arranged bookings for her through the summer of 1968, including several television appearances on the *Merv Griffin Show* (her favorite of all the talk shows), the *Mike Douglas Show,* and Virginia Graham's *Girl Talk.* Still very selective when it came to her bookings, Hazel's decisions as to where she would appear had to correspond to the sophisticated image she wished to project. However, her expectations would have to change, and concessions would have to be made as opportunties became more and more limited.

Her first job was an extended engagement at the Living Room, a popular nightclub on Manhattan's East Side. Her sidemen included the bassist Chris White, formerly with Dizzy Gillespie's band, and Bob Hamilton, a former drummer for Nina Simone. The *New York Times* reviewer John Wilson commented, "At The Living Room, Miss Scott is inclined to skim blithely across the surface of her talents. . . . But when she comes to 'When the World Was Young,' this superficiality peels away. She calls into play the shading in the warm, throaty lower range of her voice and, particularly in the passages that she sings in French, the artist in Miss Scott takes command."[25] New York audiences were happy to have her back. She played to packed houses every night. "The crowds were beautiful, wonderful," she said.[26] "They really made me happy to be back. It was a hard engagement in that I had to do three shows nightly and five on Saturdays. But, I thrive on hard work and I had a ball."[27]

Accompanied by stellar musicians, Grady Tate on drums and Milt Hinton on bass, Hazel wowed the crowd at Plaza-9, playing old tunes and new, from "12th Street Rag" to "Little Green Apples." At the end of the show, she even took requests. "Anything, even if I can't play it," she told the crowd. Critics called the combo an "exquisitely subtle jazz trio."

Although her concerts were well received, Hazel's life and career in New York were unsettled. Work was sporadic, and being idle never suited her. When she wasn't performing, she worked on her memoir, wrote poetry, and reconnected with old friends.

Mary Lou Williams's manager, Fr. Peter O'Brien, remembered meeting Hazel around this time as Hazel made frequent visits to Mary Lou's thrift shop in Harlem. "I went down to get her out of the cab. And she sweeps out of the cab and into the building," he said, leaving him to pay the cab fare. He remembered how beautifully dressed she was and her magnificent jewels. "That day, she had on a large pink ring," he said. "I asked her what it was, and she said it was a beryl. 'My jeweler designed it for me.'"[28] He was awed by her presence. "Hazel just had this terrific public presentation."[29] He got a kick out of watching Hazel and Mary Lou together. "Now, you would think, 'oh, here's two divas in the room,' but it was nothing like that at all. They enjoyed one another."[30] One memory in particular stood out above all others. "Mary was having a benefit or something. And she was walking around town with nails and a hammer, tacking up signs. And she got arrested for not having the proper permit. Well, her one phone call was to Hazel, who put on a show! Hazel came down to the precinct, you know, with the whole, big, dramatic entrance. She walked in screaming, 'THAT WOMAN IS A SAINT!' What are you doing to her?' Then Mary said, 'By that time I was having a ball playing cards with the whores. I didn't want to leave!'"[31]

Both women were living a parallel existence in New York at that time, trying to stay afloat in the jazz world. Mary Lou was struggling financially. She still performed in nightclubs but relied mostly on her thrift shop for income. And, while Hazel played hotels, supper clubs, and lounges, she was hopeful but realistic about the music industry. "The music business is just like every other business," she said. "You're exploited or you're the exploiter. People who are sufficiently independent to be able to negotiate and to manage their own destinies are few and far between."[32] She found it a sad and unfortunate truth that so many artists had to make choices contrary to their own wishes simply because they needed to "pay the rent and survive."

After several months of regular nightclub engagements at clubs such as the Downbeat, Jimmy Weston's, the Ali Baba, and the Rainbow Grill, Hazel booked a job on a cruise ship, the *Queen Mary,* sailing through the Panama Canal and winding up in Los Angeles. Once the gig was over, she decided to visit Mabel Howard in Los Angeles. While there, Hazel revisited the idea of pursuing an acting career in earnest. "Acting is what I want to do," she declared.[33] "I'm dying to get a good, meaty role."[34] Her name still carried some currency on the West Coast. But she didn't have proper representation, only what she called "an old show business musical agent."[35] Nonetheless, she landed a few roles in daytime soap operas, playing a terminal cancer victim, "Dolly Martin," on *The Bold Ones: The New Doctors.* She played an executive assistant to Barry Sullivan in a made for television movie on *CBS Playhouse* called *The Experiment,* starring Michael Douglas, John Astin, and Susan Strasberg; the teleplay, written by Ellen Violett, was nominated for an Emmy Award in 1969. Later, in New York, she would appear in two episodes of the ABC soap *One Life to Live,* where she played the piano and sang two songs that she'd written specifically for a wedding scene. But Hazel's acting career never caught on. The handful of gigs she landed, though not enough to truly satisfy her, were still a notable achievement, as even during the 1960s and 1970s black actors on television in significant roles were a rarity.

Hazel's work as an actress in Los Angeles wrapped up with two appearances on Diahann Carroll's series, *Julia*. She played her next door neighbor. *Julia* was a groundbreaking achievement for Carroll, who became the first African American actress to star in her own television series. During one of her tapings, Hazel had an unexpected run-in with one of the actresses, who had been on the set of *The Heat's On* all those years ago when Hazel staged a strike and left production early. As Hazel recalled the chance reunion, the woman "looked at me in some amusement. 'Do you remember when you left town before your picture was finished?' She looked at my startled reaction and laughed. 'I remember it well because they used me for your long shots! The camera was so far away that no one could tell the difference!' "[36]

Hazel found work in a few small Los Angeles lounges and had an extended run at the Playboy Club. But after three years Hazel gave up on Hollywood. Returning to New York, she signed with a new agent, George Scheck, and hoped for the best. Scheck was diligent and committed. He worked hard to secure nightclub bookings for Hazel along the Eastern seaboard but found it challenging. "Of course, her career wasn't where it was supposed to be. Every artist always wants to do more. It really was hard for her," recalled Hazel's friend Betsey Crawford.[37] Hazel bounced around, staying with friends until she could afford a place of her own.

Around this time, Adam III had been courting the daughter of a prominent Newport, Rhode Island, family, Beryl Slocum. Naturally, Hazel was thrilled.

On May 30, 1969, the young couple married, exchanging vows in an extravagant wedding ceremony held in Saint Mary's Chapel at the Washington National Cathedral.

Hazel arrived at the ceremony escorted by a friend, Wesley Carter. In a stunning lime green chiffon dress with a matching chapeau, Hazel's presence was not to be missed. Only the father of the groom could upstage her, as he strutted down the aisle in all his ministerial regalia, the black robe with the bright medallion hanging around his neck (a gift from Ethiopian emperor Haile Selassie). Corrine Huff, Powell's girlfriend, accompanied him, feeling somewhat embarrassed by his display. "He looked like a fool up there in his robe," she said.[38] Powell told the minister presiding over the ceremony that he'd like to say a few words, but his request was denied. The minister intended to adhere to an Episcopalian litany without interruption.

Intrigued by the union of these two prominent families, the national media descended on the ceremony. *Time* reported, "The reception in the Slocum's Georgetown home included certainly one of the most varied guests lists in that exclusive community."[39] Among the well-wishers were people from New England's social register; Powell's friends from Harlem; Hazel's celebrity friends from the entertainment world; and ambassadors from Peru, Belgium, the Netherlands, and Switzerland. "Despite the fact that it was a wedding reception, everybody wanted to talk to Adam," journalist and close family friend Mike Wallace remembered. "He had such a ball. He was so proud of the marriage and his boy."[40]

While Hazel gave an impromptu performance at the piano during the wedding reception, Powell Jr. was a social butterfly. Wherever he sauntered in the house, the crowd followed. "Mrs. Hugh D. Auchincloss waited patiently, while he joked with a friend, to pluck at his robed sleeve and tell him she was the mother of Jacqueline Kennedy Onassis," wrote the *Washington Post*.[41] "I knew Jackie before President Kennedy did," Powell told her. "She used to follow us around on the Hill with her camera when she was an inquiring photographer. A lovely girl."[42]

Family friends, Mabel Howard and Pearl Swangin were also in attendance, and both were interviewed by the press. Mabel was proud, but it wasn't her nature to be boisterous. Pearl, on the other hand, was completely caught up in the moment. She told a *Washington Post* reporter that Adam III "was always quiet and reserved."[43] Then she added that her surname, in case they wanted the correct spelling, was a combination of swan soap and gin, "And honey, I use both!"[44]

After a two-week honeymoon in Russia, Adam III returned to work as a CBS television news producer. Beryl, a Radcliffe graduate, worked as a freelance writer. Adam and his new wife set up house on Manhattan's Upper West Side.

Over the next few years, they would become the proud parents of two sons, Adam Clayton Powell IV and Sherman Powell.

Hazel Scott would be a grandmother—the job she loved most of all.

CHAPTER SIXTEEN

Reverie

Strolling down 52nd Street, Hazel revisited her past: playing as an intermission pianist at the Yacht Club, standing in for Art Tatum at the Famous Door, being chased into the subway by Billie Holiday. These days she performed mostly in New York, traveling little. She played smaller rooms than in the old days; some were classy, some were not. "She was working to a small and not particularly attentive clientele at the King Cole Room in the St. Regis–Sheraton Hotel," said Leonard Feather, recalling the last time he saw Hazel perform. "She did not even bother to hush the audience. With no adoring crowds to salute her, no newspaper headlines, it seemed as though she was simply working for a living instead of performing for the sheer joy of communication. The volatile, tempestuous Hazel Scott of the past now somehow was strangely becalmed."[1]

So many others around her had gone on to terrific careers, achieving not only commercial success but longevity. And longevity was what Hazel had hoped for. "Whenever one of Leonard Bernstein's concerts with the New York Philharmonic was televised on CBS," Hazel's son recalled, "she would say, 'Oh, I can't believe it. Skinny Lenny. Look how he turned out. I remember he used to hang out backstage . . . and her voice would trail off, as if she was saying, 'I should be up there.' "[2]

Hazel's abiding love for jazz and classical music never diminished. She found inspiration in the work of other great pianists. Arthur Rubinstein and Vladimir Horowitz she held in the highest regard. Of Rubinstein, she would say, "His passion! I don't know how he does it."[3] Horowitz, she believed, was totally unreachable. Adam III remembered:

> When Horowitz came out of retirement, he performed a live concert at Carnegie Hall. CBS broadcast it on a Sunday night from nine to ten, "Live from Carnegie Hall: Horowitz in Concert," without commercials. This was Bill Paley's production. There were articles in the newspapers about how there were chalk marks all over the floor of the stage so as they rolled the cameras around to take different shots they could avoid certain spots that might creak. It was an hour-long special. It was just him walking out and sitting down and playing the piano. That was it. And Horowitz, of course, a showman, was taking all the great pianistic leaps. Live on national television. At the end, when the credits rolled, my phone rang, and I knew who it was. She didn't say hello, she said: "*Your mother* has just slit her wrists." I asked her if she recorded it, and she said, "Why? *To extend my misery?*"[4]

Throughout the 1970s, Hazel remained active on the circuit, continually looking for ways to stay in the game, refusing to fade slowly into retirement. Artistically, she had many interests. "She was always curious," her son said. "Sometimes she'd say 'I want to write a novel' or 'I'd like to write a really long jazz piece, a jazz suite.' And she would begin work on it then abandon it and go on to something else." [5] Hazel even considered composing an opera or a sacred work. She had always wanted to record calypso music but produced only two sides on the Decca label of the popular calypsos "Carnaval" and "Take Me, Take Me."

During a seven-week engagement at the St. Regis Hotel, tired of waiting for a response from record companies, she attempted to self-produce a live recording of the last two shows. With a rhythm section that included Martin "Fangs" Rivera and Bill English, Hazel made "twelve excellent sides" that she felt truly reflected her sound.

"For the first time I am satisfied with how I sound on a record," she said.[6] "When I heard it, I said, 'That's my voice, and that's the way I sound on the piano.'"[7] But *Hazel Scott: Live at the St. Regis* was not released or distributed for reasons unknown. "When people say Hazel Scott, they haven't got a clue as to what I do, because there are no records for them to listen to," she once remarked.[8] All of her recordings from the 1940s were by now rare and no longer in circulation.

Whenever Hazel looked back on the way her career had unfolded, she still believed that being blacklisted, her hearing before the House Un-American Activities Committee all those years ago had caused irreparable damage, the controversy eventually leading to her expatriation and disappearance from the American music scene. She said, "At times, it has almost been overwhelming, the fact that my career was stopped."[9]

In June of 1969, the Supreme Court finally ruled that the actions of the House of Representatives had been unconstitutional in the corruption case against Adam Powell. He was able to regain his seat in Congress. His penalty was steep, however, a fine of twenty-five thousand dollars and the loss of twenty-two years' seniority. "I could not refuse the terms," he wrote in his memoir. "If I had been the only one involved, I would have fought forever. But the people of Harlem had been without representation in Congress for two years and I could not allow them to be forced into suffering another two without a voice."[10]

His return to politics was brief. Just one year later Congressman Powell lost his bid for reelection to Charles B. Rangel, his first loss since becoming Harlem's representative in 1945. Harlem had given him its unwavering support for decades, but Powell had been absent in recent years. He had spent much time away from the district, and with crime and overcrowding, police corruption, and drug activity plaguing their neighborhoods his constituents needed someone they could lay eyes on.

In 1971, Powell would resign as pastor of the Abyssinian Baptist Church.

Through it all, the legislative victories and personal defeats, Powell maintained that history would tell the real tale. As Harlem's congressman from 1945 to 1971, Powell's legislative efforts drove the desegregation of public schools and the United States military; as chairman of the Education and Labor committee he introduced the minimum wage, set standards for work hours and wage increases, and passed a record number of over fifty bills, which led to the establishment of numerous social programs that are still intact to this day. "When you come to the end of your journey of life," he preached, "you won't have to answer to any city judge, any board of education or any Supreme Court. You will answer only to God, and God is going to say, 'Well done. Well done.'"[11]

On April 4, 1972, Adam Clayton Powell Jr. died in a Florida hospital, succumbing to prostate cancer. He was sixty-three years old. Thousands gathered from all over the world to attend his memorial service at Abyssinian Baptist Church.

Unlike the rest of his family, all of whom were buried in the family plot in Flushing Cemetery in Queens, Adam Powell Jr. requested that his body be cremated. Carrying out his father's wishes, Adam III took his father's ashes aboard a chartered plane and let them loose over the island of Bimini.

With her son on her arm, Hazel orchestrated a march on the streets of Harlem the day of the funeral, leading the way to Abyssinian's church doors. Highly emotional over his death, Hazel was extremely angry about how Powell Jr. had been treated during the last years of his career. She wrote:

> His devotion to his people, however, was not appreciated, in any real sense. At the time of his death, I marveled at the paeans of praise that came forth from almost every corner. At the time I could not help thinking how extraordinary it would have been if only a little of that praise had been his. . . . A great deal of inexplicable behavior, on his part, a lot of defensive overcompensating could have been avoided. The dignity of the man could have been more intact. Those of us who knew him truly well knew how much pain lay behind that toothy grin with which he faced the world.[12]

Adam III handled his father's estate. There were still some out-standing tax issues. To help settle the debt, Hazel gave her son permission to auction some of her most prized possessions, gifts from her former husband—several pieces of fine diamond jewelry and the Steinway piano.

Only later in life would Hazel confess that she had been the one to walk away from her marriage to Adam Powell. She was the one who had insisted on the divorce. "It was unfortunate," she said.[13] "I should have been a little stronger and a little older in the head and not quite so child-like."[14] Many of the personal details of their eleven-year marriage that she'd kept private for years Hazel shared openly as she got older. "Adam was a wonderful father to Skippy, which is what we used to call our boy," she said. "They'd play ball together out in the snow and when I was away on tour, I knew Adam would make a special effort to be home at night to take care of his son."[15] She blamed herself for having allowed Powell to control her career choices. "I ruined my own career, really," she said. "Adam said in his book that subconsciously he must have resented my career. Actually, there was nothing subconscious about it. Any woman who has stature of her own—that's what attracts the man and then, all of a sudden, it's kill, kill, kill, kill."[16]

Having spent years fighting for civil rights, her interest now centered on issues pertaining specifically to black women. After two failed marriages, Hazel decided that she no longer believed in marriage, telling an interviewer that "the day they find an institution that protects the woman's children and doesn't make the man her enemy, I'll go for it."[17] Although she did not join the feminist movement in the 1970s ("I am a Black feminist and there is a difference"), she was outspoken about what she considered "a conspiracy of silence on the suffering of Black women." She was quoted as saying, "Any woman who has a great deal to offer the world is in trouble. And if she's a black woman, she's in deep trouble."[18] She even wrote an article on the subject of "black women being unappreciated" for *Cosmopolitan* entitled "It Would Be Nice to Be Cherished."[19]

In the end, she cast no aspersions on Adam Powell Jr. or the years they shared together. Hazel chose to focus on those aspects of the man that she loved and admired, writing:

> The fact that I got to know him as a man took nothing away from the greatness of his drive, his contribution or his achievements. Whatever he lacked as a husband, he more than made up for in his efforts to gain justice for his people.[20]

With the help of her son and his family, Hazel settled into a nice, quiet existence, babysitting her grandsons a few days a week when they came home from school, then making a club appearance in the evenings. She complained about her weight (her figure was now more plump than svelte), but overall she was content. Wherever Adam, Beryl, and the kids lived, Hazel always lived close by. When the family moved to a new high-rise development on Roosevelt Island, across the East River, at the suggestion of her daughter-in-law, Hazel found an apartment in the same building.

Her grandsons adored her. They visited her apartment often and remember it as filled with "all kinds of little decorations, trinkets, various things, artsy lamps."[21] There was the scent of white votive candles, which she always had burning, a small vestige of her Roman Catholic faith. Hazel had evolved in terms of her religious affiliation. When Dizzy Gillespie introduced her to the Baha'i faith and the idea of "progressive revelation," it sparked her interest in world religions. "Whenever man has been ready to absorb more knowledge," she said, "God has revealed it."[22] After years of soul-searching, Hazel realized that what she had always been was a mystic, believing that spirituality was not confined to one church or one doctrine. She began wearing a necklace of two crosses, the nine-pointed star of the Baha'i, a gold Buddha, an Egyptian symbol, and a Jewish star.

Adam IV and Sherman have fond memories of their grandmother playing the piano for them: "Whether it was just at her apartment or when we went up to Newport, Rhode Island, to visit my mother's family, she would play for huge parties, hundreds of people. My mother's parents would have these tremendous get-togethers," remembered Sherman Powell, the younger of the two grandsons.[23] As they grew older, both of them came to realize the significant artistic and social contribution their grandmother had made. "She was a pioneer in a great many ways. It's very impressive to me. Very, I suppose, inspirational, instructive," said Sherman.[24]

During a concert at the Hideaway, an intimate room inside the Waldorf-Astoria Hotel, Hazel played solo piano with no accompaniment. That night, her grandsons were in the audience. She had them join her up onstage. "I remember being maybe about seven or eight years old, and she called my brother and me to come up and sit on her lap. And she bounced us up and down on her knees as she played the piano with her arms kind of around us. It was a blast!" Adam IV remembered.[25] That particular evening Hazel sang and played everything from Leonard Bernstein's "Who Am I?" to the Beatles' "Eleanor Rigby." Music critic John Wilson observed, "She can switch to a smoky simmer on a great torch song, 'In Love in Vain.' Proving once again that less can be more, Miss Scott's solo performance is giving her work a new and broader dimension."[26]

Hazel encouraged her grandsons to play the piano (although both would follow their father's lead, obtaining degrees from MIT). "I started taking piano lessons when I was maybe three or four years old and very quickly frustrated the teacher because I didn't want to play what they wanted me to play," Adam IV recalled. "I wanted to play, you know, Scott Joplin or improvise some things. I guess that was my grandmother's influence on me musically. I wanted to play the kinds of things that I heard her play."[27]

He continued, "Her involvement in our lives, my life and my brother's, as a grandmother is what I remember most. She was a real person in her relationships, not being wrapped up in celebrity or anything else. . . . Her family really came first. And we really felt and saw and experienced and appreciated that."[28]

Always a big film buff, Hazel spent countless hours watching movies with her grandsons. She'd purchased one of the first videocassette recorders on the market, before they were a common household item, at a time when they were still very expensive. "It was something new, and unfamiliar and exciting to me. She had dozens of movies. We would always go over to watch movies with her. *Silver Streak* with Richard Pryor I think we watched sixty or seventy times," Sherman recalled.[29]

On one occasion, Hazel told her son: "My treat. I'm taking you to the movies." They walked into a newly renovated cinema on the East Side. After they took their seats, Hazel took a long look around the room, then began shouting aloud, "This is Cafe Society! That was the stage!" They reminisced, as they sat watching an obscure foreign film in the very room where Hazel had found fame.

Hazel's contributions in American cinema were finally recognized in 1978 when she was inducted into the Black Filmmakers Hall of Fame.

In March of 1975, Hazel played at Town Hall, part of their evening "Interludes" series. The reception could not have been better, and the critical praise was remarkable. These were the concerts that kept her going with steady work so hard to come by. "The truly special singer-pianist, who has been the "darling of Manhattan's Café Society" since the 1940s will present the best of her piano-singing ballads"noted the *Amsterdam News*.[30] "Hazel Scott: Red Velvet and Soul," the *New York Daily News* headline proclaimed. "As a pianist, she can swing from hard-driving jazz to concert-hall polish. As a singer, she is a combination of Park Avenue red velvet and Lenox Avenue soul."[31]

Hazel didn't go back into the studio until 1979. Within a year's time, she would complete three recordings. *Always,* a contemporary album, dedicated to her grandsons, captures the sound of the 1970s, featuring Hazel on piano and vocals and a host of musicians and background singers. The personnel includes Joel Diamond on piano, Allen Ross on saxophone and flute, Gianpaolo Biagi and Grace Millan on drums, Nabil M. Totah and Rafael Goldfeld on bass, Valerie Romanoff on guitar; Alan Roy Scott on string synthesizer, Carlos Rodriguez on congas, and Sue Hadjopoulous on percussion. Sandy Sandoval was the producer and arranger on the album. Shifting styles, Hazel performed disco-inspired renditions of her original title song, "Always," Billy Joel's "Just the Way You Are," Julie Burger's "Let Me Hold You," and "La Vita" (This is My Life) sung in Italian and English. "Be What You Are," another original composition, and the popular ballad "No Greater Love" are the only tunes that incorporate jazz and blues.

Her final albums, *Afterthoughts* and *After Hours,* are believed to have been recorded in one session in April of 1980. They would later be released in limited distribution on the Tioch label in 1980 and 1983, respectively. Here Hazel is joined by two of the jazz world's finest musicians, bass player George Duvivier—who had worked with Coleman Hawkins, Bud Powell, Jimmie Lunceford, and Sy Oliver's big band and recorded with Benny Goodman, Frank Sinatra, Clark Terry, and Count Basie—and Detroit-born drummer Oliver Jackson, who was a generation younger but who had been on the scene since the late 1940s, playing with legendary musicians Tommy Flanagan, Yusef Lateef, Earl Hines, and Lionel Hampton.

On *Afterthoughts,* the trio plays music from the popular Broadway musical *42nd Street,* which had debuted five years earlier. It is a well-executed recording that adds some swing to the legit musical numbers, featuring Hazel on piano and vocals. Yet the full essence of their well-seasoned skills is heard on *After Hours.* The album includes three original compositions written by Hazel—"Lover's Leap," "Guess I Gotta Move" (cowritten with Duvivier), and "Moving Day," along with three jazz classics, "Nancy with the Laughing Face," W. C. Handy's "St. Louis Blues," and "After Hours." "Lover's Leap" is nine minutes of pure swing, featuring Hazel's blithely original phrasing with Duvivier and Jackson given equal time to add their inimitable touch to the groove. On the slow drags "Guess I Gotta Move" and "After Hours," Hazel demonstrates her love for the down-home blues. Here, she gives a nod to Fats Waller with her use of a deliberate, strong left hand and a light-hearted right. Whether the tempo is fast or slow, her piano is bold and confident, and the rhythm accompaniment is strong and steady. Together, they play with the energy and immediacy of a live performance. The *San Francisco Chronicle* wrote that the performance was "forceful, melodic, embellished but not busy, sometimes Oscar Peterson, sometimes Erroll Garner, sometimes Art Tatum, always Hazel Scott."

Younger musicians loved accompanying Hazel. "She's beautiful," said drummer Ray Mosca, who played with her on a gig at the Ali Baba. "It's a ball. . . . She's a challenge musically. You never know what she's going to do next. She might come up with anything from anywhere."[32] Her bassist, Jamil Nasser, agreed: "She's everything I thought she would be and more. Hazel is one of our queens. She's an original. A genius who defies category."[33] But Nasser felt she suffered from unappreciative audiences: "We as a people do not rally to our performers who are geniuses now. Our people are led away by Madison Avenue, which often picks mediocre talent to constantly expose and promote."[34]

In early 1981, Hazel found out that Mary Lou Williams had been diagnosed with cancer. Having accepted a teaching position at Duke University, Mary Lou was living in Durham, North Carolina. They spoke often by phone. When Hazel realized that the illness was becoming progressively worse, she made a trip down south to visit her friend. Just a few months later, on May 18, 1981, Mary Lou Williams died at the age of seventy-one.

At a Town Hall tribute concert, Hazel played the spirited tune "KoolBonga" and the hymn "St. Martin de Porres" from Mary Lou's seminal work *Black Christ of the Andes*. Father O'Brien remembered, "Hazel was really devastated at the funeral, but she played those two songs and really knocked me out."[35]

Of her beloved musician friends who had passed away, Hazel said, "The people that I loved—I've had to adjust to their going, and it hasn't been easy, as philosophical as I try to be about it, but nobody dies, if you continue to love them."[36]

In summer of 1981, Hazel called her son at work with thrilling news. "I've got great news. This is fantastic news. *Your mother* has her dream job. Joe Kipnus says he's going to open a new room on 45th Street and he wants to name it after me. I can play as many weeks a year as I want. I don't have to be there all the time. So I can play maybe twenty, twenty-five weeks. I'll make more than enough money to live happily. And it will be a long-term deal. It'll be years and years. This will be great."[37] Ecstatic, she began rattling off big plans for herself and the family. "Let's all plan to go to Trinidad. I want my grandchildren to see Trinidad. I haven't been in years and years and years. Goodness knows I want to go back. And maybe we can even go for Carnival," she said.[38]

"Then I sort of remember she stopped," Adam said. "And I asked, 'What's the matter?' She replied: 'Well, you know the superstition. When you get your dream job, you're going to die.'"

Adam laughed it off, believing this to be just another one of his mother's dramatic moments. Yet, during her first week at Kippy's Pier 44, Hazel felt a crippling pain in her stomach. "But she was so happy. She was getting good reviews. 'This is Hazel's place' they were saying, and on and on. And she really could call up and say, 'I want to do two shows on this night, five days here, I want to take next week off.' It was the kind of luxury that few performers have unless they own the place. She performed even though she was in pain. She insisted on playing. She kept saying 'It's my room.' So she kept on playing. Finally, the pain was unbearable, she was taken to . . . I think it was Mount Sinai, after her show. Within twenty-four hours, they discovered she had pancreatic cancer."[39]

A few weeks after her diagnosis, Hazel Scott languished in the hospital, given little chance of recovery. Friends and family gathered around her bed, sharing stories, lightening the mood with recollections of something she'd once said or something outrageous she did.

On October 2, 1981, Hazel Scott passed away as Dizzy Gillespie played a soft trumpet solo of one of her favorite songs, "Alone Together." She was sixty-one years old.

Adam began the arduous task of packing away his mother's belongings. While sifting through her personal papers, he found page after page of journal writings, poems, and passages that his mother had wanted to include in her memoir. Among the many papers, he came across a small slip of paper, a receipt issued from a Paris bank. He took it and filed it away. "It wasn't until at least three years later, maybe four years later, that I went to Paris and tried to access to these accounts," he recalled.[40] He found the bank in one of the oldest sections of the city. "And here's this bank sitting there, and it's really a sixteenth-century building. So I go in with this slip. They bring out these big ledgers. There wasn't even an electric typewriter in this bank. Everything was on paper," Adam said.[41] He presented her death certificate and the other necessary documents to prove that he was in charge of Hazel's estate. They took him back to an old vault and opened a security deposit box that had belonged to her. Rifling through it, Adam found it full of old sheet music, playbills, and some tax documents. But underneath all that paper were jewels. A pair of sapphire and diamond clips mounted in platinum lay at the bottom of the metal box. Each clip had two round sapphires bordered by twenty oval-shaped sapphires and 48 marquise-shaped diamonds weighing nearly three carats. There was a matching pair of platinum and diamond pendant earrings with four triangular diamonds, two carats each, and a platinum and diamond necklace, collar length, prong set with seventy-seven round diamonds, weighing thirty-one carats, designed by Cartier.

"She was photographed in these pieces quite often, and you'll recognize it as soon as you see it if you've seen a lot of photographs of her from the late forties and early fifties," he said.[42] It is still unclear to him why she never retrieved them before returning to the States. Perhaps pride kept her from selling the pieces even when she was living hand-to-mouth in Paris. Maybe it was sentimentality, for some of these jewels had been gifts from the men in her life. The pieces may have been tucked away safely for future use. Surely, she must have hoped that her career would return to its former glory, where fine jewelry would be needed to complete her glamorous image.

But the jewels were not an heirloom Adam would be able to keep. Having inherited his mother's substantial tax dept, he was forced to auction them at Sotheby's.

At her personal request, Hazel's funeral was held at the Abyssinian Baptist Church. That day the church was filled to capacity. "As different people came in," Betsey Crawford said, "I had this urge that I wanted to get to a phone and tell Hazel all about it." The dynamic pianist was remembered by a host of artists, musicians, entertainers, politicians, and journalists. "She was gregarious. And sweet . . . She really *lived*," journalist Mike Wallace said.

It was a beautiful service befitting the incomparable pianist. And from his father's pulpit Adam III read a few stanzas of a Langston Hughes poem in his mother's honor:

TO BE SOMEBODY

Little girl
Dreaming of a baby grand piano
(Not knowing there's a Steinway bigger, bigger)
Dreaming of a baby grand to play
That stretches paddle-tailed across the floor,
Not standing upright
Like a bad boy in the corner,
But sending music
Up the stairs and down the stairs
And out the door
To confound even Hazel Scott
Who might be passing!

Oh![43]

Hazel Scott was buried in Flushing Cemetery in Queens, New York.

Hazel loved deeply and fought bitterly for what she believed in. Her artistic journey was a courageous one. While she never stopped reinventing herself, she never stopped being who she was, fiercely original—pianist, vocalist, actress, poet, dancer, activist, wife, mother, and grandmother.

A renegade, Hazel Scott achieved many firsts but found it hard to resist the challenge of exploring every aspect of her creative self. In one of her final interviews, when asked what was most important to her in life, Hazel simply replied:

The important part? When I have been able to transmit that which I have been singularly gifted with . . . to move an audience to their feet.[44]

ACKNOWLEDGMENTS

As with all projects that take years to come to fruition, this work has been helped along by the support and assistance of very special people. Foremost, I would like to extend my sincerest thanks and gratitude to Adam Clayton Powell III, whose extraordinary generosity, input, and support helped make this project possible. Many thanks go, as well, to Dr. Adam Clayton Powell IV and Sherman Scott Powell for graciously sharing special memories of their grandmother.

Many thanks to my agent, Michelle Tessler, for championing this work (in the "ninth hour!"), and to my editor, Chris Hebert, for his insight, guidance, and meticulous attention. I am deeply grateful to the friends, fellow musicians, artists, and associates of Hazel Scott, who gave so generously of their time, and whose personal recollections have been an invaluable contribution to this biography: Betsey Crawford, Murray Horwitz, Mike Wallace, Fr. Peter F. O'Brien, Ezio Bedin and Christina Cassal, Melvin Van Pebbles, Marian McPartland, Dick Hyman, Dr. Matthew Kennedy, Esther McCall, Doug Yeager and Oscar Brand.

My heartfelt thanks go to my entire family for their boundless love and encouragement, especially my parents, Richard and Telia Chilton; my brothers, Richard Chilton, Jr. and Steven Chilton; my sister and brother-in-law, Kim and Howard Griffith; my nephews, Howard and Houston Griffith; my niece, Stephanie Chilton; and my cousins, Ferial and Joseph Bishop.

And a special thanks to Lewis Hamilton for your enduring support and patience throughout this journey.

I would also like to gratefully acknowledge the help and support of Herald "Chip" Johnson, Kenneth L. Roberson, Aston Penn, Lawrence Hamilton, and Stephonne Smith for sharing not only their friendship but their expertise. A hearty thanks is also in order to Ingrid Grimes-Myles, Michelle Robinson, Gloria Lynne, Byron Easley, Janice Bailey, Charles Randolph-Wright, Sharon Wilkins, Judi Edwards, Beverly L. Jones, Shirley Walls, Inell Chapman Peck, Ryan Fleck and Anna Boden, Marc Damon Johnson, Joe James, Andre Blake, Frank Mariglia, Pam Cardwell, Geoffrey O'Connor, Helen Benedict, Cliff Terry, Farah Jasmine Griffin, Jay-Me Brown, William McDaniel, Hazel and Darien Hendricks, Michael Chertok, Sidra Rausch, Allan Duncan, Nancy Nigrosh, Martha Hopewell, Judith Maysles, and Susan Dowling.

Many thanks to the archivists and librarians at the following institutions for their research assistance: Ann Kuebler at the Rutgers University Institute of Jazz Studies; the New York Public Library for the Performing Arts; the New York Public Library's Humanities and Social Sciences Library; the Schomburg Center for Research in Black Culture; the Carnegie Hall Archives; the Julliard School; the U.S. National Archives and Records Administration; the National Archives of Trinidad and Tobago; the Smithsonian Institution; Emily Davis at Sotheby's; and Henry Z. Steinway at Steinway Hall.

RIGHTS AND PERMISSIONS

NOTES

INTRO

1. *Essence,* November 1978.

CHAPTER 1

1. Hazel Scott, Personal Papers.
2. Hazel Scott, Personal Papers.
3. Hazel Scott, Personal Papers.
4. Hazel Scott, Personal Papers.
5. Hazel Scott, Personal Papers.
6. Luther Davis and John Cleveland, "Hi, Hazel!" *Collier's,* April 18, 1942.
7. Luther Davis and John Cleveland, "Hi, Hazel!" *Collier's,* April 18, 1942.
8. Lyrics from the traditional hymn "Gentle Jesus."
9. Hazel Scott, Personal Papers.
10. Hazel Scott, Personal Papers.
11. Hazel Scott, Personal Papers.

CHAPTER 2

1. Hazel Scott, Personal Papers.
2. Hazel Scott, Personal Papers.
3. Hazel Scott, Personal Papers.
4. The term *Jim Crow* originated with the performances of Thomas Dartmouth "Daddy" Rice, an English immigrant who was one of the first to popularize the use of blackface. He wrote the song "Jump Jim Crow" based on a tune he'd heard an old black slave singing, and minstrelsy was born. The Jim Crow caricature, a shuffling, backwoods black man, became a regular character in many minstrel shows. The laws of segregation in the South between 1876 and 1965, which mandated "separate but equal" status between the races took on the name and were commonly referred to as the Jim Crow laws.
5. Hazel Scott, Personal Papers.
6. Hazel Scott, Personal Papers.
7. Hazel Scott, Personal Papers.
8. Hazel Scott, Personal Papers.
9. Hazel Scott, Personal Papers.
10. Hazel Scott, Personal Papers.

11. "Hazel Scott Comes Home to the Action," *Ebony,* March 1968.

12. "Hazel Scott Comes Home to the Action," *Ebony,* March 1968.

13. Hazel Scott, Personal Papers.

14. Hazel Scott, Personal Papers.

15. Hazel Scott, Personal Papers.

CHAPTER 3

1. Hazel Scott, Personal Papers.

2. Hazel Scott, Personal Papers.

3. Hazel Scott, Personal Papers.

4. Hazel Scott, Personal Papers.

5. Hazel Scott, Personal Papers.

6. Hazel Scott, Personal Papers.

7. Hazel Scott, Personal Papers.

8. Hazel Scott, Personal Papers.

9. Hazel Scott, Personal Papers.

10. Arthur Taylor, *Notes and Tones: Musician-to-Musician Interviews* (New York: Da Capo, 1977), 255.

11. *Collier's,* April 18, 1942. Many references in biographical articles refer to Hazel's Juilliard instructor as Paul Wagner. However, the Juilliard archives have no record of a Paul Wagner ever having taught at the institution. Oscar Wagner was on the staff during the 1920s–1930s and is the name that Hazel referenced in her personal journal entries, as well as in some live radio and television interviews.

12. *Collier's,* April 18, 1942.

13. Hazel Scott, Personal Papers.

14. Hazel Scott, Personal Papers.

15. Hazel Scott, Personal Papers.

16. Hazel Scott, Personal Papers.

17. Hazel Scott, Personal Papers.

18. Hazel Scott, Personal Papers.

19. Hazel Scott, Personal Papers.

CHAPTER 4

1. Hazel Scott, Personal Papers.

2. Hazel Scott, Personal Papers.

3. Hazel Scott, Personal Papers.

4. Hazel Scott, Personal Papers.

5. Hazel Scott, Personal Papers.

6. D. Antoinette Handy, *Black Women in American Bands and Orchestras,* 40. Lovie Austin also went by the name Cora Calhoun. (New Jersey: Scarecrow Press, 1981), 40.

7. The International Sweethearts of Rhythm, an all-women band of fourteen to seventeen members between the ages of fourteen to nineteen, was established in Piney Woods, Mississippi, at the Piney Woods Country Life

School. The president and founder of the school, Laurence C. Jones, acted as the band's manager and guided the young women to a level of fame and success that was unprecedented at that time. The band functioned from 1937 through 1948 and is considered one of the most talented all-women jazz bands of the twentieth century. A comprehensive study of the band was written by D. Antoinette Handy, *The International Sweethearts of Rhythm: The Ladies Jazz Band from Piney Woods Country Life School* (Scarecrow Press, 1983).

8. Hazel Scott, Personal Papers.

9. Hazel Scott, Personal Papers.

10. Hazel Scott, Personal Papers.

11. Hazel Scott, Personal Papers.

12. Hazel Scott, Personal Papers.

13. Hazel Scott, Personal Papers.

14. Rusty E. Frank, *Tap! The Greatest Tap Dance Stars and Their Stories, 1900–1955* (DiCapo Press, 1995), 158.

15. Hazel Scott, Personal Papers.

16. Linda Dahl, *Stormy Weather: The Music and Lives of a Century of Jazz Women* (New York: Pantheon, 1984), 47.

17. "Great Scott!" *Ms.*, November 1974.

18. "Great Scott!" *Ms.*, November 1974.

19. "Great Scott!" *Ms.*, November 1974. In her personal journal Hazel mentions Margaret Kennerly Upshur as a terrific influence in her life. In the passage she writes, "I will tell more about this lovely woman further on." However, nothing more was mentioned in her journal, and no further information on Mrs. Upshur was found.

CHAPTER 5

1. Hazel Scott, Personal Papers.

2. Hazel Scott, Personal Papers.

3. Hazel Scott, Personal Papers.

4. Hazel Scott, Personal Papers.

5. Hazel Scott, Personal Papers.

6. Hazel Scott, Personal Papers.

7. Hazel Scott, Personal Papers.

8. Hazel Scott, Personal Papers.

9. Arthur Taylor, *Notes and Tones: Musician-to-Musician Interviews* (New York: Da Capo, 1977), 255.

10. Hazel Scott, Personal Papers.

11. Hazel Scott, Personal Papers.

12. Hazel Scott, Personal Papers.

13. Hazel Scott, Personal Papers.

14. Hazel Scott, Personal Papers.

15. Hazel Scott, Personal Papers.

16. Hazel Scott, Personal Papers.

17. Hazel Scott, Personal Papers. Chick Webb's most notable female hire

was the seventeen-year-old vocalist Ella Fitzgerald, who joined the band in 1935. Together they recorded over sixty songs, including the immensely popular "Tisket-a-Tasket." After Webb's early death in 1939, Ella Fitzgerald acted as the bandleader until the band dissolved in 1942.

18. Hazel Scott, Personal Papers.

19. "Great Scott!" *Ms.*, November 1974.

20. Hazel Scott, Personal Papers.

21. Hazel Scott, Personal Papers.

22. Hazel Scott, Personal Papers.

23. Hazel Scott, Personal Papers.

24. Hazel Scott, Personal Papers.

25. Hazel Scott, Personal Papers.

26. *Collier's,* April, 18,1942.

27. Mike Wallace, interview with Hazel Scott, CBS Radio, 1978.

28. Mike Wallace, interview with Hazel Scott, CBS Radio, 1978.

29. Hazel Scott, Personal Papers.

30. *Nation,* January 22, 1936.

31. Hazel Scott, Personal Papers.

32. Hazel Scott, Personal Papers.

33. Hazel Scott, Personal Papers.

34. Hazel Scott, Personal Papers.

35. Hazel Scott, Personal Papers.

36. Hazel Scott, Personal Papers.

37. The James Van Der Zee photo, entitled "Hazel Scott in 1936," appears on the recent release *Hazel Scott: 1939–1945* on the Classics Chronological Series label.

38. "Franklin D. Roosevelt Jones," lyrics by Harold J. Rome, from the Broadway musical *Sing Out the News.*

39. *Ms.*, November 1974.

40. *Ms.*, November 1974.

41 Dick Hyman, interview with the author.

42. Marian McPartland, interview with the author.

43. Matthew Kennedy, interview with the author.

44. Hazel Scott, Personal Papers.

45. Quoted in James Lester, *Too Marvelous for Words: The Life and Genius of Art Tatum* (New York: Oxford University Press, 1994), 76.

46. Performing Arts Library, New York Public Library, Hazel Scott clippings file, publication unknown, 1938.

47. *Collier's,* April, 18, 1942.

48. *Ebony,* May 1956.

CHAPTER 6

1. Helen Lawrenson, *Whistling Girl* (New York: Doubleday, 1978), 89.

2. Helen Lawrenson, *Whistling Girl* (New York: Doubleday, 1978), 86.

3. Helen Lawrenson, *Whistling Girl* (New York: Doubleday, 1978), 86.

4. *New York Times,* September 30, 1988.

5. Helen Lawrenson, *Whistling Girl* (New York: Doubleday, 1978), 88.

6. "Strange Fruit," lyrics by Lewis Allan [Abel Meeropool].

7. Geoffrey C. Ward and Ken Burns, *Jazz: A History of America's Music* (New York: Knopf, 2000), 270.

8. David Margolick, *Strange Fruit: Billie Holiday, Café Society and an Early Cry for Civil Rights,* 78.

9. David Margolick, *Strange Fruit: Billie Holiday, Café Society and an Early Cry for Civil Rights* (Philadelphia: Running Press, 2000), 78.

10. Helen Lawrenson, *Whistling Girl* (New York: Doubleday, 1978), 86.

11. Helen Lawrenson, *Whistling Girl* (New York: Doubleday, 1978), 86.

12. *Time,* October 5, 1942.

13. Hazel Scott, Personal Papers.

14. *Los Angeles Times,* October 11, 1981.

15. "Mighty Like the Blues," lyrics by Leonard Feather.

16. Institute of Jazz Studies, Rutgers University, Hazel Scott clippings file, publication unknown, December 1, 1939.

17. *Los Angeles Times,* October 11, 1981.

18. *Time,* October 11, 1981.

19. *Collier's,* April, 18, 1942.

20. *Collier's,* April, 18, 1942.

21. *Washington Post,* May 18, 1947.

22. Linda Dahl, *Morning Glory: A Biography of Mary Lou Williams* (Berkeley: University of California Press, 1999), 142.

23. Linda Dahl, *Morning Glory: A Biography of Mary Lou Williams* (Berkeley: University of California Press, 1999), 142.

24. Hazel Scott, Personal Papers.

25. *Marian McPartland's Piano Jazz,* National Public Radio, interview with Hazel Scott. November 26, 1979.

26. Helen Lawrenson, *Whistling Girl* (New York: Doubleday, 1978), 94.

27. Helen Lawrenson, *Whistling Girl* (New York: Doubleday, 1978), 94.

28. *Los Angeles Times,* October 11, 1981.

29. Performing Arts Library, New York Public Library, Hazel Scott clippings file.

30. *Collier's,* April, 18, 1942.

31. *Collier's,* April, 18, 1942.

32. *Collier's,* April, 18, 1942.

33. Marian McPartland, interview with the author.

34. *Time,* May 5, 1941.

35. *New York Herald Tribune,* Performing Arts Library, New York Public Library, Hazel Scott clippings file, date unknown.

36. *Newsweek,* November 29, 1943.

37. *Washington Post,* July 4, 1942.

38. *Newsweek,* November 29, 1943.

39. *Time,* July 26, 1943.

40. *Marian McPartland's Piano Jazz,* National Public Radio, interview with Hazel Scott. November 26, 1979.

41. *Newsweek,* November 29, 1943.

42. *Los Angeles Times,* October 11, 1981.

43. Peter O'Brien, interview with the author.

44. *Current Biography,* 1943. Quoted in *Current Biography,* 1943.

45. "Biography of Concert Star Hazel Scott," program notes, Program Publishing Company, New York.

46. "Biography of Concert Star Hazel Scott," program notes, Program Publishing Company, New York.

47. Hazel Scott, Personal Papers.

48. Hazel Scott, Personal Papers.

49. Hazel Scott, Personal Papers.

50. Hazel Scott, Personal Papers.

51. Hazel Scott, Personal Papers.

52. Hazel Scott, Personal Papers.

53. *Collier's,* April, 18, 1942.

CHAPTER 7

1. Donald Bogle, *Toms, Coons, Mulattoes, Mammies, and Bucks: An Interpretative History of Blacks in American Films* (New York: Continuum, 1973), 93.

2. Hazel Scott, Personal Papers.

3. Hazel Scott, Personal Papers.

4. Hazel Scott, Personal Papers.

5. Adam Powell III, interview with the author.

6. Hazel Scott, Personal Papers.

7. Lines taken from the script of *Something to Shout About.*

8. Hazel Scott, Personal Papers.

9. Hazel Scott, Personal Papers.

10. *Washington Post,* April 17, 1943.

11. *Washington Post,* April 17, 1943.

12. *Look,* December 15, 1942.

13. *Time,* October 5, 1942.

14. *Time,* October 5, 1942.

15. *Ebony,* May 1956.

16. Donald Bogle, *Bright Boulevards, Bold Dreams: The Story of Black Hollywood* (New York: One World/Ballantine, 2005), 218.

17. Jill Watts, *Hattie McDaniel: Black Ambition, White Hollywood* (New York: HarperCollins, 2005), inside cover.

18. Hazel Scott, Personal Papers.

19. *Washington Post,* October 15, 1943.

20. *Current Biography,* 1943.

21. *Chicago Daily Tribune,* August 15, 1942.

22. Hazel Scott, Personal Papers.

23. Hazel Scott, Personal Papers.

24. Hazel Scott, Personal Papers.

25. Hazel Scott, Personal Papers.

26. Hazel Scott, Personal Papers.

27. Hazel Scott, Personal Papers.
28. Hazel Scott, Personal Papers.
29. Hazel Scott, Personal Papers.
30. Hazel Scott, Personal Papers.
31. Hazel Scott, Personal Papers.
32. Hazel Scott, Personal Papers.
33. Hazel Scott, Personal Papers.
34. Hazel Scott, Personal Papers.
35. Hazel Scott, Personal Papers.
36. Hazel Scott, Personal Papers.
37. Hazel Scott, Personal Papers.
38. Hazel Scott, Personal Papers.
39. Hazel Scott, Personal Papers.
40. Hazel Scott, Personal Papers.
41. Hazel Scott, Personal Papers.
42. *Ebony*, November, 1945.
43. *Los Angeles Times*, October 11, 1981.
44. *Army/Navy Screen,* no. 8.
45. "The Powells," *Ebony,* May 1946.
46. *Newsweek,* November 29, 1943.

CHAPTER 8

1. Adam C. Powell, Jr., *Adam by Adam: The Autobiography of Adam Clayton Powell Jr.* (New York: Dial, 1971), 48.
2. Adam C. Powell, Jr., *Adam by Adam: The Autobiography of Adam Clayton Powell Jr.* (New York: Dial, 1971), 24.
3. Adam C. Powell, Jr., *Adam by Adam: The Autobiography of Adam Clayton Powell Jr.* (New York: Dial, 1971), 24.
4. Wil Haygood, *King of the Cats: The Life and Times of Adam Clayton Powell Jr.* (New York: Houghton Mifflin, 1993), 1.
5. Adam Clayton Powell Jr., *Adam by Adam: The Autobiography of Adam Clayton Powell Jr.* (New York: Dial, 1971), 30.
6. Adam Clayton Powell Jr., *Adam by Adam: The Autobiography of Adam Clayton Powell Jr.* (New York: Dial, 1971), 31.
7. Wil Haygood, *King of the Cats: The Life and Times of Adam Clayton Powell Jr.* (New York: Houghton Mifflin, 1993), 10.
8. Wil Haygood, *King of the Cats: The Life and Times of Adam Clayton Powell Jr.* (New York: Houghton Mifflin, 1993), 32.
9. Wil Haygood, *King of the Cats: The Life and Times of Adam Clayton Powell Jr.* (New York: Houghton Mifflin, 1993), 12.
10. Adam Clayton Powell Jr., *Adam by Adam: The Autobiography of Adam Clayton Powell Jr.* (New York: Dial, 1971), 34.
11. Adam Clayton Powell Jr., *Adam by Adam: The Autobiography of Adam Clayton Powell Jr.* (New York: Dial, 1971), 35.
12. Adam Clayton Powell Jr., *Adam by Adam: The Autobiography of Adam Clayton Powell Jr.* (New York: Dial, 1971), 57.

13. Adam Clayton Powell Jr., *Adam by Adam: The Autobiography of Adam Clayton Powell Jr.* (New York: Dial, 1971), 56.

14. Adam Clayton Powell Jr., *Adam by Adam: The Autobiography of Adam Clayton Powell Jr.* (New York: Dial, 1971), 60.

15. Adam Clayton Powell Jr., *Adam by Adam: The Autobiography of Adam Clayton Powell Jr.* (New York: Dial, 1971), 37.

16. Adam Clayton Powell Jr., *Adam by Adam: The Autobiography of Adam Clayton Powell Jr.* (New York: Dial, 1971), 57.

17. Adam Clayton Powell Jr., *Adam by Adam: The Autobiography of Adam Clayton Powell Jr.* (New York: Dial, 1971), 59.

18. Adam Clayton Powell Jr., *Adam by Adam: The Autobiography of Adam Clayton Powell Jr.* (New York: Dial, 1971), 64.

19. Adam Clayton Powell Jr., *Adam by Adam: The Autobiography of Adam Clayton Powell Jr.* (New York: Dial, 1971), 64.

20. Esther McCall, interview with the author.

21. Wil Haygood, *King of the Cats: The Life and Times of Adam Clayton Powell Jr.* (New York: Houghton Mifflin, 1993), 78.

22. Wil Haygood, *King of the Cats: The Life and Times of Adam Clayton Powell Jr.* (New York: Houghton Mifflin, 1993), 119.

INTERMEZZO

1. "Adam, According to Hazel," *New York Daily News,* January 29, 1967.

2. Adam Clayton Powell Jr., *Adam by Adam: The Autobiography of Adam Clayton Powell Jr.* (New York: Dial, 1971), 225.

3. Hazel Scott, Personal Papers.

4. Hazel Scott, Personal Papers.

5. Hazel Scott, Personal Papers.

6. Hazel Scott, Personal Papers.

7. Hazel Scott, Personal Papers.

8. *Essence,* November 1978.

9. Adam Clayton Powell Jr., "My Life with Hazel Scott," *Ebony,* January 1949.

10. Hazel Scott, Personal Papers.

11. Hazel Scott, Personal Papers.

12. Hazel Scott, Personal Papers.

13. *Essence,* November 1978.

14. *Essence,* November 1978.

15. *Essence,* November 1978.

CHAPTER 9

1. Wil Haygood, *King of the Cats: The Life and Times of Adam Clayton Powell Jr.* (New York: Houghton Mifflin, 1993), 101.

2. Adam Clayton Powell Jr., *Adam by Adam: The Autobiography of Adam Clayton Powell Jr.* (New York: Dial, 1971), 70.

3. Adam Clayton Powell Jr., *Adam by Adam: The Autobiography of Adam Clayton Powell Jr.* (New York: Dial, 1971), 93.

4. Adam Clayton Powell Jr., *Adam by Adam: The Autobiography of Adam Clayton Powell Jr.* (New York: Dial, 1971), 93.

5. Wil Haygood, *King of the Cats: The Life and Times of Adam Clayton Powell Jr.* (New York: Houghton Mifflin, 1993), 95.

6. Wil Haygood, *King of the Cats: The Life and Times of Adam Clayton Powell Jr.* (New York: Houghton Mifflin, 1993), 101.

7. *Time,* November 27, 1944.

8. *New York Daily News,* November 21, 1944.

9. "Hazel Scott Remembers," WPIX-TV, New York, 1980.

10. Adam Clayton Powell Jr., *Adam by Adam: The Autobiography of Adam Clayton Powell Jr.* (New York: Dial, 1971), 72.

11. Wil Haygood, *King of the Cats: The Life and Times of Adam Clayton Powell Jr.* (New York: Houghton Mifflin, 1993), 114.

12. Esther McCall, interview with author.

13. *Essence,* November 1978.

14. *Essence,* November 1978.

15. Adam Clayton Powell Jr., *Adam by Adam: The Autobiography of Adam Clayton Powell Jr.* (New York: Dial, 1971), 225.

16. *Tan Confessions,* December 1951.

17. Adam Clayton Powell Jr., *Adam by Adam: The Autobiography of Adam Clayton Powell Jr.* (New York: Dial, 1971), 225.

18. Adam Clayton Powell Jr., *Adam by Adam: The Autobiography of Adam Clayton Powell Jr.* (New York: Dial, 1971), 224.

19. Adam Clayton Powell Jr., *Adam by Adam: The Autobiography of Adam Clayton Powell Jr.* (New York: Dial, 1971), 224.

20. *New York Daily News,* January 29, 1967.

21. *New York Daily News,* January 29, 1967.

22. Quoted in Wil Haygood, *King of the Cats: The Life and Times of Adam Clayton Powell Jr.* (New York: Houghton Mifflin, 1993), 231.

23. *Time,* August 13, 1945.

CHAPTER 10

1. *Ebony,* May 1956.

2. *Ebony,* January 1949.

3. *Ebony,* January 1949.

4. *Ebony,* January 1949.

5. *Ebony,* January 1949.

6. *Ebony,* November 1945.

7. *New York Post Weekend Magazine,* February 8, 1947.

8. *New York Post Weekend Magazine,* February 8, 1947.

9. *New York Post Weekend Magazine,* February 8, 1947.

10. *New York Post,* February 9, 1947.

11. Performing Arts Library, New York Public Library, Hazel Scott clippings file, publication unknown, July 31, 1946.

12. *New York Times,* August 4, 1981.

13. *Ebony,* January 1949.

14. *Ebony*, January 1949.

15. *Ebony*, January 1949.

16. *Ebony*, January 1949.

17. Hazel Scott, Personal Papers.

18. Hazel Scott, "I Found God in Show Business," *Ebony*, May 1953.

19. *Ebony*, November 1945.

20. *Ebony*, January 1949.

21. *Ebony*, January 1949.

22. *Ebony*, November, 1945.

23. *Essence*, November 1978.

24. James Agee, *Agee on Film: Criticism and Comment on the Movies* (New York: McDowell, Oblensky, 1958), 432.

25. James Agee, *Agee on Film: Criticism and Comment on the Movies* (New York: McDowell, Oblensky, 1958), 435.

26. James Agee, *Agee on Film: Criticism and Comment on the Movies* (New York: McDowell, Oblensky, 1958), 435.

27. Arthur Taylor, *Notes and Tones: Musician-to-Musician Interviews* (New York: Da Capo, 1977), 264.

28. *New York Herald Tribune*, October 2, 1945.

29. Adam Clayton Powell Jr., *Adam by Adam: The Autobiography of Adam Clayton Powell Jr.* (New York: Dial, 1971), 79.

30. *New York Herald Tribune*, October 2, 1945.

31. Truman Papers, "168 Letter to Representative Powell of New York," October 12, 1945.

32. *New York Times*, October 11, 1945.

33. *New York Times*, October 13, 1945.

34. Robert J. Donovan, *Conflict and Crisis: The Presidency of Harry S. Truman, 1945–1948* (New York: Norton, 1977), 147.

35. *New York Times*, January 10, 1967.

36. *New York Times*, January 10, 1967.

37. *Time*, October 22, 1945.

38. *Time*, November 2, 1945.

39. *New York Herald Tribune*, October 2, 1945.

40. *New York Herald Tribune*, October 2, 1945.

41. *New York Herald Tribune*, October 2, 1945.

42. *New York Herald Tribune*, October 2, 1945.

43. *New York Herald Tribune*, October 2, 1945.

44. *New York Herald Tribune*, October 2, 1945.

45. *Washington Post*, November 11, 1945.

46. *Washington Post*, November 11, 1945.

47. *New York Times*, November 10, 1945.

48. *New York Times*, November 10, 1945.

49. Arthur Taylor, *Notes and Tones: Musician-to-Musician Interviews* (New York: Da Capo, 1977), 257.

50. *The Chicago Sun*, November 10, 1945.

51. *Chicago Tribune*, November 12, 1945.

52. *Chicago Sun,* November 10, 1945.

53. *New York Herald Tribune,* November 27, 1945.

54. *New York Times,* November 27, 1945.

55. Hazel Scott Concert press release, Metropolitan Musical Bureau, Division of Columbia Concerts, Inc.

56. Hazel Scott Concert Press release, Metropolitan Musical Bureau, Division of Columbia Concerts, Inc.

57. *Amsterdam News,* December 1, 1945.

58. *Ebony,* May 1953.

59. Powell Christmas Card text with photo, Institute of Jazz Studies, Rutgers University, Hazel Scott clippings file.

60. Arthur Taylor, *Notes and Tones: Musician-to-Musician Interviews* (New York: Da Capo, 1977), 260.

61. Charles V. Hamilton, *Adam Clayton Powell Jr: The Political Biography of American Dilemma* (New York: Scribners, 1991), 183.

62. Charles V. Hamilton, *Adam Clayton Powell Jr: The Political Biography of American Dilemma* (New York: Scribners, 1991), 183.

63. Adam Clayton Powell Jr., *Adam by Adam: The Autobiography of Adam Clayton Powell Jr.* (New York: Dial, 1971), 226.

64. *Ebony,* May 1953.

65. *Ebony,* January 1949.

66. *Ebony,* January 1949.

67. *Ebony,* January 1949.

68. *Chicago Daily Tribune,* May 16, 1948.

69. *New York Times,* June 21, 1948.

70. Adam Powell III, interview with the author.

71. Interview with Adam Powell III.

72. *Ebony,* May 1953.

73. *Ebony,* May 1953.

74. *Ebony,* January 1949.

75. *Essence,* November 1978.

CHAPTER 11

1. Wil Haygood, *King of the Cats: The Life and Times of Adam Clayton Powell Jr.* (New York: Houghton Mifflin, 1993), 157–58, quoted from U.S. Department of Records, #442.112, dated December 19, 1949.

2. *Time,* November 29, 1948.

3. Adam C. Powell III, interview with the author.

4. "Hazel Scott Remembers," WPIX-TV, New York, 1980.

5. "Hazel Scott Remembers," WPIX-TV, New York, 1980.

6. "Hazel Scott Remembers," WPIX-TV, New York, 1980.

7. "Hazel Scott Remembers," WPIX-TV, New York, 1980.

8. *Washington Post,* February 18, 1949.

9. Quoted in Dwayne Mack, "Hazel Scott: A Career Curtailed," *Journal of African American History* 91, no. 2, Spring 2006. The Association for the Study of African American Life and History.

10. *Spokane Daily News,* April 18, 1950.

11. "Hazel Scott Remembers," WPIX-TV, New York, 1980.

12. Although the *Hazel Scott Show* was the first television program to be hosted by a black performer, Nat King Cole's show, which aired six years later, in 1956, has often been given that honor, largely due to its longevity and popularity. In fact, the next show to be hosted by a black entertainer after Hazel Scott was the *Billy Daniels Show,* which ran for two months on ABC in 1952. In November 1956, the *Nat King Cole Show* debuted on NBC; it aired for fifty weeks.

13. Donald Bogle, *Primetime Blues: African Americans on Network Television* (New York: Farrar, Straus Giroux, 2001), 16.

14. Donald Bogle, *Primetime Blues: African Americans on Network Television* (New York: Farrar, Straus Giroux, 2001), 16.

15. "How's your Hooper?" was a catchphrase of the 1940s, during which time the C. E. Hooper Company tracked radio and television ratings. In the 1950s, the company was purchased by A. C. Nielsen.

16. Adam Powell III, interview with the author.

17. *Variety,* April 19, 1950.

18. *Red Channels: The Report of Communist Influence in Radio and Television* (1950), 129–30 (New York: American Business Consultants).

19. *Scandalize My Name: Stories from the Blacklist,* written and directed by Alexandra Isles, Encore Media Group, 1999.

20. *Scandalize My Name: Stories from the Blacklist,* written and directed by Alexandra Isles, Encore Media Group, 1999.

21. Wil Haygood, *King of the Cats: The Life and Times of Adam Clayton Powell Jr.* (New York: Houghton Mifflin, 1993), 147.

22. Wil Haygood, *King of the Cats: The Life and Times of Adam Clayton Powell Jr.* (New York: Houghton Mifflin, 1993), 147.

23. Hazel Scott, Personal Papers.

24. Hazel Scott, Personal Papers.

25. *Scandalize My Name: Stories from the Blacklist,* written and directed by Alexandra Isles, Encore Media Group, 1999.

26. *Scandalize My Name: Stories from the Blacklist,* written and directed by Alexandra Isles, Encore Media Group, 1999.

27. Testimony of Hazel Scott Powell, transcripts from the Hearing before the Committee on Un-American Activities, House of Representatives, 81st Cong., 2nd sess., September 22, 1950, 3612.

28. Testimony of Hazel Scott Powell, transcripts from the Hearing before the Committee on Un-American Activities, House of Representatives, 81st Cong., 2nd sess., September 22, 1950, 3612.

29. Testimony of Hazel Scott Powell, transcripts from the Hearing before the Committee on Un-American Activities, House of Representatives, 81st Cong., 2nd sess., September 22, 1950, 3612.

30. Testimony of Hazel Scott Powell, transcripts from the Hearing before the Committee on Un-American Activities, House of Representatives, 81st Cong., 2nd sess., September 22, 1950, 3612.

31. Testimony of Hazel Scott Powell, transcripts from the Hearing before the Committee on Un-American Activities, House of Representatives, 81st Cong., 2nd sess., September 22, 1950, 3624.

32. Testimony of Hazel Scott Powell, transcripts from the Hearing before the Committee on Un-American Activities, House of Representatives, 81st Cong., 2nd sess., September 22, 1950, 3624.

33. Testimony of Hazel Scott Powell, transcripts from the Hearing before the Committee on Un-American Activities, House of Representatives, 81st Cong., 2nd sess., September 22, 1950, 3624.

34. Testimony of Hazel Scott Powell, transcripts from the Hearing before the Committee on Un-American Activities, House of Representatives, 81st Cong., 2nd sess., September 22, 1950, 3617.

35. Testimony of Hazel Scott Powell, transcripts from the Hearing before the Committee on Un-American Activities, House of Representatives, 81st Cong., 2nd sess., September 22, 1950, 3617.

36. Testimony of Hazel Scott Powell, transcripts from the Hearing before the Committee on Un-American Activities, House of Representatives, 81st Cong., 2nd sess., September 22, 1950, 3617.

37. Testimony of Hazel Scott Powell, transcripts from the Hearing before the Committee on Un-American Activities, House of Representatives, 81st Cong., 2nd sess., September 22, 1950, 3617.

38. Testimony of Hazel Scott Powell, transcripts from the Hearing before the Committee on Un-American Activities, House of Representatives, 81st Cong., 2nd sess., September 22, 1950, 3617.

39. Testimony of Hazel Scott Powell, transcripts from the Hearing before the Committee on Un-American Activities, House of Representatives, 81st Cong., 2nd sess., September 22, 1950, 3617.

40. Testimony of Hazel Scott Powell, transcripts from the Hearing before the Committee on Un-American Activities, House of Representatives, 81st Cong., 2nd sess., September 22, 1950, 3617.

41. Testimony of Hazel Scott Powell, transcripts from the Hearing before the Committee on Un-American Activities, House of Representatives, 81st Cong., 2nd sess., September 22, 1950, 3617.

42. Elijah Ward, *Josh White: Society Blues* (New York: Routledge, June 2002), 192.

43. James Gavin, *Intimate Nights: The Golden Age of New York Cabaret* (New York: Grove, 1991), 84–85.

44. Peter O'Brien, interview with the author.

CHAPTER 12

1. Hazel Scott promotional materials, distributed by Columbia Artists Management.

2. Interview with Hazel Scott, *Dial M for Music*, WCBS-TV Community Services, Department of Education, City of New York.

3. Adam C. Powell III, interview with the author.

4. Adam C. Powell III, interview with the author.

5. "Adam According to Hazel," *New York Daily News,* January 29, 1967.
6. *Ebony,* January 1949.
7. *Ebony,* May 1953.
8. Adam C. Powell III, interview with the author.
9. Adam C. Powell III, interview with the author.
10. *Ebony,* May 1953.
11. "Gravely Ill, Hazel Scott Flown Home from Paris," *Jet,* October 1951.
12. "Gravely Ill, Hazel Scott Flown Home from Paris," *Jet,* October 1951.
13. Adam C. Powell III, interview with the author.
14. *Ebony,* May 1953.
15. *Ebony,* May 1953.
16. *Ebony,* May 1953.
17. *Ebony,* May 1953.
18. Adam C. Powell III, interview with the author.
19. Adam C. Powell III, interview with the author.
20. *Ebony,* April 1954.
21. *Ebony,* April 1954.
22. *Ebony,* May 1953.
23. *Ebony,* May 1953.
24. *Ebony,* May 1953.
25. *Ebony,* May 1953.
26. *Essence,* November 1978.
27. *Essence,* November 1978.
28. *Essence,* November 1978.
29. Adam Clayton Powell Jr., *Adam by Adam: The Autobiography of Adam Clayton Powell Jr.* (New York: Dial, 1971), 228.
30. *New York Times,* July 3, 1955.
31. Wil Haygood, *King of the Cats: The Life and Times of Adam Clayton Powell Jr.* (New York: Houghton Mifflin, 1993), 196.
32. *Chicago Tribune,* December 17, 1954.
33. *New York Times,* July 4, 1956.
34. Murray Horwitz, interview with the author.
35. "Hazel Scott's Pianobatics Add Life to Pops Concert," Performing Arts Library, New York Public Library, Hazel Scott clippings file, publication unknown, January 19, 1955.
36. "Hazel Scott's Pianobatics Add Life to Pops Concert," Performing Arts Library, New York Public Library, Hazel Scott clippings file, publication unknown, January 19, 1955.
37. Brian Priestly, *Chasin' the Bird: The Life and Legacy of Charlie Parker* (Oxford: Oxford University Press, 2005), 37. The Charlie Parker—Hazel Scott duet "Embraceable You" is available, remastered, on Stash Records (ST 260, STCD 535).
38. Adam C. Powell III, interview with the author.
39. *Ms.,* November 1974.

40. Hazel Scott, "The Truth about Me," *Ebony,* September 1960.
41. *Ms.,* November 1974.
42. Adam C. Powell III, interview with the author.
43. Adam C. Powell III, personal writings.

CHAPTER 13

1. Hazel Scott, "The Truth about Me," *Ebony,* September 1960.
2. Hazel Scott, "The Truth about Me," *Ebony,* September 1960.
3. Adam C. Powell III, interview with the author.
4. Hazel Scott, "The Truth about Me," *Ebony,* September 1960.
5. Hazel Scott, "The Truth about Me," *Ebony,* September 1960.
6. *Amsterdam News,* November 1957.
7. *Amsterdam News,* November 1957.
8. *Amsterdam News,* November 1957.
9. *Amsterdam News,* November 1957.
10. *Ebony,* "The Truth About Me," September 1960.
11. *Ebony,* "The Truth About Me," September 1960.
12. Adam C. Powell III, personal writings.
13. *Ebony,* September 1960.
14. *Ebony,* September 1960.
15. *Ebony,* September 1960.
16. Adam C. Powell III, interview with the author.
17. Hazel Scott, Personal Papers.
18. Hazel Scott, Personal Papers.
19. Adam C. Powell III, interview with the author.
20. Adam C. Powell III, interview with the author.
21. *Los Angeles Times,* January 1968.
22. *Sepia,* September 1960.
23. *Sepia,* September 1960.
24. *Ebony,* September 1960.
25. "Hazel Scott Remembers," WPIX-TV, New York, 1980.
26. "Hazel Scott Remembers," WPIX-TV, New York, 1980.
27. *Los Angeles Times,* January 21, 1968.
28. *Ebony,* September 1960.
29. Arthur Taylor, *Notes and Tones: Musician-to-Musician Interviews* (New York: Da Capo, 1977), 255.
30. *New York Post,* July 18, 1980.
31. *Ebony,* September 1960.
32. Adam C. Powell III, interview with the author.
33. *Ebony,* September 1960.
34. *National Enquirer,* April 13, 1958.
35. *National Enquirer,* April 13, 1958.
36. Ezio Bedin, interview with the author.
37. Ezio Bedin, interview with the author.

38. *New York Times,* May 18, 1958.
39. *Time,* March 21, 1960.
40. *Time,* March 21, 1960.
41. *Washington Post,* March 11, 1960.
42. *New York Times,* March 25, 1960.
43. *Washington Post,* March 15, 1960.
44. Wil Haygood, *King of the Cats: The Life and Times of Adam Clayton Powell Jr.* (New York: Houghton Mifflin, 1993), 261.
45. *New York Post,* November 8, 1960.
46. *New York Post,* November 8, 1960.
47. *New York Post,* November 8, 1960.
48. *New York Post,* November 8, 1960.
49. *Variety,* June 8, 1960.
50. Adam C. Powell III, interview with the author.
51. *Pittsburgh Courier,* October 1, 1960.
52. *Pittsburgh Courier,* October 1, 1960.
53. *Sepia,* September 1960.
54. *New York Times,* March 15, 1962.
55. Ezio Bedin, interview with the author.

CHAPTER 14

1. James Baldwin, *Notes of a Native Son* (Boston: Beacon, 1953), 117.
2. James Baldwin, "The New Lost Generation," *Esquire,* July 1961.
3. John Bainbridge, *Another Way of Living: A Gallery of Americans Who Choose to Live in Europe* (New York: Holt, Rinehart and Winston, 1968), 281.
4. Ezio Bedin, interview with the author.
5. John Bainbridge, *Another Way of Living: A Gallery of Americans Who Choose to Live in Europe,* 282–83.
6. John Bainbridge, *Another Way of Living: A Gallery of Americans Who Choose to Live in Europe* (New York: Holt, Rinehart and Winston, 1968), 280.
7. Ezio Bedin, interview with the author.
8. Ezio Bedin, interview with the author.
9. Ezio Bedin, interview with the author.
10. *Los Angeles Times,* January 21, 1968.
11. *Essence,* November 1978.
12. *Washington Post,* July 4, 1970.
13. Letter from Hazel Scott to Mary Lou Williams, Institute for Jazz Studies, Rutgers University, Mary Lou Williams Archive Collection.
14. *Sepia,* September 1960.
15. Letter from Hazel Scott to Mary Lou Williams, Institute for Jazz Studies, Rutgers University, Mary Lou Williams Archive Collection.
16. Letter from Hazel Scott to Mary Lou Williams, Institute for Jazz Studies, Rutgers University, Mary Lou Williams Archive Collection.
17. Letter from Hazel Scott to Mary Lou Williams, Institute for Jazz Studies, Rutgers University, Mary Lou Williams Archive Collection.
18. Letter from Hazel Scott to Mary Lou Williams, Institute for Jazz Studies, Rutgers University, Mary Lou Williams Archive Collection.

19. Letter from Hazel Scott to Mary Lou Williams, Institute for Jazz Studies, Rutgers University, Mary Lou Williams Archive Collection.

20. Letter from Hazel Scott to Mary Lou Williams, Institute for Jazz Studies, Rutgers University, Mary Lou Williams Archive Collection.

21. Letter from Hazel Scott to Mary Lou Williams, Institute for Jazz Studies, Rutgers University, Mary Lou Williams Archive Collection.

22. Letter from Hazel Scott to Mary Lou Williams, Institute for Jazz Studies, Rutgers University, Mary Lou Williams Archive Collection.

23. Letter from Hazel Scott to Mary Lou Williams, Institute for Jazz Studies, Rutgers University, Mary Lou Williams Archive Collection.

24. *Los Angeles Times,* January 21, 1968.

25. *Los Angeles Times,* January 21, 1968.

26. Letter from Hazel Scott to Mary Lou Williams, Institute for Jazz Studies, Rutgers University, Mary Lou Williams Archive Collection.

27. Letter from Hazel Scott to Mary Lou Williams, Institute for Jazz Studies, Rutgers University, Mary Lou Williams Archive Collection.

28. Letter from Hazel Scott to Mary Lou Williams, Institute for Jazz Studies, Rutgers University, Mary Lou Williams Archive Collection.

29. Letter from Hazel Scott to Mary Lou Williams, Institute for Jazz Studies, Rutgers University, Mary Lou Williams Archive Collection.

30. Letter from Hazel Scott to Mary Lou Williams, Institute for Jazz Studies, Rutgers University, Mary Lou Williams Archive Collection.

31. Letter from Hazel Scott to Mary Lou Williams, Institute for Jazz Studies, Rutgers University, Mary Lou Williams Archive Collection.

32. Letter from Hazel Scott to Mary Lou Williams, Institute for Jazz Studies, Rutgers University, Mary Lou Williams Archive Collection.

33. Letter from Hazel Scott to Mary Lou Williams, Institute for Jazz Studies, Rutgers University, Mary Lou Williams Archive Collection.

34. Letter from Hazel Scott to Mary Lou Williams, Institute for Jazz Studies, Rutgers University, Mary Lou Williams Archive Collection.

35. Letter from Hazel Scott to Mary Lou Williams, Institute for Jazz Studies, Rutgers University, Mary Lou Williams Archive Collection.

36. Letter from Hazel Scott to Mary Lou Williams, Institute for Jazz Studies, Rutgers University, Mary Lou Williams Archive Collection.

37. Letter from Hazel Scott to Mary Lou Williams, Institute for Jazz Studies, Rutgers University, Mary Lou Williams Archive Collection.

38. Letter from Hazel Scott to Mary Lou Williams, Institute for Jazz Studies, Rutgers University, Mary Lou Williams Archive Collection.

39. *Jet,* June 2, 1966.

40. *Jet,* June 2, 1966.

CHAPTER 15

1. *Ebony,* March 1968.

2. *Ebony,* March 1968.

3. *Ebony,* March 1968.

4. *Ebony,* March 1968.

5. *Ebony,* March 1968.

6. *Ebony,* March 1968.

7. *Ebony,* March 1968.

8. John Bainbridge, *Another Way of Living: A Gallery of Americans Who Choose to Live in Europe* (New York: Holt, Rinehart and Winston, 1968), 282.

9. *Los Angeles Times,* January 21, 1968.

10. *Ebony,* March 1968.

11. Hazel Scott, Personal Papers.

12. Hazel Scott, Personal Papers.

13. Hazel Scott, Personal Papers.

14. *New York Daily News,* January 13, 1967.

15. *Jet,* February 9, 1967.

16. Adam C. Powell III, interview with the author.

17. Adam C. Powell III, interview with the author.

18. Adam C. Powell III, interview with the author.

19. Adam C. Powell III, interview with the author.

20. Adam C. Powell III, interview with the author.

21. *Washington Post,* July 4, 1970.

22. *Jet,* February 9, 1967.

23. *Essence,* November 1978.

24. *New York Sun,* January 23, 2006.

25. *New York Times,* January 13, 1967.

26. *Jet,* February 9, 1967.

27. *Jet,* February 9, 1967.

28. Father Peter O'Brien, interview with the author.

29. Father Peter O'Brien, interview with the author.

30. Father Peter O'Brien, interview with the author.

31. Father Peter O'Brien, interview with the author.

32. Arthur Taylor, *Notes and Tones: Musician-to-Musician Interviews* (New York: Da Capo, 1977), 258.

33. Arthur Taylor, *Notes and Tones: Musician-to-Musician Interviews* (New York: Da Capo, 1977), 267.

34. *New York Herald Tribune,* September 9, 1973.

35. Arthur Taylor, *Notes and Tones: Musician-to-Musician Interviews* (New York: Da Capo, 1977), 260.

36. Hazel Scott, Personal Papers.

37. Betsey Crawford, interview with the author.

38. Wil Haygood, *King of the Cats: The Life and Times of Adam Clayton Powell Jr.* (New York: Houghton Mifflin, 1993), 389.

39. *Time,* June 6, 1969.

40. Mike Wallace, interview with the author.

41. *Washington Post,* May 31, 1969.

42. *Washington Post,* May 31, 1969.

43. *Washington Post,* May 31, 1969.

44. *Washington Post,* May 31, 1969.

CHAPTER 16

1. *Los Angeles Times,* October 2, 1981.
2. Adam C. Powell III, interview with the author.
3. Adam C. Powell III, interview with the author.
4. Adam C. Powell III, interview with the author.
5. Adam C. Powell III, interview with the author.
6. Arthur Taylor, *Notes and Tones: Musician-to-Musician Interviews* (New York: Da Capo, 1977), 257.
7. Arthur Taylor, *Notes and Tones: Musician-to-Musician Interviews* (New York: Da Capo, 1977), 257.
8. Arthur Taylor, *Notes and Tones: Musician-to-Musician Interviews* (New York: Da Capo, 1977), 256.
9. *Essence,* November 1978.
10. Adam Clayton Powell Jr., *Adam by Adam: The Autobiography of Adam Clayton Powell Jr.* (New York: Dial, 1971), 236.
11. *New York Times,* January 10, 1967.
12. Hazel Scott, Personal Papers.
13. *Essence,* November 1978.
14. *Essence,* November 1978.
15. "Adam According to Hazel," *New York Daily News,* January 29, 1967.
16. *Essence,* November 1978.
17. *Ms.,* November 1974.
18. *Ms.,* November 1974.
19. *Cosmopolitan,* July 1972.
20. *Ms.,* November 1974.
21. Adam C. Powell IV, interview with the author.
22. Arthur Taylor, *Notes and Tones: Musician-to-Musician Interviews* (New York: Da Capo, 1977), 258.
23. Sherman Powell, interview with the author.
24. Sherman Powell, interview with the author.
25. Adam Powell IV, interview with the author.
26. *New York Yimes,* February 2, 1981.
27. Adam C. Powell IV, interview with the author.
28. Adam C. Powell IV, interview with the author.
29. Sherman Powell, interview with the author.
30. *Amsterdam News,* March 29, 1975.
31. *New York Daily News,* June 11, 1975.
32. *New York Daily News,* June 11, 1975.
33. *New York Daily News,* June 11, 1975.
34. *New York Daily News,* June 11, 1975.
35. Father Peter O'Brien, interview with the author.
36. *Essence,* November 1978.
37. Adam C. Powell III, interview with the author.
38. Adam C. Powell III, interview with the author. There is little evidence that Hazel Scott ever performed in her native Trinidad. The country's na-

tional archives have no record of it, although in some published articles in the United States there is mention of at least one concert in Port of Spain. Unfortunately, for the most part her musical legacy is scarcely documented in the country. Younger generations of Trinidadians have little or no knowledge of Hazel Scott.

39. Adam C. Powell III, interview with the author.

40. Adam C. Powell III, interview with the author.

41. Adam C. Powell III, interview with the author.

42. Adam C. Powell III, interview with the author.

43. Langston Hughes, "To Be Somebody." *The Collected Poems of Langston Hughes* (New York: Knopf, 1994), 374. Used by permission of Alfred A. Knopf, a Division of Random House, Inc.

44. *Essence,* November 1978.

SELECTED DISCOGRAPHY AND
FILMOGRAPHY

SEXTET OF THE RHYTHM CLUB OF LONDON (*BLUEBIRD*)

Calling All Bars *(Feather)*
Mighty Like the Blues *(Feather)*
You Gave Me the Go-By *(Feather)*
Why Didn't William Tell *(Feather)*

Hazel Scott (piano, vocals); Danny Polo (clarinet); Pete Brown (alto saxophone);
Albert Harris (guitar); Pete Barry (bass); Arthur Herbert (drums)
    Recorded in New York City, December 1, 1939

SWINGING THE CLASSICS (*DECCA*) *NO. A–212*

Valse in D-flat Major *(Chopin)*
Country Gardens *(Grainger)*
Ritual Fire Dance *(De Falla)*
Prelude in C-sharp Minor *(Rachmaninoff)*
Two-Part Invention in A Minor *(Bach)*
Hungarian Rhapsody No. 2 *(Liszt)*

Hazel Scott (piano); J. C. Heard (drums)
    Recorded in New York City, December 11, 1940

HAZEL SCOTT, VOL. 2 (*DECCA*) *NO. A–321*

Embraceable You *(Gershwin/Gershwin)*
Hazel's Boogie-Woogie *(Scott)*
Blues in B-Flat *(Scott)*
Hallelujah *(Youmans/Robin/Grey)*
Dark Eyes *(Traditional)*
Three Little Words *(Ruby/Kalmar)*

Hazel Scott (piano); J. C. Heard (drums)
    Recorded in New York City, February 27, 1942

HAZEL SCOTT (V-DISCS)

Body and Soul *(Sour/Heyman/Green)*
People Will Say We're in Love *(Rodgers/Hammerstein)*

Hazel Scott (piano; vocals)
  Recorded in New York City, August 27, 1943

(V-Discs were special recordings made specifically for servicemen abroad during World War II.)

HAZEL SCOTT AND SID CATLETT (V-DISCS)

Honeysuckle Rose *(Waller/Razaf)*
"C" Jam Blues *(Ellington)*

Hazel Scott (piano); Sid Catlett (drums)
  Recorded in New York City, August 27, 1943

HAZEL SCOTT WITH TOOTS CAMARATA'S ORCHESTRA (*DECCA*)

Take Me in Your Arms *(Markush/Parish)*
I've Got the World on a String *(Koehler/Arlen)*
On the Sunny Side of the Street *(Fields/McHugh)*
Butterfly Kick *(Scott)*
Ich Vil Sich Spielen *(Green)*

Hazel Scott (piano, vocals) with orchestra; Toots Camarata (arranger, conductor)
  Recorded in New York City, March, 1945

I'm Glad There's You *(Madeira/Dorsey)*
Fascinating Rhythm *(Gershwin/Gershwin)*
The Man I Love *(Gershwin/Gershwin)*

Hazel Scott (piano, vocals) with orchestra; Toots Camarata (arranger, conductor)
  Recorded in New York City, May 3, 1945

HAZEL SCOTT: A PIANO RECITAL (*SIGNATURE*)

A Rainy Night in G *(Scott)*
How High the Moon *(Hamilton/Lewis)*
I Guess I'll Have to Change My Plans *(Dietz/Schwartz)*
Valse in C-sharp Minor (Opus 64. no. 2) *(Chopin)*
Nocturne in B-flat Minor (Opus 9, no. 1) *(Chopin)*
Fantasie Impromptu (Opus 66) *(Chopin)*
Sonata in C Minor *(Scarlatti)*
Toccata *(Paradisi)*
Idyll *(Scott)*

Hazel Scott (piano) solo
  Recorded in New York City, 1946

GREAT SCOTT! (*COLUMBIA*)

Emaline *(Parish-Perkins)*

Nightmare Blues *(Scott)*
Mary Lou *(Lyman/Waggner/Robinson)*
Soon *(Gershwin)*
Brown Bee Boogie *(Scott)*
Love Me or Leave Me *(Kahn/Donaldson)*
Love Will Find a Way *(Sissle/Blake)*
Dancing on the Ceiling *(Rodgers/Hart)*

Hazel Scott (piano); with rhythm accompaniment (personnel unknown)
Recorded in New York City, 1948

HAZEL SCOTT (*DECCA*)

Body and Soul *(Sour/Heyman/Green)*
St. Louis Blues *(Handy)*
La Ronde *(Strauss/Ducreux)*
The One I Love Belongs to Somebody Else *(Jones/Kahn)*
Tea for Two *(Youmans/Colline/Merry)*
How Blue Can You Get? *(Scott)*

Hazel Scott (piano, vocals); Georges Hadjo (bass); Gerard "Dave" Pochonet (drums)
Recorded in Paris, 1951

HAZEL SCOTT'S LATE SHOW (*CAPITOL*)

The Girl Friend *(Arlen/Mercer)*
The Way You Look Tonight *(Kern/Fields)*
Thou Swell *(Rodgers/Hart)*
I Get a Kick Out of You *(Porter)*
S'Wonderful *(Gershwin/Gershwin)*
I'll Be Around *(Wilder)*
I'm Yours *(Mellin)*
That Old Black Magic *(Arlen/Mercer)*

Hazel Scott (piano); Red Callender (bass); Lee Young (drums)
Recorded in Hollywood, California, 1953

RELAXED PIANO MOODS (*DEBUT*)

Like Someone in Love *(Van Heusen/Burke)*
Peace of Mind *(Scott)*
Lament *(Johnson)*
The Jeep Is Jumpin' *(Ellington/Hodges)*
Git Up from There *(Scott)*
A Foggy Day *(Gershwin/Gershwin)*
Mountain Greenery *(Rodgers/Hart)*
Git Up from There (alternate)
Lament (alternate)

Selections 7–9 previously released as part of the boxed set Charles Mingus: The Complete Debut Recordings.

Hazel Scott (piano); Charles Mingus (bass); Max Roach (drums)
   Recorded in Hackensack, New Jersey, January 21, 1955

'ROUND MIDNIGHT (*DECCA*)

'Round Midnight *(Monk/Williams/Hanighen)*
Just Imagine *(DeSylva/Brown/Henderson)*
It's You or No One *(Styne/Cahn)*
It's Easy to Remember *(Rodgers/Hart)*
Lucky to Be Me *(Bernstein/Comden/Green)*
Maybe *(Gershwin/Gershwin)*
I Wish I Didn't Love You So *(Loesser)*
(In the) Wee Small Hours (of the Morning) *(Mann/Hillard)*
Warm All Over *(Loesser)*
Love Is the Time *(Washington/Young)*
Ev'ry Time *(Martin/Blane)*
For You, for Me, Forevermore *(Gershwin/Gershwin)*

Hazel Scott (piano); rhythm accompaniment unknown
   Recorded in New York 1956

'ROUND MIDNIGHT (*UNIVERSAL INTERNATIONAL*)

Digitally remastered and re-released by Universal International in Audio compact disc format. (Import) November 3, 2003

HAZEL SCOTT: JOUE ET CHANTE (*POLYDOR*)

Venez donc chez moi *(Misraki-Feline)*
Réponds-moi *(Winkler-Rench-Plante)*
L'homme que j'aime (The Man I Love) *(Gershwin-Lambert)*
Avril à Paris (April in Paris) *(Duke-Henneve-Palex)*

   Recorded in Paris, 1958

ALWAYS (*IMAGE*)

Always *(Scott)*
Spend Some Time with Me *(Corbo)*
Be What You Are *(Scott)*
No Greater Love *(Lewis)*
Let Me Hold You *(Burger)*
La Vita (This Is My Life) *(Newall/Canfora)*
Just the Way You Are *(Joel)*
Do You Feel Alright? *(Scott)*

   Recorded in New York City, 1979

AFTER HOURS: THE HAZEL SCOTT TRIO (*TIOCH*)

Lover's Leap *(Scott)*
After Hours *(Parrish/Bruce/Feyne)*
Nancy with the Laughing Face *(van Heusen/Silvers)*
Moving Day *(Scott)*
Guess I Gotta Move *(Scott/Duvivier)*
St. Louis Blues *(Handy)*

Hazel Scott (piano); George Duvivier (bass); Oliver Jackson (drums)
  Recorded in New York City, April 14, 1980

HAZEL SCOTT: 1939–1945 (*MELODIE JAZZ CLASSIC*)

Calling All Bars *(Feather)*
Mighty Like the Blues *(Feather)*
You Gave Me the Go-By *(Feather)*
Why Didn't William Tell? *(Feather)*
Valse in "D" Flat Major, Op. 64 No. 1 (Minute) *(Chopin)*
Country Gardens *(Grainger)*
Ritual Fire Dance *(De Falla)*
Prelude in "C" Sharp Minor *(Rachmaninoff)*
Two Part Invention in "A" Minor *(Bach)*
Hungarian Rhapsody No. 2 in "C" Sharp Minor *(Liszt)*
Embraceable You *(Gershwin/Gershwin)*
Hazel's Boogie-Woogie *(Scott)*
Blues in B Flat *(Scott)*
Hallelujah! *(Youmans/Robin/Grey)*
Dark Eyes *(Traditional)*
Three Little Words *(Ruby/Kalmar)*
Body and Soul *(Sour/Heyman/Green)*
People Will Say We're in Love *(Rodgers/Hammerstein)*
Honeysuckle Rose *(Waller/Razaf)*
"C" Jam Blues *(Ellington)*

Hazel Scott (piano, vocals) with various instrumental accompaniment
  Released August 26, 2003

ORIGINAL COMPOSITIONS

Blues in B Flat
Brown Bee Boogie
Caribbean Fete
Carnaval
Dark Eyes
Do You Feel Alright?
Everybody Rock
Git Up from There
Hazel's Boogie Woogie

Here You Are
Home Cookin' Mama
Hungarian Rhapsody No. 2 (swing arrangement)
Nightmare Blues
Prelude in C Minor Op. 3 (swing arrangement)
A Rainy Night in G
Sidewalks of New York
Twelve O'Clock
Until We Learn

COMPILATIONS

Jazz Ladies (Warner, 2004)—"The Jeep Is Jumpin'"
Can't Stop Playing That Boogie (Jasmine, 2002)—"Brown Bee Boogie"
The Debut/Period: Original Jazz Classics Sampler (Original Jazz Classics, 2002)—"Peace of Mind"
Blues Roots, Vol. 2 (BMG, 2000)—"Mighty Like the Blues"
Hollywood Swing and Jazz: Hot Numbers from Classic MGM, Warner Brothers, and RKO Films (Rhino, 2000)—"Body and Soul"
You're Sensational: Cole Porter in the 20s, 40s and 50s (Koch, 1999)—"Through Thick and Thin"
Fascinating Rhythm (Avid, 1998)—"Fascinating Rhythm"
Rhapsody in Blue—Original Soundtrack (Great Movie Themes, 1997)—"The Man I Love"
Forty Years of Women in Jazz (Jass,1989)— "'Round Midnight"
The Debut Records Story (Debut, 1957)—"A Foggy Day," "Mountain Greenery"
The Women: Classic Female Jazz Artists, 1939–1952 (Bluebird, 1955)—"Calling All Bars;" "Mighty Like the Blues"
The Feminine Touch (Decca, 1953)—"Blues in B Flat"

FILMOGRAPHY

Something to Shout About (Columbia Pictures)
I Dood It (MGM)
Broadway Rhythm (MGM)
The Heat's On (Columbia Pictures)
Rhapsody in Blue (Warner Bros.)
Le Desorde et la Nuit ("The Night Affair") (Orex)
Une Balle dans le Canon ("A Bullet in the Gun Barrel") (Filmatec)
The Hazel Scott Show (DuMont Television Network)
CBS Playhouse "The Experiment" (CBS)
The Bold Ones: The New Doctors (NBC)
One Life to Live (ABC)

BIBLIOGRAPHY

Agee, James. *Agee on Film: Criticism and Comment on the Movies.* New York: McDowell, Oblensky, 1958.

Armstrong, Louis. *Louis Armstrong: In His Own Words.* New York: Oxford University Press, 1999.

Bainbridge, John. *Another Way of Living: A Gallery of Americans Who Choose to Live in Europe.* New York: Holt, Rinehart and Winston, 1968.

Baldwin, James. *Notes of a Native Son.* Boston: Beacon, 1953.

Bogle, Donald. *Bright Boulevards, Bold Dreams: The Story of Black Hollywood.* New York: One World/ Ballantine, 2005.

Bogle, Donald. *Brown Sugar: Eighty Years of America's Black Female Superstars.* New York: Harmony, 1980.

Bogle, Donald. *Primetime Blues: African Americans on Network Television.* New York: Farrar, Straus Giroux, 2001.

Bogle, Donald. *Toms, Coons, Mulattoes, Mammies, and Bucks: An Interpretative History of Blacks in American Films.* New York: Continuum, 1973.

Cowley, John. *Carnival, Canboulay, and Calypso: Traditions in the Making.* Cambridge: Cambridge University Press, 1996.

Dahl, Linda. *Morning Glory: A Biography of Mary Lou Williams.* Berkeley: University of California Press, 1999.

Dahl, Linda. *Stormy Weather: The Music and Lives of a Century of Jazz Women.* New York: Pantheon, 1984.

Dickerson, James. L. *Just for a Thrill: Lil Hardin Armstrong, First Lady of Jazz.* New York: Cooper Square, 2002.

Donovan, Robert J. *Conflict and Crisis: The Presidency of Harry S. Truman, 1945–1948.* New York: Norton, 1977.

Duberman, Martin. *Paul Robeson: A Biography.* New York: Knopf, 1988.

Ellington, Duke. *Music Is My Mistress.* New York: Da Capo, 1976.

Feather, Leonard, and Ira Gitler. *The Biographical Encyclopedia of Jazz.* New York: Oxford University Press, 1999.

Fried, Albert. *McCarthyism: The Great American Red Scare.* New York: Oxford University Press, 1997.

Gabler, Neil. *An Empire of Their Own: How the Jews Invented Hollywood.* New York: Crown , 1998.

Gitler, Ira. *Swing to Bop: An Oral History of the Transition in Jazz in the 1940s.* New York: Oxford University Press, 1985.

Griffin, Farah Jasmine. *If You Can't Be Free, Be a Mystery: In Search of Billie Holiday*. New York: Free Press, 2001.

Hamilton, Charles V. *Adam Clayton Powell Jr: The Political Biography of American Dilemma*. New York: Scribners, 1991.

Handy, D. Antoinette. *Black Women in American Bands & Orchestras*. Metuchen, N.J.: Scarecrow Press, 1981.

Handy, D. Antoinette. *The International Sweethearts of Rhythm: The Ladies Jazz Band from Piney Woods Country Life School*. Metuchen, N.J.: Scarecrow Press, 1983.

Haskins, James. *Adam Clayton Powell: Portrait of a Marching Black*. New York: Dial, 1974.

Haygood, Wil. *King of the Cats: The Life and Times of Adam Clayton Powell Jr*. New York: Houghton Mifflin, 1993.

Hill, Donald R. *Calypso Calaloo: Early Carnival Music in Trinidad*. Gainesville: University Press of Florida, 1993.

Hughes, Langston. *The Collected Poems of Langston Hughes*. New York: Knopf, 1994.

Jones, Leroi. *Blues People: Negro Music in White America*. New York: Morrow, 1963.

Keiler, Allan. *Marian Anderson: A Singer's Journey*. New York: Lisa Drew/Scribners, 2000.

Kirkeby, Ed. *Ain't Misbehavin*. New York: Da Capo, 1966.

Lawrenson, Helen. *Whistling Girl*. New York: Doubleday, 1978.

Lester, James. *Too Marvelous for Words: The Life and Genius of Art Tatum*. New York: Oxford University Press, 1994.

Lewis, David Levering. *When Harlem Was in Vogue*. New York: Knopf, 1981.

Lieberman, Richard K. *Steinway and Sons*. New Haven: Yale University Press, 1995.

Mac, Dwayne. "Hazel Scott: A Career Curtailed." *The Journal of African American History*, 91. no. 2, Spring. Washington, DC: The Association for the Study of African American Life and History, 2006.

Osofsky, Gilbert. *Harlem: The Making of a Ghetto*. New York: Harper and Row, 1968.

Ottley, Roi. *New World a-Coming*. Boston: Houghton Mifflin, 1943.

Powell, Adam Clayton, Jr. *Adam by Adam: The Autobiography of Adam Clayton Powell Jr*. New York: Dial, 1971.

Priestly, Brian. *Chasin' the Bird: The Life and Legacy of Charlie Parker*. Oxford: Oxford University Press, 2005.

Red Channels: The Report of Communist Influence in Radio and Television. New York: American Business Consultants, 1950.

Robeson, Paul. *Paul Robeson Speaks: Writings, Speeches, and Interviews, 1914–1978*. Edited by Philip S. Foner. New York: Brunner/Mazel, 1978.

Scott, Hazel. "I Found God in Show Business." *Ebony*, May 1953.

Scott, Hazel. "The Truth about Me." *Ebony*, September 1960.

Southern, Eileen. *The Music of Black Americans: A History*. New York: Norton, 1997.

Stovall, Tyler. *Paris Noir: African Americans in the City of Light.* Boston: Houghton Mifflin, 1996.

Taylor, Arthur. *Notes and Tones: Musician-to-Musician Interviews.* New York: Da Capo, 1977.

Wald, Elijah. *Josh White: Society Blues.* New York: Routledge, 2000.

Ward, Geoffrey and Ken Burns. *Jazz: A History of American's Music.* New York: Knopf, 2000.

Watkins-Owens, Irma. *Blood Relations: Caribbean Immigrants and the Harlem Community (1900–1930).* Bloomington: Indiana University Press, 1996.

Watts, Jill. *Hattie McDaniel: Black Ambition, White Hollywood.* New York: HarperCollins, 2005.

Wilson Teddy, with Arie Ligthart and Humphrey van Loo. *Teddy Wilson Talks Jazz.* Great Britain: Cassell/Bayou, 1996.

Zinn, Howard. *A People's History of the United States.* New York: HarperCollins, 1995.

INDEX

Abyssinian Baptist Church, 90, 93, 94, 95, 96, 101, 103, 104, 105, 108, 130, 131, 151, 165, 166, 200, 206, 207, 217, 218, 226
Academy Award, 75, 77
Adam, Young, 159
Addams, Charles, 134
African, 1, 4, 5, 14, 23, 27, 88, 91, 115, 205, 212
African Americans, 23, 88, 115, 212
Al Casey Trio: "A Salute to Thomas 'Fats' Waller," 88
Alda, Robert: *Rhapsody in Blue*, 86
Allan, Lewis: "Strange Fruit," 53
Alhambra Theater, 27, 34, 173
Allen, Henry "Red," 63
Ambrose, Bert, 55
Ameche, Don: *Something to Shout About*, 74, 75
American Communist Party, 54
American Creolians, 39, 40, 43
American Federation of Musicians, 40
American Labor Party, 102
Amerindians, 4
Ammons, Albert, 51, 58, 63; "Boogie-Woogie Piano Playing," 52
Ammons, Gene, 51
Amsterdam News, 34, 57, 129, 174, 200, 222
Anderson, Eddie "Rochester": *Broadway Rhythm*, 79
Anderson, Edward, 47
Anderson, Marian, 118, 163
Apollo Theater, 33, 56, 58, 67, 102, 187, 197
Arlen, Harold, 160; "Get Happy," 63
Armstrong, Lil Hardin, 32, 34, 39
Armstrong, Louis, 31, 32, 74, 112, 117;

"Hot Five," 32; "Hot Seven," 32; *Rhapsody in Black and Blue*, 72
The Army/Navy Screen Magazine, 88
Arthur Murray Party, 140
Artist Front to Win the War, 143
Associated Press, 120
Astin, John, 211
Atkinson, Brooks, 66, 69
Austin, Lovie: Blues Serenaders, 28
Austin, TX, 138
Avedon, Richard, 192

Bacall, Lauren, 80
Bach, Johann Sebastian, 58, 63, 67, 68, 80, 108, 112, 123, 125, 128, 161, "Invention No. 1 in C-Major," 86; Inventions, 46; "Jesu, Joy of Man's Desiring," 19, 132, 134; Prelude and Fugue in C-sharp Minor; Prelude in C sharp, 6; Two-Part Invention in A minor, 62; Well-Tempered Clavier, 133
Bacon, Peggy, 50
Bailey, Mildred, 60; "A Salute to Thomas 'Fats' Waller," 88–89
Bailey, Pearl, 169
Bainbridge, John: *Another Way of Living*, 191
Baldwin, James, 180, 190, 192
Baker, Josephine, 27, 31
Bardot, Brigitte, 178
Bardot, Mijanou: *Une Balle dans le Canon* (A Bullet in the Gun Barrel), 178
Barnet, Charlie: Orchestra, 59
Barry, Pete, 55
Barthe, Richmond, 162

Plunkett, Walter: *Gone with the Wind,*
83; *The Heat's On,* 83
Pochonet, Gerard "Dave," 155
Poitier, Sidney: *Paris Blues,* 178
Polo, Danny, 55
Polydor Records, 178
Port of Spain, 3, 4, 5, 162
Porter, Charlie, 91–92
Porter, Cole, 155, 160; "Begin the Be-
guine," 45, 63; "Hasta Luego," 76; "I
Always Knew," 75; "Just One of
Those Things," 45; "Lotus Bloom,"
76; *Something to Shout About,* 74, 77,
82; "Something to Shout About,"
76; "Through Thick and Thin," 76;
"You'd Be So Nice To Come Home
To," 75
Portuguese, 4
Powell, Adam Clayton, IV, 188, 214
Powell, Adam Clayton, Jr., 90–99,
101–8, 110–37, 139, 143, 144, 151,
153, 154–55, 156, 161–66, 172, 174,
175–77, 181, 183–87, 188, 189, 199,
206–8, 213, 217–19; *Adam by Adam,*
92; civil rights, 94, 95, 96, 111, 139;
education, 92–93, 95; politics, 96,
99, 101–5, 108, 119–20, 122, 144, 151,
154, 162, 165–66, 206–7, 217, 218;
tax fraud, 183–85
Powell, Adam Clayton, Sr., 90–96,
106, 107, 126, 161
Powell, Adam Clayton, III "Skipper,"
130, 135, 137, 143, 151, 153, 155, 160,
161, 163, 175, 186, 187, 191–92, 208,
212–13, 219
Powell, Blanche, 90, 91, 161
Powell, Bud, 70, 128, 223; Trio, 167
Powell, Eleanor, 78
Powell, Isabel Washington, 98, 106, 107
Powell, Mattie Shaefer, 90, 161
Powell, Preston, 98
Powell, Sherman, 214, 220
Powell, Yvette, 188
Powell-Buchanan Publishing Com-
pany, 130
Priestly, Brian, 167
Pryor, Richard: *Silver Streak,* 222
Puerto de los Hispanioles, 4

Queens, NY, 161, 165, 218, 227

Queen's Royal College, 3
Quinn, Anthony, 179
Rachmaninoff, Sergei, 112, 123, 125;
Prelude in C Sharp Minor, 22; *Sec-
ond Piano Concerto,* 135
racism, 91, 129, 149, 204
Radio City Music Hall, 31
Rainey, "Ma," 28
Randolph, A. Philip, 192
Rangel, Charles B., 217
Rapper, Irving: *Rhapsody in Blue,* 86
Ratoff, Gregory, 80, 85; *The Heat's On,*
81–82, 85, 212; *Something to Shout
About,* 74, 77, 82
Ravel, Maurice, 123
Raye, Nora Holt: *Rhapsody on Negro
Themes,* 34
Red Channels, 143, 144, 145, 146, 147
Refregier, Anton, 50, 58
Reinhardt, Ad, 50
Republicans, 102, 129, 184
Reynolds, Grant, 129–30; *Marching
Blacks,* 129
Rhapsody in Black, 30
Rhinelander, Leonard "Kip," 15–16
Richmond, VA, 130
Riobamba, 70
Ritt, Martin: *Paris Blues,* 178
Ritz-Carlton, 64
Rivera, Martin "Fangs," 216
RKO Pictures, 73–74
Roach, Hal: *Our Gang Comedies,* 31
Roach, Max, 167, 168
Robbins, Jerome, 148
Robeson, Paul, 49, 55, 102, 107, 118,
148; "Othello," 117
Robinson, Bill "Bojangles," 72–73,
107
Rockefeller, Nelson, 49
Rodgers, Richard, 134, 160; "Mountain
Greenery," 168
Rodriguez, Carlos, 222
Roe, Willard J., 139
Roman Catholic Church, 3, 162, 188
Romanoff, Valerie, 222
Rome, Harold, *Sing Out the News,* 45
Rome, Italy, 181, 182
Rooney, Mickey: *On the Town,* 194
Roosevelt, Eleanor, 49, 55, 102
Roosevelt Island, 220

Printed and bound by CPI Group (UK) Ltd, Croydon, CR0 4YY

09/06/2025

14685648-0003